THE
LAW OF
SUCCESS

IN SIXTEEN LESSONS

Teaching, for the First Time in the History of the World, the True Philosophy upon which all Personal Success is Built.

∙∙⟨∙∙⟩∙∙

BY

NAPOLEON HILL

∙∙⟨∙∙⟩∙∙

1928

PUBLISHED BY
The RALSTON UNIVERSITY PRESS
MERIDEN, CONN.

FACSIMILE EDITION
Published by
WILSHIRE BOOK COMPANY
2000

This book is a facsimile of the complete and original edition of *The Law of Success in Sixteen Lessons* by Napoleon Hill, originally published by Ralston University Press in 1928 and now in the public domain.

This facsimile edition, published by Wilshire Book Company with an original cover design by Peter Thorpe and Melvin Powers, is not sponsored or endorsed by, or otherwise affiliated with, Napoleon Hill or his family and heirs, the Napoleon Hill Foundation, The Ralston University Press, or any other person or entity.

FACSIMILE EDITION
Published by
WILSHIRE BOOK COMPANY
12015 Sherman Road
No. Hollywood, CA 91605
2000

General Introduction

to the

LAW OF SUCCESS

COURSE

By Napoleon Hill

Dedicated to

ANDREW CARNEGIE

who suggested the writing of the course, and to

HENRY FORD

whose astounding achievements form the foundation for practically all of the Sixteen Lessons of the course, and to

EDWIN C. BARNES

a business associate of Thomas A. Edison, whose close personal friendship over a period of more than fifteen years served to help the author "carry on" in the face of a great variety of adversities and much temporary defeat met with in organizing the course.

WHO said it could not be done? And what great victories has he to his credit which qualify h i m to judge others accurately?

—*Napoleon Hill.*

A PERSONAL STATEMENT BY THE AUTHOR

Some thirty years ago a young clergyman by the name of Gunsaulus announced in the newspapers of Chicago that he would preach a sermon the following Sunday morning entitled:

"WHAT I WOULD DO IF I HAD A MILLION DOLLARS!"

The announcement caught the eye of Philip D. Armour, the wealthy packing-house king, who decided to hear the sermon.

In his sermon Dr. Gunsaulus pictured a great school of technology where young men and young women could be taught how to succeed in life by developing the ability to THINK in practical rather than in theoretical terms; where they would be taught to "learn by doing." "If I had a million dollars," said the young preacher, "I would start such a school."

After the sermon was over Mr. Armour walked down the aisle to the pulpit, introduced himself, and said, "Young man, I believe you could do all you said you could, and if you will come down to my office tomorrow morning I will give you the million dollars you need."

There is always plenty of capital for those who can create practical plans for using it.

That was the beginning of the Armour Institute of Technology, one of the very practical schools of the country. The school was born in the "imagination" of a young man who never would have been heard of outside of the community in which he preached had it not been for the "imagination," plus the capital, of Philip D. Armour.

Every great railroad, and every outstanding financial institution and every mammoth business enterprise, and every great invention, began in the imagination of some one person.

F. W. Woolworth created the Five and Ten Cent

Store Plan in his "imagination" before it became a reality and made him a multimillionaire.

Thomas A. Edison created the talking machine and the moving picture machine and the incandescent electric light bulb and scores of other useful inventions, in his own "imagination," before they became a reality.

During the Chicago fire scores of merchants whose stores went up in smoke stood near the smoldering embers of their former places of business, grieving over their loss. Many of them decided to go away into other cities and start over again. In the group was Marshall Field, who saw, in his own "imagination," the world's greatest retail store, standing on the selfsame spot where his former store had stood, which was then but a ruined mass of smoking timbers. That store became a reality.

Fortunate is the young man or young woman who learns, early in life, to use imagination, and doubly so in this age of greater opportunity.

Imagination is a faculty of the mind which can be cultivated, developed, extended and broadened by use. If this were not true, this course on the Fifteen Laws of Success never would have been created, because it was first conceived in the author's "imagination," from the mere seed of an idea which was sown by a chance remark of the late Andrew Carnegie.

Wherever you are, whoever you are, whatever you may be following as an occupation, there is room for you to make yourself more useful, and in that manner more productive, by developing and using your "imagination."

Success in this world is always a matter of individual effort, yet you will only be deceiving yourself if you believe that you can succeed without the co-operation of other people. Success is a matter of individual effort only to the extent that each person must decide, in his or her own mind, what is wanted. This involves the use of "imagination." From this point on, achieving success is a matter of skillfully and tactfully inducing others to co-operate.

Before you can secure co-operation from others; nay, before you have the right to ask for or expect co-operation from other people, you must first show a willingness to co-operate with them. For this reason the eighth lesson of this course, THE HABIT OF DOING MORE THAN PAID FOR, is one which should have your serious and thoughtful attention. The law upon which this lesson is based, would, of itself, practically insure success to all who practice it in all they do.

In the back pages of this Introduction you will observe a Personal Analysis Chart in which ten well known men have been analyzed for your study and comparison. Observe this chart carefully and note the "danger points" which mean failure to those who do not observe these signals. Of the ten men analyzed eight are known to be successful, while two may be considered failures. Study, carefully, the reason why these two men failed.

Then, study yourself. In the two columns which have been left blank for that purpose, give yourself a rating on each of the Fifteen Laws of Success at the beginning of this course; at the end of the course rate yourself again and observe the improvements you have made.

The purpose of the Law of Success course is to enable you to find out how you may become more capable in your chosen field of work. To this end you will be analyzed and all of your qualities classified so you may organize them and make the best possible use of them.

You may not like the work in which you are now engaged.

There are two ways of getting out of that work. One way is to take but little interest in what you are doing, aiming merely to do enough with which to "get by." Very soon you will find a way out, because the demand for your services will cease.

The other and better way is by making yourself so useful and efficient in what you are now doing that you will attract the favorable attention of those who have the power to promote you into more responsible work that is more to your liking.

It is your privilege to take your choice as to which way you will proceed.

Again you are reminded of the importance of Lesson Nine of this course, through the aid of which you may avail yourself of this "better way" of promoting yourself.

Thousands of people walked over the great Calumet Copper Mine without discovering it. Just one lone man used his "imagination," dug down into the earth a few feet, investigated, and discovered the richest copper deposit on earth.

You and every other person walk, at one time or another, over your "Calumet Mine." Discovery is a matter of investigation and use of "imagination." This course on the Fifteen Laws of Success may lead the way to your "Calumet," and you may be surprised when you discover that you were standing right over this rich mine, in the work in which you are now engaged. In his lecture on "Acres of Diamonds," Russell Conwell tells us that we need not seek opportunity in the distance; that we may find it right where we stand! THIS IS A TRUTH WELL WORTH REMEMBERING!

NAPOLEON HILL,
Author of the Law of Success.

This course is the result of careful analysis of the life-work of over one hundred men and women who have achieved unusual success in their respective callings.

The author of the course has been more than twenty years in gathering, classifying, testing and organizing the Fifteen Laws upon which the course is based. In his labor he has received valuable assistance either in person or by studying the life-work of the following men:

Henry Ford	Edward Bok
Thomas A. Edison	Cyrus H. K. Curtis
Harvey S. Firestone	George W. Perkins
John D. Rockefeller	Henry L. Doherty
Charles M. Schwab	George S. Parker
Woodrow Wilson	Dr. C. O. Henry
Darwin P. Kingsley	General Rufus A. Ayers
Wm. Wrigley, Jr.	Judge Elbert H. Gary
A. D. Lasker	William Howard Taft
E. A. Filene	Dr. Elmer Gates
James J. Hill	John W. Davis

The Law of Success

Captain George M. Alexander (To whom the author was formerly an assistant)

Hugh Chalmers

Dr. E. W. Strickler

Edwin C. Barnes

Robert L. Taylor (Fiddling Bob)

George Eastman

E. M. Statler

Andrew Carnegie

John Wanamaker

Marshall Field

Samuel Insul

F. W. Woolworth

Judge Daniel T. Wright (One of the author's law instructors)

Elbert Hubbard

Luther Burbank

O. H. Harriman

John Burroughs

E. H. Harriman

Charles P. Steinmetz

Frank Vanderlip

Theodore Roosevelt

Wm. H. French

Dr. Alexander Graham Bell (To whom the author owes credit for most of Lesson One).

Of the men named, perhaps Henry Ford and Andrew Carnegie should be acknowledged as having contributed most toward the building of this course, for the reason that it was Andrew Carnegie who first suggested the writing of the course and Henry Ford whose life-work supplied much of the material out of which the course was developed.

Some of these men are now deceased, but to those who are still living the author wishes to make here grateful acknowledgment of the service they have rendered, without which this course never could have been written.

The author has studied the majority of these men at close range, in person. With many of them he enjoys, or did enjoy before their death, the privilege of

Acknowledgment

close personal friendship which enabled him to gather from their philosophy facts that would not have been available under other conditions.

The author is grateful for having enjoyed the privilege of enlisting the services of the most powerful men on earth, in the building of the Law of Success course. That privilege has been remuneration enough for the work done, if nothing more were ever received for it.

These men have been the back-bone and the foundation and the skeleton of American business, finance, industry and statesmanship.

The Law of Success course epitomizes the philosophy and the rules of procedure which made each of these men a great power in his chosen field of endeavor. It has been the author's intention to present the course in the plainest and most simple terms available, so it could be mastered by very young men and young women, of the high-school age.

With the exception of the psychological law referred to in Lesson One as the "Master Mind," the author lays no claim to having created anything basically new in this course. What he has done, however, has been to organize old truths and known laws into PRACTICAL, USABLE FORM, where they may be properly interpreted and applied by the workaday man whose needs call for a philosophy of simplicity.

In passing upon the merits of the Law of Success Judge Elbert H. Gary said: "Two outstanding features connected with the philosophy impress me most. One is the simplicity with which it has been presented, and the other is the fact that its soundness is so obvious to all that it will be immediately accepted."

The student of this course is warned against passing

judgment upon it before having read the entire sixteen lessons. This especially applies to this Introduction, in which it has been necessary to include brief reference to subjects of a more or less technical and scientific nature. The reason for this will be obvious after the student has read the entire sixteen lessons.

The student who takes up this course with an open mind, and sees to it that his or her mind remains "open" until the last lesson shall have been read, will be richly rewarded with a broader and more accurate view of life as a whole.

Contents of This Introductory Lesson

1. POWER—what it is and how to create and use it.
2. CO-OPERATION—the psychology of co-operative effort and how to use it constructively.
3. THE MASTER MIND—how it is created through harmony of purpose and effort, between two or more people.
4. HENRY FORD, THOMAS A. EDISON and HARVEY S. FIRESTONE—the secret of their power and wealth.
5. THE "BIG SIX"—how they made the law of the "Master Mind" yield them a profit of more than $25,000,000.00 a year.
6. IMAGINATION—how to stimulate it so that it will create practical plans and new ideas.
7. TELEPATHY—how thought passes from one mind to another through the ether. Every brain both a broadcasting and a receiving station for thought.
8. HOW SALESMEN and PUBLIC SPEAKERS "sense" or "tune in" on the thoughts of their audiences.
9. VIBRATION—described by Dr. Alexander Graham Bell, inventor of the Long Distance Telephone.
10. AIR and ETHER—how they carry vibrations.
11. HOW and WHY ideas "flash" into the mind from unknown sources.

The Law of Success

12. HISTORY of the Law of Success Philosophy, covering a period of over twenty-five years of scientific research and experimentation.
13. JUDGE ELBERT H. GARY reads, approves and adopts the Law of Success course.
14. ANDREW CARNEGIE responsible for beginning of Law of Success course.
15. LAW OF SUCCESS TRAINING—helps group of salespeople earn $1,000,000.00.
16. SO-CALLED "SPIRITUALISM" explained.
17. ORGANIZED EFFORT the source of all power.
18. HOW TO ANALYZE yourself.
19. HOW A SMALL FORTUNE was made from an old, worked-out, worthless (?) farm.
20. THERE'S A GOLD MINE in your present occupation if you will follow directions and dig for it.
21. THERE'S PLENTY OF READY CAPITAL for development of any practical idea or plan you may create.
22. SOME REASONS why people fail.
23. WHY HENRY FORD is the most powerful man on earth, and how others may use the principles which give him his power.
24. WHY SOME PEOPLE antagonize others without knowing it.
25. THE EFFECT of sexual contact as a mind stimulant and health builder.
26. WHAT happens in the religious orgy known as the "revival."
27. WHAT we have learned from "Nature's Bible."
28. CHEMISTRY of the mind; how it will make or destroy you.

Introduction

TIME is a Master Worker that heals the wounds of temporary defeat, and equalizes the inequalities and rights the wrongs of the world. There is nothing "Impossible" with time!

THE LAW OF SUCCESS

Lesson One

THE MASTER MIND

"You Can Do It if You Believe You Can!"

THIS is a course on the fundamentals of Success.

Success is very largely a matter of adjusting one's self to the ever-varying and changing environments of life, in a spirit of harmony and poise. Harmony is based upon understanding of the forces constituting one's environment; therefore, this course is in reality a blueprint that may be followed straight to success, because it helps the student to interpret, understand and make the most of these environmental forces of life.

Before you begin reading the Law of Success lessons you should know something of the history of the course. You should know exactly what the course promises to those who follow it until they have assimilated the laws and principles upon which it is based. You should know its limitations as well as its possibilities as an aid in your fight for a place in the world.

From the viewpoint of entertainment the Law of Success course would be a poor second for most any of the monthly periodicals of the "Snappy Story" variety which may be found upon the news stands of today.

The course has been created for the serious-minded person who devotes at least a portion of his or her time to the business of succeeding in life. The author of the Law of Success course has not intended to compete with those who write purely for the purpose of entertaining.

The author's aim, in preparing this course, has been of a two-fold nature, namely, first—to help the earnest student find out what are his or her weaknesses, and, secondly—to help create a DEFINITE PLAN for bridging those weaknesses.

The most successful men and women on earth have had to correct certain weak spots in their personalities before they began to succeed. The most outstanding of these weaknesses which stand between men and women and success are INTOLERANCE, CUPIDITY, GREED, JEALOUSY, SUSPICION, REVENGE, EGOTISM, CONCEIT, THE TENDENCY TO REAP WHERE THEY HAVE NOT SOWN, and the HABIT OF SPENDING MORE THAN THEY EARN.

All of these common enemies of mankind, and many more not here mentioned, are covered by the Law of Success course in such a manner that any person of reasonable intelligence may master them with but little effort or inconvenience.

You should know, at the very outset, that the Law of Success course has long since passed through the experimental state; that it already has to its credit a record of achievement that is worthy of serious thought and analysis. You should know, also, that the Law of Success course has been examined and endorsed by some of the most practical minds of this generation.

The Law of Success course was first used as a lecture, and was delivered by its author in practically every city and in many of the smaller localities, throughout the United States, over a period of more than seven years. Perhaps you were one of the many hundreds of thousands of people who heard this lecture.

During these lectures the author had assistants located in the audiences for the purpose of interpreting the reaction of those who heard the lecture, and in this manner he learned exactly what effect it had upon people. As a result of this study and analysis many changes were made.

The first big victory was gained for the Law of Success philosophy when it was used by the author as the basis of a course with which 3,000 men and women were trained as a sales army. The majority of these people were without previous experience, of any sort, in the field of selling. Through this training they were enabled to earn more than One Million Dollars ($1,000,000.00) for themselves and paid the author $30,000.00 for his services, covering a period of approximately six months.

The individuals and small groups of salespeople who have found success through the aid of this course are too numerous to be mentioned in this Introduction, but the number is large and the benefits they derived from the course were definite.

The Law of Success philosophy was brought to the

attention of the late Don R. Mellett, former publisher of the Canton (Ohio) Daily News, who formed a partnership with the author of the course and was preparing to resign as publisher of the Canton Daily News and take up the business management of the author's affairs when he was assassinated on July 16, 1926.

Prior to his death Mr. Mellett had made arrangements with Judge Elbert H. Gary, who was then Chairman of the Board of the United States Steel Corporation, to present the Law of Success course to every employee of the Steel Corporation, at a total cost of something like $150,000.00. This plan was halted because of Judge Gary's death, but it proves that the author of the Law of Success has produced an educational plan of an enduring nature. Judge Gary was eminently prepared to judge the value of such a course, and the fact that he analyzed the Law of Success philosophy and was preparing to invest the huge sum of $150,000.00 in it is proof of the soundness of all that is said in behalf of the course.

You will observe, in this General Introduction to the course, a few technical terms which may not be plain to you. Do not allow this to bother you. Make no attempt at first reading to understand these terms. They will be plain to you after you read the remainder of the course. This entire Introduction is intended only as a background for the other fifteen lessons of the course, and you should read it as such. You will not be examined on this Introduction, but you should read it many times, as you will get from it at each reading a thought or an idea which you did not get on previous readings.

In this Introduction you will find a description of a newly discovered law of psychology which is the very foundation stone of all outstanding personal achievements. This law has been referred to by the author as the "Master Mind," meaning a mind that is developed through the harmonious co-operation of two or more people who ally themselves for the purpose of accomplishing any given task.

If you are engaged in the business of selling you may profitably experiment with this law of the "Master Mind" in your daily work. It has been found that a group of six or seven salespeople may use the law so effectively that their sales may be increased to unbelievable proportions.

Life Insurance is supposed to be the hardest thing on earth to sell. This ought not to be true, with an established necessity such as life insurance, but it is. Despite this fact, a small group of men working for the Prudential Life Insurance Company, whose sales are mostly small policies, formed a little friendly group for the purpose of experimenting with the law of the "Master Mind," with the result that every man in the group wrote more insurance during the first three months of the experiment than he had ever written in an entire year before.

What may be accomplished through the aid of this principle, by any small group of intelligent life-insurance salesmen who have learned how to apply the law of the "Master Mind" will stagger the imagination of the most highly optimistic and imaginative person.

The same may be said of other groups of salespeople who are engaged in selling merchandise and other

N

O MAN HAS A CHANCE TO EN-JOY PERMANENT SUCCESS UNTIL HE BEGINS TO LOOK IN A MIRROR FOR THE REAL CAUSE OF ALL HIS MISTAKES.

—*Napoleon Hill.*

more tangible forms of service than life insurance. Bear this in mind as you read this Introduction to the Law of Success course and it is not unreasonable to expect that this Introduction, alone, may give you sufficient understanding of the law to change the entire course of your life.

It is the personalities back of a business which determine the measure of success the business will enjoy. Modify those personalities so they are more pleasing and more attractive to the patrons of the business and the business will thrive. In any of the great cities of the United States one may purchase merchandise of similar nature and price in scores of stores, yet you will find there is always one outstanding store which does more business than any of the others, and the reason for this is that back of that store is a man, or men, who has attended to the personalities of those who come in contact with the public. People buy personalities as much as merchandise, and it is a question if they are not influenced more by the personalities with which they come in contact than they are by the merchandise.

Life insurance has been reduced to such a scientific basis that the cost of insurance does not vary to any great extent, regardless of the company from which one purchases it, yet out of the hundreds of life insurance companies doing business less than a dozen companies do the bulk of the business of the United States.

Why? Personalities! Ninety-nine people out of every hundred who purchase life insurance policies do not know what is in their policies and, what seems more startling, do not seem to care. What they really purchase is the pleasing personality of some man or woman who knows the value of cultivating such a personality.

Your business in life, or at least the most important part of it, is to achieve success. Success, within the meaning of that term as covered by this course on the Fifteen Laws of Success, is "the attainment of your Definite Chief Aim without violating the rights of other people." Regardless of what your major aim in life may be, you will attain it with much less difficulty after you learn how to cultivate a pleasing personality and after you have learned the delicate art of allying yourself with others in a given undertaking without friction or envy.

One of the greatest problems of life, if not, in fact, the greatest, is that of learning the art of harmonious negotiation with others. This course was created for the purpose of teaching people how to negotiate their way through life with harmony and poise, free from the destructive effects of disagreement and friction which bring millions of people to misery, want and failure every year.

With this statement of the purpose of the course you should be able to approach the lessons with the feeling that a complete transformation is about to take place in your personality.

You cannot enjoy outstanding success in life without power, and *you can never enjoy power without sufficient personality to influence other people to co-operate with you in a spirit of harmony*. This course shows you step by step how to develop such a personality.

Lesson by lesson, the following is a statement of

that which you may expect to receive from the Fifteen Laws of Success:

I. A DEFINITE CHIEF AIM will teach you how to save the wasted effort which the majority of people expend in trying to find their life-work. This lesson will show you how to do away forever with aimlessness and fix your heart and hand upon some definite, well conceived purpose as a life-work.

II. SELF-CONFIDENCE will help you master the six basic fears with which every person is cursed—the fear of Poverty, the fear of Ill Health, the fear of Old Age, the fear of Criticism, the fear of Loss of Love of Someone and the fear of Death. It will teach you the difference between egotism and real self-confidence which is based upon definite, usable knowledge.

III. HABIT OF SAVING will teach you how to distribute your income systematically so that a definite percentage of it will steadily accumulate, thus forming one of the greatest known sources of personal power. No one may succeed in life without saving money. There is no exception to this rule, and no one may escape it.

IV. INITIATIVE AND LEADERSHIP will show you how to become a leader instead of a follower in your chosen field of endeavor. It will develop in you the instinct for leadership which will cause you gradually to gravitate to the top in all undertakings in which you participate.

V. IMAGINATION will stimulate your mind so that you will conceive new ideas and develop new plans which will help you in attaining the object of your Definite Chief Aim. This lesson will teach you how to "build new houses out of old stones," so to speak. It will show you how to create new ideas out of old, well known concepts, and how to put old ideas to *new uses*. This one lesson, alone, is the equivalent of a very practical course in salesmanship, and it is sure to prove a veritable gold mine of knowledge to the person who is in earnest.

VI. ENTHUSIASM will enable you to "saturate" all with whom you come in contact with interest in you and in your ideas. Enthusiasm is the foundation of a Pleasing Personality, and you must have such a personality in order to influence others to co-operate with you.

VII. SELF-CONTROL is the "balance wheel" with which you control your enthusiasm and direct it where you wish it to carry you. This lesson will teach you, in a most practical manner, to become "the master of your fate, the Captain of your Soul."

VIII. THE HABIT OF DOING MORE THAN PAID FOR is one of the most important lessons of the Law of Success course. It will teach you how to take advantage of the Law of Increasing Returns, which will eventually insure you a return in money far out of proportion to the service you render. No one may become a real leader in any walk of life without practicing the habit of doing more work and better work than that for which he is paid.

IX. PLEASING PERSONALITY is the "fulcrum" on which you must place the "crow-bar" of your efforts, and when so placed, with intelligence, it will enable you to remove mountains of obstacles. This one lesson, alone, has made scores of Master Salesmen. It has developed leaders over night. It will teach you how to transform your personality so that you may adapt yourself to any environment, or to any other personality, in such a manner that you may easily dominate.

X. ACCURATE THINKING is one of the important foundation stones of all enduring success. This lesson teaches you how to separate "facts" from mere "information." It teaches you how to organize known facts into two classes: the "important" and the "unimportant." It teaches you how to determine what is an "important" fact. It teaches you how to build definite working plans, in the pursuit of any calling, out of FACTS.

XI. CONCENTRATION teaches you how to focus your attention upon one subject at a time until you have worked out practical plans for mastering that subject. It will teach you how to ally yourself with others in such a manner that you may have the use of their entire knowledge to back you up in your own plans and purposes. It will give you a practical working knowledge of the forces around you, and show you how to

If you must slander someone don't speak it—but write it—write it in the sand, near the water's edge!

—*Napoleon Hill.*

harness and use these forces in furthering your own interests.

XII. CO-OPERATION will teach you the value of team-work in all you do. In this lesson you will be taught how to apply the law of the "Master Mind" described in this Introduction and in Lesson Two of this course. This lesson will show you how to co-ordinate your own efforts with those of others, in such a manner that friction, jealousy, strife, envy and cupidity will be eliminated. You will learn how to make use of all that other people have learned about the work in which you are engaged.

XIII. PROFITING BY FAILURE will teach you how to make stepping stones out of all of your past and future mistakes and failures. It will teach you the difference between "failure" and "temporary defeat," a difference which is very great and very important. It will teach you how to profit by your own failures and by the failures of other people.

XIV. TOLERANCE will teach you how to avoid the disastrous effects of racial and religious prejudices which mean defeat for millions of people who permit themselves to become entangled in foolish argument over these subjects, thereby poisoning their own minds and closing the door to reason and investigation. This lesson is the twin sister of the one on ACCURATE THOUGHT, for the reason that no one may become an Accurate Thinker without practicing tolerance. Intolerance closes the book of Knowledge and writes on the cover, "Finis!

I have learned it all!"   Intolerance makes enemies of those who should be friends.   It
destroys opportunity and fills the mind with
doubt, mistrust and prejudice.

XV. PRACTICING THE GOLDEN RULE will
teach you how to make use of this great universal law of human conduct in such a manner
that you may easily get harmonious co-operation from any individual or group of individuals.   Lack of understanding of the law upon
which the Golden Rule philosophy is based is
one of the major causes of failure of millions
of people who remain in misery, poverty and
want all their lives.   This lesson has nothing
whatsoever to do with religion in any form,
nor with sectarianism, nor have any of the other
lessons of this course on the Law of Success.

When you have mastered these Fifteen Laws and
made them your own, as you may do within a period
of from fifteen to thirty weeks, you will be ready to
develop sufficient personal power to insure the attainment of your Definite Chief Aim.

The purpose of these Fifteen Laws is to develop
or help you organize all the knowledge you have, and
all you acquire in the future, so you may turn this
knowledge into POWER.

You should read the Law of Success course with a
note-book by your side, for you will observe that ideas
will begin to "flash" into your mind as you read, as
to ways and means of using these laws in advancing
your own interests.

You should also begin teaching these laws to those

in whom you are most interested, as it is a well known fact that the more one tries to teach a subject the more he learns about that subject. A man who has a family of young boys and girls may so indelibly fix these Fifteen Laws of Success in their minds that this teaching will change the entire course of their lives. The man with a family should interest his wife in studying this course with him, for reasons which will be plain before you complete reading this Introduction.

POWER is one of the three basic objects of human endeavor.

POWER is of two classes—that which is developed through co-ordination of natural physical laws, and that which is developed by organizing and classifying KNOWLEDGE.

POWER growing out of organized knowledge is the more important because it places in man's possession a tool with which he may transform, redirect and to some extent harness and use the other form of power.

The object of this reading course is to mark the route by which the student may safely travel in gathering such facts as he may wish to weave into his fabric of KNOWLEDGE.

There are two major methods of gathering knowledge, namely, by studying, classifying and assimilating facts which have been organized by other people, and through one's own process of gathering, organizing and classifying facts, generally called "personal experience."

This lesson deals mainly with the ways and means of studying the facts and data gathered and classified by other people.

.   .   .   .

The state of advancement known as "civilization" is but the measure of knowledge which the race has accumulated. This knowledge is of two classes— mental and physical.

Among the useful knowledge organized by man, he has discovered and catalogued the eighty-odd physical elements of which all material forms in the universe consist.

By study and analysis and accurate measurements man has discovered the "bigness" of the material side of the universe as represented by planets, suns and stars, some of which are known to be over ten million times as large as the little earth on which he lives.

On the other hand, man has discovered the "littleness" of the physical forms which constitute the universe by reducing the eighty-odd physical elements to molecules, atoms, and, finally, to the smallest particle, the electron. An electron cannot be seen; it is but a center of force consisting of a positive or a negative. The electron is the beginning of everything of a physical nature.

MOLECULES, ATOMS AND ELECTRONS: To understand both the detail and the perspective of the process through which knowledge is gathered, organized and classified, it seems essential for the student to begin with the smallest and simplest particles of physical matter, because these are the A B C's with which Nature has constructed the entire frame-work of the physical portion of the universe.

The molecule consists of atoms, which are said to be little invisible particles of matter revolving continuously with the speed of lightning, on exactly the same principle that the earth revolves around the sun.

These little particles of matter known as atoms, which revolve in one continuous circuit, in the molecule, are said to be made up of electrons, the smallest particles of physical matter. As already stated, the electron is nothing but two forms of force. The electron is uniform, of but one class, size and nature; thus in a grain of sand or a drop of water the entire principle upon which the whole universe operates is duplicated.

How marvelous! How stupendous! You may gather some slight idea of the magnitude of it all the next time you eat a meal, by remembering that every article of food you eat, the plate on which you eat it, the tableware and the table itself are, in final analysis, but a collection of ELECTRONS.

In the world of physical matter, whether one is looking at the largest star that floats through the heavens or the smallest grain of sand to be found on earth, the object under observation is but an organized collection of molecules, atoms and electrons revolving around one another at inconceivable speed.

Every particle of physical matter is in a continuous state of highly agitated motion. Nothing is ever still, although nearly all physical matter may appear, to the physical eye, to be motionless. There is no "solid" physical matter. The hardest piece of steel is but an organized mass of revolving molecules, atoms and electrons. Moreover, the electrons in a piece of steel are of the same nature, and move at the same rate of speed as the electrons in gold, silver, brass or pewter.

The eighty-odd forms of physical matter appear to be different from one another, and they are different,

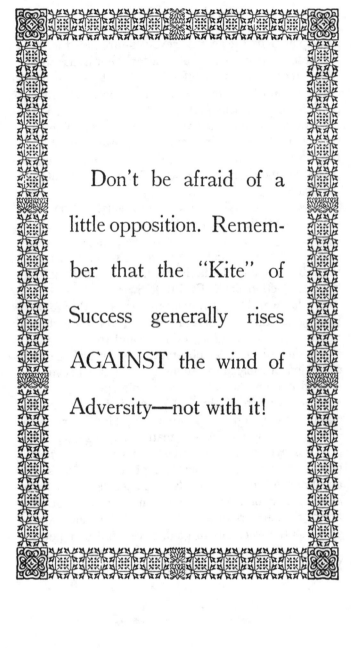

Don't be afraid of a little opposition. Remember that the "Kite" of Success generally rises AGAINST the wind of Adversity—not with it!

because they are made up of different combinations of atoms (although the electrons in these atoms are always the same, except that some electrons are positive and some are negative, meaning that some carry a positive charge of electrification while others carry a negative charge).

Through the science of chemistry, matter may be broken up into atoms which are, within themselves, unchangeable. The eighty-odd elements are created through and by reason of combining and changing of the positions of the atoms. To illustrate the modus operandi of chemistry through which this change of atomic position is wrought, in terms of modern science:

"Add four electrons (two positive and two negative) to the hydrogen atom, and you have the element lithium; knock out of the lithium atom (composed of three positive and three negative electrons) one positive and one negative electron, and you have one atom of helium (composed of two positive and two negative electrons)."

Thus it may be seen that the eighty-odd physical elements of the universe differ from one another only in the number of electrons composing their atoms, and the number and arrangement of those atoms in the molecules of each element.

As an illustration, an atom of mercury contains eighty positive charges (electrons) in its nucleus, and eighty negative outlying charges (electrons). If the chemist were to expel two of its positive electrons it would instantly become the metal known as platinum. If the chemist could then go a step further and take from it a negative ("planetary") electron, the mercury atom would then have lost two positive electrons and one negative; that is, one positive charge on the whole; hence it would retain seventy-nine positive charges in the nucleus and seventy-nine outlying negative electrons, thereby becoming GOLD!

The formula through which this electronic change might be produced has been the object of diligent search by the alchemists all down the ages, and by the modern chemists of today.

It is a fact known to every chemist that literally tens of thousands of synthetic substances may be composed out of only four kinds of atoms, viz.: hydrogen, oxygen, nitrogen and carbon.

"Differences in the number of electrons in atoms confer upon them qualitative (chemical) differences, though all atoms of any one element are chemically alike. Differences in the number and spacial arrangement of these atoms (in groups of molecules) constitute both physical and chemical differences in substances, i.e., in compounds. Quite different substances are produced by combinations of precisely the same kinds of atoms, but in different proportions.

"Take from a molecule of certain substances one single atom, and they may be changed from a compound necessary to life and growth into a deadly poison. Phosphorus is an element, and thus contains but one kind of atoms; but some phosphorus is yellow and some is red, varying with the spacial distribution of the atoms in the molecules composing the phosphorus."

It may be stated as a literal truth that the atom is the universal particle with which Nature builds all material forms, from a grain of sand to the largest star that floats through space. The atom is Nature's "building block" out of which she erects an oak tree or a pine, a rock of sandstone or granite, a mouse or an elephant.

Some of the ablest thinkers have reasoned that the earth on which we live, and every material particle on the earth, began with two atoms which attached themselves to each other, and through hundreds of millions of years of flight through space, kept contacting and accumulating other atoms until, step by step, the earth was formed. This, they point out, would account for the various and differing strata of the earth's substances, such as the coal beds, the iron ore deposits, the gold and silver deposits, the copper deposits, etc.

They reason that, as the earth whirled through space, it contacted groups of various kinds of nebulæ, or atoms, which it promptly appropriated, through the law of magnetic attraction. There is much to be seen, in the earth's surface composition, to support this theory, although there may be no positive evidence of its soundness.

These facts concerning the smallest analyzable particles of matter have been briefly referred to as a starting point from which we shall undertake to ascertain how to develop and apply the law of POWER.

It has been noticed that all matter is in a constant state of vibration or motion; that the molecule is made up of rapidly moving particles called atoms, which, in turn, are made up of rapidly moving particles called electrons.

THE VIBRATING FLUID OF MATTER: In every particle of matter there is an invisible "fluid" or force which causes the atoms to circle around one another at an inconceivable rate of speed.

This "fluid" is a form of energy which has never been analyzed. Thus far it has baffled the entire scientific world. By many scientists it is believed to be the same energy as that which we call electricity. Others prefer to call it vibration. It is believed by some investigators that the rate of speed with which this force (call it whatever you will) moves determines to a large extent the nature of the outward visible appearance of the physical objects of the universe.

One rate of vibration of this "fluid energy" causes what is known as sound. The human ear can detect only the sound which is produced through from 32,000 to 38,000 vibrations per second.

As the rate of vibrations per second increases above that which we call sound they begin to manifest themselves in the form of heat. Heat begins with about 1,500,000 vibrations per second.

Still higher up the scale vibrations begin to register in the form of light. 3,000,000 vibrations per second create violet light. Above this number vibration sheds ultra-violet rays (which are invisible to the naked eye) and other invisible radiations.

And, still higher up the scale—just how high no one at present seems to know—vibrations create the power with which man THINKS.

It is the belief of the author that the "fluid" portion of all vibration, out of which grow all known forms of energy, is universal in nature; that the "fluid" portion of sound is the same as the "fluid" portion of light, the difference in effect between sound and light being only a difference in rate of vibration, also that the "fluid" portion of thought is exactly the same as that in sound, heat and light, excepting the number of vibrations per second.

Just as there is but one form of physical matter, of which the earth and all the other planets—suns and stars—are composed—the electron—so is there but one form of "fluid" energy, which causes all matter to remain in a constant state of rapid motion.

AIR AND ETHER: The vast space between the suns, moons, stars and other planets of the universe is filled with a form of energy known as ether. It is this author's belief that the "fluid" energy which keeps all particles of matter in motion is the same as the universal "fluid" known as ether which fills all the space of the universe. Within a certain distance of the earth's surface, estimated by some to be about fifty miles, there exists what is called air, which is a gaseous substance composed of oxygen and nitrogen. Air is a conductor of sound vibrations, but a non-conductor of light and the higher vibrations, which are carried by the ether. The ether is a conductor of all vibrations from sound to thought.

Air is a localized substance which performs, in the main, the service of feeding all animal and plant life with oxygen and nitrogen, without which neither could exist. Nitrogen is one of the chief necessities of plant life and oxygen one of the mainstays of animal life. Near the top of very high mountains the air becomes very light, because it contains but little nitrogen, which is the reason why plant life cannot exist there. On the other hand, the "light" air found in high altitudes

Render more service
than that for which you
are paid and you will soon
be paid for more than
you render. The law
of "Increasing Returns"
takes care of this.

consists largely of oxygen, which is the chief reason why tubercular patients are sent to high altitudes.

.   .   .   .

Even this brief statement concerning molecules, atoms, electrons, air, ether and the like, may be heavy reading to the student, but, as will be seen shortly, this introduction plays an essential part as the foundation of this lesson.

Do not become discouraged if the description of this foundation appears to have none of the thrilling effects of a modern tale of fiction. You are seriously engaged in finding out what are your available powers and how to organize and apply these powers. To complete this discovery successfully you must combine determination, persistency and a well defined DESIRE to gather and organize knowledge.

.   .   .   .

The late Dr. Alexander Graham Bell, inventor of the long distance telephone and one of the accepted authorities on the subject of vibration, is here introduced in support of this author's theories concerning the subject of vibration:

"Suppose you have the power to make an iron rod vibrate with any desired frequency in a dark room. At first, when vibrating slowly, its movement will be indicated by only one sense, that of touch. As soon as the vibrations increase, a low sound will emanate from it and it will appeal to two senses.

"At about 32,000 vibrations to the second the sound will be loud and shrill, but at 40,000 vibrations it will be silent and the movements of the rod will not be perceived by touch. Its movements will be perceived by no ordinary human sense.

"From this point up to about 1,500,000 vibrations per second, we have no sense that can appreciate any effect of the intervening vibrations. After that stage is reached, movement is indicated first by the sense of temperature and then, when the rod becomes red hot, by the sense of sight. At 3,000,000 it sheds violet light. Above that it sheds ultra-violet rays and other invisible radiations, some of which can be perceived by instruments and employed by us.

"Now it has occurred to me that there must be a great deal to be learned about the effect of those vibrations in the great gap where the ordinary human senses are unable to hear, see or feel the movement. The power to send wireless messages by ether vibrations lies in that gap, but the gap is so great that it seems there must be much more. You must make machines practically to supply new senses, as the wireless instruments do.

"Can it be said, when you think of that great gap, that there are not many forms of vibrations that may give us results as wonderful as, or even more wonderful than, the wireless waves? It seems to me that in this gap lie the vibrations which we have assumed to be given off by our brains and nerve cells when we think. But then, again, they may be higher up, in the scale beyond the vibrations that produce the ultra-violet rays. [AUTHOR'S NOTE: The last sentence suggests the theory held by this author.]

"Do we need a wire to carry these vibrations? Will they not pass through the ether without a wire, just as the wireless waves do? How will they be perceived by the recipient? Will he hear a series of signals or will he find that another man's thoughts have entered into his brain?

"We may indulge in some speculations based on what we know of the wireless waves, which, as I have said, are all we can recognize of a vast series of vibrations which theoretically must exist. If the thought waves are similar to the wireless waves, they must pass from the brain and flow endlessly around the world and the universe. The body and the skull and other solid obstacles would form no obstruction to their passage, as they pass through the ether which surrounds the molecules of every substance, no matter how solid and dense.

"You ask if there would not be constant interference and confusion if other people's thoughts were flowing through our brains and setting up thoughts in them that did not originate with ourselves?

"How do you know that other men's thoughts are not interfering with yours now? I have noticed a good many phenomena of mind disturbances that I have never been able to explain. For instance, there is the inspiration or the discouragement that a speaker feels in addressing an audience. I have experienced this many times in my life and have never been able to define exactly the physical causes of it.

"Many recent scientific discoveries, in my opinion, point to a day not far distant perhaps, when men will read one another's thoughts, when thoughts will be conveyed directly from brain to brain without intervention of speech, writing or any of the present known methods of communication.

"It is not unreasonable to look forward to a time

when we shall see without eyes, hear without ears and talk without tongues.

"Briefly, the hypothesis that mind can communicate directly with mind rests on the theory that thought or vital force is a form of electrical disturbance, that it can be taken up by induction and transmitted to a distance either through a wire or simply through the all-pervading ether, as in the case of wireless telegraph waves.

"There are many analogies which suggest that thought is of the nature of an electrical disturbance. A nerve, which is of the same substance as the brain, is an excellent conductor of the electric current. When we first passed an electrical current through the nerves of a dead man we were shocked and amazed to see him sit up and move. The electrified nerves produced contraction of the muscles very much as in life.

"The nerves appear to act upon the muscles very much as the electric current acts upon an electromagnet. The current magnetizes a bar of iron placed at right angles to it, and the nerves produce, through the intangible current of vital force that flows through them, contraction of the muscular fibers that are arranged at right angles to them.

"It would be possible to cite many reasons why thought and vital force may be regarded as of the same nature as electricity. The electric current is held to be a wave motion of the ether, the hypothetical substance that fills all space and pervades all substances. We believe that there must be ether because without it the electric current could not pass through a vacuum, or sunlight through space. It is reasonable to believe that only a wave motion of a similar character can produce the phenomena of thought and vital force. We may assume that the brain cells act as a battery and that the current produced flows along the nerves.

"But does it end there? Does it not pass out of the body in waves which flow around the world unperceived by our senses, just as the wireless waves passed unperceived before Hertz and others discovered their existence?"

EVERY MIND BOTH A BROADCASTING AND A RECEIVING STATION: This author has proved, times too numerous to enumerate, to his own satisfaction at least, that every human brain is both a broadcasting and a receiving station for vibrations of thought frequency.

If this theory should turn out to be a fact, and methods of reasonable control should be established, imagine the part it would play in the gathering, classifying and organizing of knowledge. The possibility, much less the probability, of such a reality, staggers the mind of man!

Thomas Paine was one of the great minds of the American Revolutionary Period. To him more, perhaps, than to any other one person, we owe both the beginning and the happy ending of the Revolution, for it was his keen mind that both helped in drawing up the Declaration of Independence and in persuading the signers of that document to translate it into terms of reality.

In speaking of the source of his great storehouse of knowledge, Paine thus described it:

"Any person, who has made observations on the

Every failure is a bless-
ing in disguise, providing
it teaches some needed
lesson one could not have
learned without it. Most
so-called Failures a r e
only temporary defeats.

state of progress of the human mind, by observing his own, cannot but have observed that there are two distinct classes of what are called Thoughts: those that we produce in ourselves by reflection and the act of thinking, and those that bolt into the mind of their own accord. I have always made it a rule to treat these voluntary visitors with civility, taking care to examine, as well as I was able, if they were worth entertaining; and it is from them I have acquired almost all the knowledge that I have. As to the learning that any person gains from school education, it serves only like a small capital, to put him in the way of beginning learning for himself afterwards. Every person of learning is finally his own teacher, the reason for which is, that principles cannot be impressed upon the memory; their place of mental residence is the understanding, and they are never so lasting as when they begin by conception."

In the foregoing words Paine, the great American patriot and philosopher, described an experience which at one time or another is the experience of every person. Who is there so unfortunate as not to have received positive evidence that thoughts and even complete ideas will "pop" into the mind from outside sources?

What means of conveyance is there for such visitors except the ether? Ether fills the boundless space of the universe. It is the medium of conveyance for all known forms of vibration such as sound, light and heat. Why should it not be, also, the medium of conveyance of the vibration of Thought?

Every mind, or brain, is directly connected with every other brain by means of the ether. Every thought released by any brain may be instantly picked up and interpreted by all other brains that are "en rapport" with the sending brain. This author is as sure of this fact as he is that the chemical formula H_2O will produce water. Imagine, if you can, what a part this principle plays in every walk of life.

Nor is the probability of ether being a conveyor of thought from mind to mind the most astounding of its performances. It is the belief of this author that every thought vibration released by any brain is picked up by the ether and kept in motion in circuitous wave lengths corresponding in length to the intensity of the energy used in their release; that these vibrations remain in motion forever; that they are one of the two sources from which thoughts which "pop" into one's mind emanate, the other source being direct and immediate contact through the ether with the brain releasing the thought vibration.

Thus it will be seen that if this theory is a fact the boundless space of the whole universe is now and will continue to become literally a mental library wherein may be found all the thoughts released by mankind.

The author is here laying the foundation for one of the most important hypotheses enumerated in the lesson Self-confidence, a fact which the student should keep in mind as he approaches that lesson.

This is a lesson on Organized Knowledge. Most of the useful knowledge to which the human race has become heir has been preserved and accurately recorded in Nature's Bible. By turning back the pages of this unalterable Bible man has read the story of the terrific struggle through and out of which the present civilization has grown. The pages of this Bible are made up of the physical elements of which this earth and the other planets consist, and of the ether which fills all space.

By turning back the pages written on stone and covered near the surface of this earth on which he lives, man has uncovered the bones, skeletons, footprints and other unmistakable evidence of the history of animal life on this earth, planted there for his enlightenment and guidance by the hand of Mother Nature throughout unbelievable periods of time. The evidence is plain and unmistakable. The great stone pages of Nature's Bible found on this earth and the endless pages of that Bible represented by the ether wherein all past human thought has been recorded, constitute an authentic source of communication between the Creator and man. This Bible was begun before man had reached the thinking stage; indeed, before man had reached the amœba (one-cell animal) stage of development.

This Bible is above and beyond the power of man to alter. Moreover, it tells its story not in the ancient dead languages or hieroglyphics of half savage races, but in universal language which all who have eyes may read. Nature's Bible, from which we have derived all the knowledge that is worth knowing, is one that no man may alter or in any manner tamper with.

The most marvelous discovery yet made by man is that of the recently discovered radio principle, which operates through the aid of ether, an important portion of Nature's Bible. Imagine the ether picking up the ordinary vibration of sound, and transforming that vibration from audio-frequency into radio-frequency, carrying it to a properly attuned receiving station and there transforming it back into its original form of audio-frequency, all in the flash of a second. It should surprise no one that such a force could gather up the vibration of thought and keep that vibration in motion forever.

The established and known fact of instantaneous transmission of sound, through the agency of the ether, by means of the modern radio apparatus, removes the theory of transmission of thought vibration from mind to mind from the possible to the probable.

THE MASTER MIND: We come, now, to the next step in the description of the ways and means by which one may gather, classify and organize useful knowledge, through harmonious alliance of two or more minds, out of which grows a Master Mind.

The term "Master Mind" is abstract, and has no counterpart in the field of known facts, except to a small number of people who have made a careful study of the effect of one mind upon other minds.

This author has searched in vain through all the textbooks and essays available on the subject of the human mind, but nowhere has been found even the slightest reference to the principle here described as the "Master Mind." The term first came to the attention of the author through an interview with Andrew Carnegie, in the manner described in Lesson Two.

CHEMISTRY OF THE MIND: It is this author's belief that the mind is made up of the same universal "fluid" energy as that which constitutes the ether which fills the universe. It is a fact as well known to the layman as to the man of scientific investigation, that some minds clash the moment they come in contact with each other, while other minds show a natural affinity for each other. Between the two extremes of natural antagonism and natural affinity growing out of the meeting or contacting of minds there is a wide range of possibility for varying reactions of mind upon mind.

Some minds are so naturally adapted to each other that "love at first sight" is the inevitable outcome of the contact. Who has not known of such an experience? In other cases minds are so antagonistic that violent mutual dislike shows itself at first meeting. These results occur without a word being spoken, and without the slightest signs of any of the usual causes for love and hate acting as a stimulus.

It is quite probable that the "mind" is made up of a fluid or substance or energy, call it what you will, similar to (if not in fact the same substance as) the ether. When two minds come close enough to each other to form a contact, the mixing of the units of this "mind stuff" (let us call it the electrons of the ether) sets up a chemical reaction and starts vibrations which affect the two individuals pleasantly or unpleasantly.

The effect of the meeting of two minds is obvious to even the most casual observer. Every effect must have a cause! What could be more reasonable than to suspect that the cause of the change in mental attitude between two minds which have just come in close contact is none other than the disturbance of the electrons or units of each mind in the process of rearranging themselves in the new field created by the contact?

TO BELIEVE IN
THE HEROIC
MAKES HEROES.

—*Disraeli.*

For the purpose of establishing this lesson upon a sound foundation we have gone a long way toward success by admitting that the meeting or coming in close contact of two minds sets up in each of those minds a certain noticeable "effect" or state of mind quite different from the one existing immediately prior to the contact. While it is desirable it is not essential to know what is the "cause" of this reaction of mind upon mind. That the reaction takes place, in every instance, is a known fact which gives us a starting point from which we may show what is meant by the term "Master Mind."

A Master Mind may be created through the bringing together or blending, in a spirit of perfect harmony, of two or more minds. Out of this harmonious blending the chemistry of the mind creates a third mind which may be appropriated and used by one or all of the individual minds. This Master Mind will remain available as long as the friendly, harmonious alliance between the individual minds exists. It will disintegrate and all evidence of its former existence will disappear the moment the friendly alliance is broken.

This principle of mind chemistry is the basis and cause for practically all the so-called "soul-mate" and "eternal triangle" cases, so many of which unfortunately find their way into the divorce courts and meet with popular ridicule from ignorant and uneducated people who manufacture vulgarity and scandal out of one of the greatest of Nature's laws.

The entire civilized world knows that the first two or three years of association after marriage are often marked by much disagreement, of a more or less petty nature. These are the years of "adjustment." If the marriage survives them it is more than apt to become a permanent alliance. These facts no experienced married person will deny. Again we see the "effect" without understanding the "cause."

While there are other contributing causes, yet, in the main, lack of harmony during these early years of marriage is due to the slowness of the chemistry of the minds in blending harmoniously. Stated differently, the electrons or units of the energy called the mind are often neither extremely friendly nor antagonistic upon first contact; but, through constant association they gradually adapt themselves in harmony, except in rare cases where association has the opposite effect of leading, eventually, to open hostility between these units.

It is a well known fact that after a man and a woman have lived together for ten to fifteen years they become practically indispensable to each other, even though there may not be the slightest evidence of the state of mind called love. Moreover, this association and relationship sexually not only develops a natural affinity between the two minds, but it actually causes the two people to take on a similar facial expression and to resemble each other closely in many other marked ways. Any competent analyst of human nature can easily go into a crowd of strange people and pick out the wife after having been introduced to her husband. The expression of the eyes, the contour of the faces and the tone of the voices of people who have long been associated in marriage, become similar to a marked degree.

So marked is the effect of the chemistry of the human mind that any experienced public speaker may quickly interpret the manner in which his statements are accepted by his audience. Antagonism in the mind of but one person in an audience of one thousand may be readily detected by the speaker who has learned how to "feel" and register the effects of antagonism. Moreover, the public speaker can make these interpretations without observing or in any manner being influenced by the expression on the faces of those in his audience. On account of this fact an audience may cause a speaker to rise to great heights of oratory, or heckle him into failure, without making a sound or denoting a single expression of satisfaction or dissatisfaction through the features of the face.

All "Master Salesmen" know the moment the "psychological time for closing" has arrived; not by what the prospective buyer says, but from the effect of the chemistry of his mind as interpreted or "felt" by the salesman. Words often belie the intentions of those speaking them but a correct interpretation of the chemistry of the mind leaves no loophole for such a possibility. Every able salesman knows that the majority of buyers have the habit of affecting a negative attitude almost to the very climax of a sale.

Every able lawyer has developed a sixth sense whereby he is enabled to "feel" his way through the most artfully selected words of the clever witness who is lying, and correctly interpret that which is in the witness's mind, through the chemistry of the mind. Many lawyers have developed this ability without knowing the real source of it; they possess the technique without the scientific understanding upon which it is based. Many salesmen have done the same thing.

One who is gifted in the art of correctly interpreting

the chemistry of the minds of others may, figuratively speaking, walk in at the front door of the mansion of a given mind and leisurely explore the entire building, noting all its details, walking out again with a complete picture of the interior of the building, without the owner of the building so much as knowing that he has entertained a visitor. It will be observed, in the lesson Accurate Thinking, that this principle may be put to a very practical use (having reference to the principle of the chemistry of the mind). The principle is referred to merely as an approach to the major principles of this lesson.

Enough has already been stated to introduce the principle of mind chemistry, and to prove, with the aid of the student's own every-day experiences and casual observations that the moment two minds come within close range of each other a noticeable mental change takes place in both, sometimes registering in the nature of antagonism and at other times registering in the nature of friendliness. Every mind has what might be termed an electric field. The nature of this field varies, depending upon the "mood" of the individual mind back of it, and upon the nature of the chemistry of the mind creating the "field."

It is believed by this author that the normal or natural condition of the chemistry of any individual mind is the result of his physical heredity plus the nature of thoughts which have dominated that mind; that every mind is continuously changing to the extent that the individual's philosophy and general habits of thought change the chemistry of his or her mind. These principles the author BELIEVES to be true. That any individual may voluntarily change the chemistry of his or her mind so that it will either attract or repel all with whom it comes in contact is a KNOWN FACT! Stated in another manner, any person may assume a mental attitude which will attract and please others or repel and antagonize them, and this without the aid of words or facial expression or other form of bodily movement or demeanor.

Go back, now, to the definition of a "Master Mind" —a mind which grows out of the blending and co-ordination of two or more minds, IN A SPIRIT OF PERFECT HARMONY, and you will catch the full significance of the word "harmony" as it is here used. Two minds will not blend nor can they be co-ordinated unless the element of perfect harmony is present, wherein lies the secret of success or failure of practically all business and social partnerships.

Every sales manager and every military commander and every leader in any other walk of life understands the necessity of an "esprit de corps"—a spirit of common understanding and co-operation—in the attainment of success. This mass spirit of harmony of purpose is obtained through discipline, voluntary or forced, of such a nature that the individual minds become blended into a "Master Mind," by which is meant that the chemistry of the individual minds is modified in such a manner that these minds blend and function as one.

The methods through which this blending process takes place are as numerous as the individuals engaged in the various forms of leadership. Every leader has his or her own method of co-ordinating the minds of the followers. One will use force. Another uses per-

IF YOU DO NOT BE-
LIEVE IN CO-OP-
ERATION, LOOK
WHAT HAPPENS TO
A WAGON THAT
LOSES A WHEEL.

suasion. One will play upon the fear of penalties
while another plays upon rewards, in order to reduce
the individual minds of a given group of people to
where they may be blended into a mass mind. The
student will not have to search deeply into history of
statesmanship, politics, business or finance, to discover
the technique employed by the leaders in these fields
in the process of blending the minds of individuals
into a mass mind.

The really great leaders of the world, however, have
been provided by Nature with a combination of mind
chemistry favorable as a nucleus of attraction for
other minds. Napoleon was a notable example of a
man possessing the magnetic type of mind which had
a very decided tendency to attract all minds with
which it came in contact. Soldiers followed Napoleon
to certain death without flinching, because of the impelling or attracting nature of his personality, and that
personality was nothing more nor less than the chemistry of his mind.

No group of minds can be blended into a Master
Mind if one of the individuals of that group possesses
one of these extremely negative, repellent minds. The
negative and positive minds will not blend in the sense
here described as a Master Mind. Lack of knowledge
of this fact has brought many an otherwise able leader
to defeat.

Any able leader who understands this principle of
mind chemistry may temporarily blend the minds of
practically any group of people, so that it will represent a mass mind, but the composition will disintegrate almost the very moment the leader's presence is
removed from the group. The most successful life-

insurance sales organizations and other sales forces meet once a week, or more often, for the purpose of— OF WHAT?

FOR THE PURPOSE OF MERGING THE INDIVIDUAL MINDS INTO A MASTER MIND WHICH WILL, FOR A LIMITED NUMBER OF DAYS, SERVE AS A STIMULUS TO THE INDIVIDUAL MINDS!

It may be, and generally is, true that the leaders of these groups do not understand what actually takes place in these meetings, which are usually called "pep meetings." The routine of such meetings is usually given over to talks by the leader and other members of the group, and occasionally from someone outside of the group, meanwhile the minds of the individuals are contacting and recharging one another.

The brain of a human being may be compared to an electric battery in that it will become exhausted or run down, causing the owner of it to feel despondent, discouraged and lacking in "pep." Who is so fortunate as never to have had such a feeling? The human brain, when in this depleted condition, must be recharged, and the manner in which this is done is through contact with a more vital mind or minds. The great leaders understand the necessity of this "recharging" process, and, moreover, they understand how to accomplish this result. THIS KNOWLEDGE IS THE MAIN FEATURE WHICH DISTINGUISHES A LEADER FROM A FOLLOWER!

Fortunate is the person who understands this principle sufficiently well to keep his or her brain vitalized or "recharged" by periodically contacting it with a more vital mind. Sexual contact is one of the most effective of the stimuli through which a mind may be recharged, providing the contact is intelligently made, between man and woman who have genuine affection for each other. Any other sort of sexual relationship is a devitalizer of the mind. Any competent practitioner of Psycho-therapeutics can "recharge" a brain within a few minutes.

Before passing away from the brief reference made to sexual contact as a means of revitalizing a depleted mind it seems appropriate to call attention to the fact that all of the great leaders, in whatever walks of life they have arisen, have been and are people of highly sexed natures. (The word "sex" is not an indecent word. You'll find it in all the dictionaries.)

There is a growing tendency upon the part of the best informed physicians and other health practitioners, to accept the theory that all diseases begin when the brain of the individual is in a depleted or devitalized state. Stated in another way, it is a known fact that a person who has a perfectly vitalized brain is practically, if not entirely, immune from all manner of disease.

Every intelligent health practitioner, of whatever school or type, knows that "Nature" or the mind cures disease in every instance where a cure is effected. Medicines, faith, laying on of hands, chiropractic, osteopathy and all other forms of outside stimulant are nothing more than artificial aids to NATURE, or, to state it correctly, mere methods of setting the chemistry of the mind into motion to the end that it readjusts the cells and tissues of the body, revitalizes the brain and otherwise causes the human machine to function normally.

The most orthodox practitioner will admit the truth of this statement.

What, then, may be the possibilities of the future developments in the field of mind chemistry?

Through the principle of harmonious blending of minds perfect health may be enjoyed. Through the aid of this same principle sufficient power may be developed to solve the problem of economic pressure which constantly presses upon every individual.

We may judge the future possibilities of mind chemistry by taking inventory of its past achievements, keeping in mind the fact that these achievements have been largely the result of accidental discovery and of chance groupings of minds. We are approaching the time when the professorate of the universities will teach mind chemistry the same as other subjects are now taught. Meanwhile, study and experimentation in connection with this subject open vistas of possibility for the individual student.

.   .   .   .

MIND CHEMISTRY AND ECONOMIC POWER: That mind chemistry may be appropriately applied to the workaday affairs of the economic and commercial world is a demonstrable fact.

Through the blending of two or more minds, in a spirit of PERFECT HARMONY, the principle of mind chemistry may be made to develop sufficient power to enable the individuals whose minds have been thus blended to perform seemingly superhuman feats. Power is the force with which man achieves success in any undertaking. Power, in unlimited quantities, may be enjoyed by any group of men, or men and women, who possess the wisdom with which to submerge their own personalities and their own immediate individual interests, through the blending of their minds in a spirit of perfect harmony.

Observe, profitably, the frequency with which the word "harmony" appears throughout this Introduction! There can be no development of a "Master Mind" where this element of PERFECT HARMONY does not exist. The individual units of the mind will not blend with the individual units of another mind UNTIL THE TWO MINDS HAVE BEEN AROUSED AND WARMED, AS IT WERE, WITH A SPIRIT OF PERFECT HARMONY OF PURPOSE. The moment two minds begin to take divergent roads of interest the individual units of each mind separate, and the third element, known as a "MASTER MIND," which grew out of the friendly or harmonious alliance, will disintegrate.

We come, now, to the study of some well known men who have accumulated great power (also great fortunes) through the application of mind chemistry.

Let us begin our study with three men who are known to be men of great achievement in their respective fields of economic, business and professional endeavor.

Their names are Henry Ford, Thomas A. Edison and Harvey S. Firestone.

Of the three Henry Ford is, by far, the most POWERFUL, having reference to economic and financial power. Mr. Ford is the most powerful man now living on earth. Many who have studied Mr. Ford believe him to be the most powerful man who ever

COURAGE IS THE STANDING ARMY OF THE SOUL WHICH KEEPS IT FROM CONQUEST, PILLAGE AND SLAVERY.

—*Henry van Dyke.*

lived. As far as is known Mr. Ford is the only man now living, or who ever lived, with sufficient power to outwit the money trust of the United States. Mr. Ford gathers millions of dollars with as great ease as a child fills its bucket with sand when playing on the beach. It has been said, by those who were in position to know, that Mr. Ford, if he needed it, could send out the call for money and gather in a billion dollars (a thousand million dollars) and have it available for use within one week. No one who knows of Ford's achievements doubts this. Those who know him well know that he could do it with no more effort than the average man expends in raising the money with which to pay a month's house rent. He could get this money, if he needed it, through the intelligent application of the principles on which this course is based.

While Mr. Ford's new automobile was in the process of perfection, in 1927, it is said that he received advance orders, with cash payments, for more than 375,000 cars. At an estimated price of $600.00 per car this would amount to $225,000,000.00 which he received before a single car was delivered. Such is the power of confidence in Ford's ability.

Mr. Edison, as everyone knows, is a philosopher, scientist and inventor. He is, perhaps, the keenest Bible student on earth; a student of Nature's Bible, however, and not of the myriads of man-made Bibles. Mr. Edison has such a keen insight into Mother Nature's Bible that he has harnessed and combined, for the good of mankind, more of Nature's laws than any other person now living or who ever lived. It was he who brought together the point of a needle and a piece of revolving wax, in such a way that the vibration of the human voice may be recorded and reproduced through the modern talking machine.

(And it may be Edison who will eventually enable man to pick up and correctly interpret the vibrations of thought which are now recorded in the boundless universe of ether, just as he has enabled man to record and reproduce the spoken word.)

It was Edison who first harnessed the lightning and made it serve as a light for man's use, through the aid of the incandescent electric light bulb.

It was Edison who gave the world the modern moving picture.

These are but a few of his outstanding achievements. These modern "miracles" which he has performed (not by trickery, under the sham pretense of superhuman power, but in the very midst of the bright light of science) transcend all of the so-called "miracles" described in the man-made books of fiction.

Mr. Firestone is the moving spirit in the great Firestone Tire industry, in Akron, Ohio. His industrial achievements are so well known wherever automobiles are used that no special comment on them seems necessary.

All three of these men began their careers, business and professional, without capital and with but little schooling of that type usually referred to as "education."

All three men are now well educated. All three are wealthy. All three are powerful. Now let us inquire into the source of their wealth and power. Thus far we have been dealing only with effect; the true philosopher wishes to understand the *cause* of a given effect.

It is a matter of general knowledge that Mr. Ford, Mr. Edison and Mr. Firestone are close personal friends, and have been so for many years; that in former years they were in the habit of going away to the woods once a year for a period of rest, meditation and recuperation.

But it is not generally known—it is a grave doubt if these three men themselves know it—that there exists between the three men a bond of harmony which has caused their minds to become blended into a "Master Mind" which is the real source of the power of each. This mass mind, growing out of the co-ordination of the individual minds of Ford, Edison and Firestone, has enabled these men to "tune in" on forces (and sources of knowledge) with which most men are to no extent familiar.

If the student doubts either the principle or the effects here described, let him remember that more than half the theory here set forth is a known fact. For example, it is known that these three men have great power. It is known that they are wealthy. It is known that they began without capital and with but little schooling. It is known that they form periodic mind contacts. It is known that they are harmonious and friendly. It is known that their achievements are so outstanding as to make it impossible to compare these achievements with those of other men in their respective fields of activity.

All these "effects" are known to practically every school-boy in the civilized world, therefore there can be no dispute as far as effects are concerned.

Of one fact connected with the *cause* of the achieve-ments of Edison, Ford and Firestone we may be sure, namely, that these achievements were in no way based upon trickery, deceit, the "supernatural" or so-called "revelations" or any other form of unnatural law. These men do not possess a stock of legerdemain. They work with natural laws; laws which, for the most part, are well known to all economists and leaders in the field of science, with the possible exception of the law upon which chemistry of the mind is based. As yet chemistry of the mind is not sufficiently developed to be classed, by scientific men, in their catalogue of known laws.

A "Master Mind" may be created by any group of people who will co-ordinate their minds, in a spirit of perfect harmony. The group may consist of any number from two upward. Best results appear available from the blending of six or seven minds.

It has been suggested that Jesus Christ discovered how to make use of the principle of mind chemistry, and that His seemingly miraculous performances grew out of the power He developed through the blending of the minds of His twelve disciples. It has been pointed out that when one of the disciples (Judas Iscariot) broke faith the "Master Mind" immediately disintegrated and Jesus met with the supreme catastrophe of His life.

When two or more people harmonize their minds and produce the effect known as a "Master Mind," each person in the group becomes vested with the power to contact with and gather knowledge through the "subconscious" minds of all the other members of the group. This power becomes immediately noticeable, having the effect of stimulating the mind to a higher rate of vibration, and otherwise evidencing itself in the form of a more vivid imagination and the consciousness of what appears to be a sixth sense. It is through this sixth sense that new ideas will "flash" into the mind. These ideas take on the nature and form of the subject dominating the mind of the individual. If the entire group has met for the purpose of discussing a given subject, ideas concerning that subject will come pouring into the minds of all present, as if an outside influence were dictating them. The minds of those participating in the "Master Mind" become as magnets, attracting ideas and thought stimuli of the most highly organized and practical nature, from—no one knows where!

The process of mind-blending here described as a "Master Mind" may be likened to the act of one who connects many electric batteries to a single transmission wire, thereby "stepping up" the power flowing over that line. Each battery added increases the power passing over that line by the amount of energy the battery carries. Just so in the case of blending individual minds into a "Master Mind." Each mind, through the principle of mind chemistry, stimulates all the other minds in the group, until the mind energy thus becomes so great that it penetrates to and connects with the universal energy known as ether, which, in turn, touches every atom of the entire universe.

The modern radio apparatus substantiates, to a considerable extent, the theory here expounded. Powerful sending or broadcasting stations must be erected through which the vibration of sound is "stepped up" before it can be picked up by the much higher vibrating energy of the ether and carried in all directions. A "Master Mind" made up of many individual minds,

MEN cease to interest us when we find their limitations. The only sin is limitation.   As soon as you once come up to a man's limitations, it is all over with him.

—*Emerson.*

so blended that they produce a strong vibrating energy, constitutes almost an exact counterpart of the radio broadcasting station.

Every public speaker has felt the influence of mind chemistry, for it is a well known fact that as soon as the individual minds of an audience become "en rapport" (attuned to the rate of vibration of the mind of the speaker) with the speaker, there is a noticeable increase of enthusiasm in the speaker's mind, and he often rises to heights of oratory which surprise all, including himself.

The first five to ten minutes of the average speech are devoted to what is known as "warming up." By this is meant the process through which the minds of the speaker and his audience are becoming blended in a spirit of PERFECT HARMONY.

Every speaker knows what happens when this state of "perfect harmony" fails to materialize upon part of his audience.

The seemingly supernatural phenomena occurring in spiritualistic meetings are the result of the reaction, upon one another, of the minds in the group. These phenomena seldom begin to manifest themselves under ten to twenty minutes after the group is formed, for the reason that this is about the time required for the minds in the group to become harmonized or blended.

The "messages" received by members of a spiritualistic group probably come from one of two sources, or from both, namely:

First: From the vast storehouse of the subconscious mind of some member of the group; or

Second: From the universal storehouse of the ether,

in which, it is more than probable, all thought vibration is preserved.

Neither any known natural law nor human reason supports the theory of communication with individuals who have died.

It is a known fact that any individual may explore the store of knowledge in another's mind, through this principle of mind chemistry, and it seems reasonable to suppose that this power may be extended to include contact with whatever vibrations are available in the ether, if there are any.

The theory that all the higher and more refined vibrations, such as those growing out of thought, are preserved in the ether grows out of the known fact that neither matter nor energy (the two known elements of the universe) may be either created or destroyed. It is reasonable to suppose that all vibrations which have been "stepped up" sufficiently to be picked up and absorbed in the ether, will go on forever. The lower vibrations, which do not blend with or otherwise contact the ether, probably live a natural life and die out.

All the so-called geniuses probably gained their reputations because, by mere chance or otherwise, they formed alliances with other minds which enabled them to "step up" their own mind vibrations to where they were enabled to contact the vast Temple of Knowledge recorded and filed in the ether of the universe. All of the great geniuses, as far as this author has been enabled to gather the facts, were highly sexed people. The fact that sexual contact is the greatest known mind stimulant lends color to the theory herein described.

Inquiring further into the source of economic power, as manifested by the achievements of men in the field of business, let us study the case of the Chicago group known as the "Big Six," consisting of Wm. Wrigley, Jr., who owns the chewing gum business bearing his name, and whose individual income is said to be more than Fifteen Million Dollars a year; John R. Thompson, who operates the chain of lunch rooms bearing his name; Mr. Lasker, who owns the Lord & Thomas Advertising Agency; Mr. McCullough, who owns the Parmalee Express Company, the largest transfer business in America; and Mr. Ritchie and Mr. Hertz, who own the Yellow Taxicab business.

A reliable financial reporting company has estimated the yearly income of these six men at upwards of Twenty-five Million Dollars ($25,000,000.00), or an average of more than Four Million Dollars a year per man.

Analysis of the entire group of six men discloses the fact that not one of them had any special educational advantages; that all began without capital or extensive credit; that their financial achievement has been due to their own individual plans, and not to any fortunate turn of the wheel of chance.

Many years ago these six men formed a friendly alliance, meeting at stated periods for the purpose of assisting one another with ideas and suggestions in their various and sundry lines of business endeavor.

With the exception of Hertz and Ritchie none of the six men were in any manner associated in a legal partnership. These meetings were strictly for the purpose of co-operating on the give and take basis of assisting one another with ideas and suggestions, and occasionally by endorsing notes and other securities to assist some member of the group who had met with an emergency making such help necessary.

It is said that each of the individuals belonging to this Big Six group is a millionaire many times over. As a rule there is nothing worthy of special comment on behalf of a man who does nothing more than accumulate a few million dollars. However, there is something connected with the financial success of this particular group of men that is well worth comment, study, analysis and even emulation, and that "something" is the fact that they have learned how to coordinate their individual minds by blending them in a spirit of perfect harmony, thereby creating a "Master Mind" that unlocks, to each individual of the group, doors which are closed to most of the human race.

The United States Steel Corporation is one of the strongest and most powerful industrial organizations in the world. The Idea out of which this great industrial giant grew was born in the mind of Elbert H. Gary, a more or less commonplace small-town lawyer who was born and reared in a small Illinois town near Chicago.

Mr. Gary surrounded himself with a group of men whose minds he successfully blended in a spirit of perfect harmony, thereby creating the "Master Mind" which is the moving spirit of the great United States Steel Corporation.

Search where you will, wherever you find an outstanding success in business, finance, industry or in any of the professions, you may be sure that back of the success is some individual who has applied the principle of mind chemistry, out of which a "Master

Mind" has been created. These outstanding successes often appear to be the handiwork of but one person, but search closely and the other individuals whose minds have been co-ordinated with his own may be found. Remember that two or more persons may operate the principle of mind chemistry so as to create a "Master Mind."

POWER (man-power) is ORGANIZED KNOWL-EDGE, EXPRESSED THROUGH INTELLIGENT EFFORTS!

No effort can be said to be ORGANIZED unless the individuals engaged in the effort co-ordinate their knowledge and energy in a spirit of perfect harmony. Lack of such harmonious co-ordination of effort is the main cause of practically every business failure.

An interesting experiment was conducted by this author, in collaboration with the students of a well known college. Each student was requested to write an essay on "How and Why Henry Ford Became Wealthy."

Each student was required to describe, as a part of his or her essay, what was believed to be the nature of Ford's real assets, of what these assets consisted in detail.

The majority of the students gathered financial statements and inventories of the Ford assets and used these as the basis of their estimates of Ford's wealth.

Included in these "sources of Ford's wealth" were such as cash in banks, raw and finished materials in stock, real estate and buildings, good-will, estimated at from ten to twenty-five per cent of the value of the material assets.

YOU cannot become a power in your community nor achieve enduring success in any worthy undertaking until you become big enough to blame yourself for your own mistakes and reverses.

One student out of the entire group of several hundred answered as follows:

"Henry Ford's assets consist, in the main, of two items, viz.: (1) Working capital and raw and finished materials; (2) The knowledge, gained from experience, of Henry Ford, himself, and the co-operation of a well trained organization which understands how to apply this knowledge to best advantage from the Ford viewpoint. It is impossible to estimate, with anything approximating correctness, the actual dollars and cents value of either of these two groups of assets, but it is my opinion that their relative values are:

"The organized knowledge of the Ford Organization 75%
The value of cash and physical assets of every nature, including raw and finished materials 25%"

This author is of the opinion that this statement was not compiled by the young man whose name was signed to it, without the assistance of some very analytical and experienced mind or minds.

Unquestionably the biggest asset that Henry Ford has is his own brain. Next to this would come the brains of his immediate circle of associates, for it has been through co-ordination of these that the physical assets which he controls were accumulated.

Destroy every plant the Ford Motor Company owns: every piece of machinery; every atom of raw or finished material, every finished automobile, and every dollar on deposit in any bank, and Ford would still be the most powerful man, economically, on earth. The brains which have built the Ford business could duplicate it again in short order. Capital is always available, in unlimited quantities, to such brains as Ford's.

Ford is the most powerful man on earth (economically) because he has the keenest and most practical conception of the principle of ORGANIZED KNOWLEDGE of any man on earth, as far as this author has the means of knowing.

Despite Ford's great power and financial success, it may be that he has blundered often in the application of the principles through which he accumulated this power. There is but little doubt that Ford's methods of mind co-ordination have often been crude; they must needs have been in the earlier days of this experience, before he gained the wisdom of application that would naturally go with maturity of years.

Neither can there be much doubt that Ford's application of the principle of mind chemistry was, at least at the start, the result of a chance alliance with other minds, particularly the mind of Edison. It is more than probable that Mr. Ford's remarkable insight into the laws of nature was first begun as the result of his friendly alliance with his own wife long before he ever met either Mr. Edison or Mr. Firestone. Many a man who never knows the real source of his success is made by his wife, through application of the "Master Mind" principle. Mrs. Ford is a most remarkably intelligent woman, and this author has reason to believe that it was her mind, blended with Mr. Ford's, which gave him his first real start toward power.

It may be mentioned, without in any way depriving Ford of any honor or glory, that in his earlier days of experience he had to combat the powerful enemies of illiteracy and ignorance to a greater extent than did either Edison or Firestone, both of whom were gifted by natural heredity with a most fortunate aptitude for acquiring and applying knowledge. Ford had to hew this talent out of the rough, raw timbers of his hereditary estate.

Within an inconceivably short period of time Ford has mastered three of the most stubborn enemies of mankind and transformed them into assets constituting the very foundation of his success.

These enemies are: Ignorance, illiteracy and poverty!

Any man who can stay the hand of these three savage forces, much less harness and use them to good account, is well worth close study by the less fortunate individuals.

. . . .

This is an age of INDUSTRIAL POWER in which we are living!

The source of all this POWER is ORGANIZED EFFORT. Not only has the management of industrial enterprises efficiently organized individual workers, but, in many instances, mergers of industry have been effected in such a manner and to the end that these combinations (as in the case of the United States Steel Corporation, for example) have accumulated practically unlimited power.

One may hardly glance at the news of a day's events without seeing a report of some business, industrial or financial merger, bringing under one management enormous resources and thus creating great power.

One day it is a group of banks; another day it is

a chain of railroads; the next day it is a combination of steel plants, all merging for the purpose of developing power through highly organized and co-ordinated effort.

Knowledge, general in nature and unorganized, is not POWER; it is only potential power—the material out of which real power may be developed. Any modern library contains an unorganized record of all the knowledge of value to which the present stage of civilization is heir, but this knowledge is not power because it is not organized.

Every form of energy and every species of animal or plant life, to survive, must be organized. The oversized animals whose bones have filled Nature's bone-yard through extinction have left mute but certain evidence that non-organization means annihilation.

From the electron—the smallest particle of matter —to the largest star in the universe: these and every material thing in between these two extremes offer proof positive that one of Nature's first laws is that of ORGANIZATION. Fortunate is the individual who recognizes the importance of this law and makes it his business to familiarize himself with the various ways in which the law may be applied to advantage.

The astute business man has not only recognized the importance of the law of organized effort, but he has made this law the warp and the woof of his POWER.

Without any knowledge, whatsoever, of the principle of mind chemistry, or that such a principle exists, many men have accumulated great power by merely organizing the knowledge they possessed. The majority of all who have discovered the principle of mind chemistry and developed that principle into a "MASTER MIND" have stumbled upon this knowledge by the merest of accident; often failing to recognize the real nature of their discovery or to understand the source of their power.

This author is of the opinion that all living persons who at the present time are consciously making use of the principle of mind chemistry in developing power through the blending of minds, may be counted on the fingers of the two hands, with, perhaps, several fingers left to spare.

If this estimate is even approximately true the student will readily see that there is but slight danger of the field of mind chemistry practice becoming overcrowded.

It is a well known fact that one of the most difficult tasks that any business man must perform is that of inducing those who are associated with him to co-ordinate their efforts in a spirit of harmony. To induce continuous co-operation between a group of workers, in any undertaking, is next to impossible. Only the most efficient leaders can accomplish this highly desired object, but once in a great while such a leader will rise above the horizon in the field of industry, business or finance, and then the world hears of a Henry Ford, Thomas A. Edison, John D. Rockefeller, Sr., E. H. Harriman or James J. Hill.

Power and success are practically synonomous terms!

One grows out of the other; therefore, any person who has the knowledge and the ability to develop power, through the principle of harmonious co-ordi-

NEVER, in the history of the world, has there been such abundant opportunity as there is now for the person who is willing to serve before trying to collect.

nation of effort between individual minds, or in any other manner, may be successful in any reasonable undertaking that is possible of successful termination.

.   .   .   .

It must not be assumed that a "Master Mind" will immediately spring, mushroom fashion, out of every group of minds which make pretense of co-ordination in a spirit of HARMONY!

Harmony, in the real sense of meaning of the word, is as rare among groups of people as is genuine Christianity among those who proclaim themselves Christians.

Harmony is the nucleus around which the state of mind known as "Master Mind" must be developed. Without this element of harmony there can be no "Master Mind," a truth which cannot be repeated too often.

Woodrow Wilson had in mind the development of a "Master Mind," to be composed of groups of minds representing the civilized nations of the world, in his proposal for establishing the League of Nations. Wilson's conception was the most far-reaching humanitarian idea ever created in the mind of man, because it dealt with a principle which embraces sufficient power to establish a real Brotherhood of Man on earth. The League of Nations, or some similar blending of international minds, in a spirit of harmony, is sure to become a reality.

The time when such unity of minds will take place will be measured largely by the time required for the great universities and NON-SECTARIAN institutions of learning to supplant ignorance and superstition with understanding and wisdom. This time is rapidly approaching.

THE PSYCHOLOGY OF THE REVIVAL MEETING: The old religious orgy known as the "revival" offers a favorable opportunity to study the principle of mind chemistry known as "Master Mind."

It will be observed that music plays no small part in bringing about the harmony essential to the blending of a group of minds in a revival meeting. Without music the revival meeting would be a tame affair.

During revival services the leader of the meeting has no difficulty in creating harmony in the minds of his devotees, but it is a well known fact that this state of harmony lasts no longer than the presence of the leader, after which the "Master Mind" he has temporarily created disintegrates.

By arousing the emotional nature of his followers the revivalist has no difficulty, under the proper stage setting and with the embellishment of the right sort of music, in creating a "Master Mind" which becomes noticeable to all who come in contact with it. The very air becomes charged with a positive, pleasing influence which changes the entire chemistry of all minds present.

The revivalist calls this energy "the Spirit of the Lord."

This author, through experiments conducted with a group of scientific investigators and laymen (who were unaware of the nature of the experiment), has created the same state of mind and the same positive atmosphere without calling it the Spirit of the Lord.

On many occasions this author has witnessed the

creation of the same positive atmosphere in a group of men and women engaged in the business of salesmanship, without calling it the Spirit of the Lord.

The author helped conduct a school of salesmanship for Harrison Parker, founder of the Co-operative Society, of Chicago, and, by the use of the same principle of mind chemistry which the revivalist calls the Spirit of the Lord, so transformed the nature of a group of 3,000 men and women (all of whom were without former sales experience) that they sold more than $10,000,000.00 worth of securities in less than nine months, and earned more than $1,000,000 for themselves.

It was found that the average person who joined this school would reach the zenith of his or her selling power within one week, after which it was necessary to revitalize the individual's brain through a group sales meeting. These sales meetings were conducted on very much the same order as are the modern revival meetings of the religionist, with much the same stage equipment, including music and "high-powered" speakers who exhorted the salespeople in very much the same manner as does the modern religious revivalist.

Call it religion, psychology, mind chemistry or anything you please (they are all based upon the same principle), but there is nothing more certain than the fact that wherever a group of minds are brought into contact, in a spirit of PERFECT HARMONY, each mind in the group becomes immediately supplemented and re-enforced by a noticeable energy called a "Master Mind."

For all this writer professes to know this uncharted energy may be the Spirit of the Lord, but it operates just as favorably when called by any other name.

The human brain and nervous system constitute a piece of intricate machinery which but few, if any, understand. When controlled and properly directed this piece of machinery can be made to perform wonders of achievement and if not controlled it will perform wonders fantastic and phantom-like in nature, as may be seen by examining the inmates of any insane asylum.

The human brain has direct connection with a continuous influx of energy from which man derives his power to think. The brain receives this energy, mixes it with the energy created by the food taken into the body, and distributes it to every portion of the body, through the aid of the blood and the nervous system. It thus becomes what we call life.

From what source this outside energy comes no one seems to know; all we know about it is that we must have it or die. It seems reasonable to suppose that this energy is none other than that which we call ether, and that it flows into the body along with the oxygen from the air, as we breathe.

Every normal human body possesses a first-class chemical laboratory and a stock of chemicals sufficient to carry on the business of breaking up, assimilating and properly mixing and compounding the food we take into the body, preparatory to distributing it to wherever it is needed as a body builder.

Ample tests have been made, both with man and beast, to prove that the energy known as the mind plays an important part in this chemical operation of compounding and transforming food into the required substances to build and keep the body in repair.

It is known that worry, excitement or fear will interfere with the digestive process, and in extreme cases stop this process altogether, resulting in illness or death. It is obvious, then, that the mind enters into the chemistry of food digestion and distribution.

It is believed by many eminent authorities, although it may never have been scientifically proved, that the energy known as mind or thought may become contaminated with negative or "unsociable" units to such an extent that the whole nervous system is thrown out of working order, digestion is interfered with and various and sundry forms of disease will manifest themselves. Financial difficulties and unrequited love affairs head the list of causes of such mind disturbances.

A negative environment such as that existing where some member of the family is constantly "nagging," will interfere with the chemistry of the mind to such an extent that the individual will lose ambition and gradually sink into oblivion. It is because of this fact that the old saying that a man's wife may either "make" or "break" him is literally true. In a subsequent lesson a whole chapter on this subject is addressed to the wives of men.

Any high-school student knows that certain food combinations will, if taken into the stomach, result in indigestion, violent pain and even death. Good health depends, in part at least, upon a food combination that "harmonizes." But harmony of food combinations is not sufficient to insure good health; there must be harmony, also, between the units of energy known as the mind.

A man is half whipped the minute he begins to feel sorry for himself, or to spin an alibi with which he would explain away his defects.

"Harmony" seems to be one of Nature's laws, without which there can be no such thing as ORGANIZED ENERGY, or life in any form whatsoever.

The health of the body as well as the mind is literally built around, out of and upon the principle of HARMONY! The energy known as life begins to disintegrate and death approaches when the organs of the body stop working in harmony.

The moment harmony ceases at the source of any form of organized energy (power) the units of that energy are thrown into a chaotic state of disorder and the power is rendered neutral or passive.

Harmony is also the nucleus around which the principle of mind chemistry known as a "Master Mind" develops power. Destroy this harmony and you destroy the power growing out of the co-ordinated effort of a group of individual minds.

This truth has been stated, re-stated and presented in every manner which the author could conceive, with unending repetition, for the reason that unless the student grasps this principle and learns to apply it this lesson is useless.

Success in life, no matter what one may call success, is very largely a matter of adaptation to environment in such a manner that there is harmony between the individual and his environment. The palace of a king becomes as a hovel of a peasant if harmony does not abound within its walls. Conversely stated, the hut of a peasant may be made to yield more happiness than that of the mansion of the rich man, if harmony obtains in the former and not in the latter.

Without perfect harmony the science of astronomy would be as useless as the "bones of a saint," because the stars and planets would clash with one another, and all would be in a state of chaos and disorder.

Without the law of harmony an acorn might grow into a heterogeneous tree consisting of the wood of the oak, poplar, maple and what not.

Without the law of harmony the blood might deposit the food which grows finger nails on the scalp where hair is supposed to grow, and thus create a horny growth which might easily be mistaken, by the superstitious, to signify man's relationship to a certain imaginary gentleman with horns, often referred to by the more primitive type.

Without the law of harmony there can be no organization of knowledge, for what, may one ask, is organized knowledge except the harmony of facts and truths and natural laws?

The moment discord begins to creep in at the front door harmony edges out at the back door, so to speak, whether the application is made to a business partnership or the orderly movement of the planets of the heavens.

If the student gathers the impression that the author is laying undue stress upon the importance of HARMONY, let it be remembered that lack of harmony is the first, and often the last and only, cause of FAILURE!

There can be no poetry nor music nor oratory worthy of notice without the presence of harmony.

Good architecture is largely a matter of harmony. Without harmony a house is nothing but a mass of building material, more or less a monstrosity.

Sound business management plants the very sinews of its existence in harmony.

Every well dressed man or woman is a living picture and a moving example of harmony.

With all these workaday illustrations of the important part which harmony plays in the affairs of the world—nay, in the operation of the entire universe—how could any intelligent person leave harmony out of his "Definite Aim" in life? As well have no "definite aim" as to omit harmony as the chief stone of its foundation.

.   .   .   .

The human body is a complex organization of organs, glands, blood vessels, nerves, brain cells, muscles, etc. The mind energy which stimulates to action and co-ordinates the efforts of the component parts of the body is also a plurality of ever-varying and changing energies. From birth until death there is continuous struggle, often assuming the nature of open combat, between the forces of the mind. For example, the life-long struggle between the motivating forces and desires of the human mind, which takes place between the impulses of right and wrong, is well known to everyone.

Every human being possesses at least two distinct mind powers or personalities, and as many as six distinct personalities have been discovered in one person. One of man's most delicate tasks is that of harmonizing these mind forces so that they may be organized and directed toward the orderly attainment of a given objective. Without this element of harmony no individual can become an accurate thinker.

It is no wonder that leaders in business and industrial enterprises, as well as those in politics and other fields of endeavor, find it so difficult to organize groups of people so they will function in the attainment of a given objective, without friction. Each individual human being possesses forces, within himself, which are hard to harmonize, even when he is placed in the environment most favorable to harmony. If the chemistry of the individual's mind is such that the units of his mind cannot be easily harmonized, think how much more difficult it must be to harmonize a group of minds so they will function as one, in an orderly manner, through what is known as a "Master Mind."

The leader who successfully develops and directs the energies of a "Master Mind" must possess tact, patience, persistence, self-confidence, intimate knowledge of mind chemistry and the ability to adapt himself (in a state of perfect poise and harmony) to quickly changing circumstances, without showing the least sign of annoyance.

How many are there who can measure up to this requirement?

The successful leader must possess the ability to change the color of his mind, chameleon-like, to fit every circumstance that arises in connection with the object of his leadership. Moreover, he must possess the ability to change from one mood to another without showing the slightest signs of anger or lack of self-control. The successful leader must understand the Fifteen Laws of Success and be able to put into practice any combination of these Fifteen Laws whenever occasion demands.

Without this ability no leader can be powerful, and without power no leader can long endure.

THE MEANING OF EDUCATION: There has long been a general misconception of the meaning of the word "educate." The dictionaries have not aided in the elimination of this misunderstanding, because they have defined the word "educate" as an act of imparting knowledge.

The word educate has its roots in the Latin word *educo,* which means to develop FROM WITHIN; to educe; to draw out; to grow through the law of USE.

Nature hates idleness in all its forms. She gives continuous life only to those elements which are in use. Tie up an arm, or any other portion of the body, taking it out of use, and the idle part will soon atrophy and become lifeless. Reverse the order, give an arm more than normal use, such as that engaged in by the blacksmith who wields a heavy hammer all day long, and that arm (developed from within) grows strong.

Power grows out of ORGANIZED KNOWLEDGE, but, mind you, it "grows out of it" through application and use!

A man may become a walking encyclopædia of knowledge without possessing any power of value. This knowledge becomes power only to the extent that it is organized, classified and put into action. Some of the best educated men the world has known possessed much less general knowledge than some who have been known as fools, the difference between the two being that the former put what knowledge they possessed into use while the latter made no such application.

An "educated" person is one who knows how to acquire everything he needs in the attainment of his main purpose in life, without violating the rights of

SEEK the counsel of men who will tell you the truth about yourself, even if it hurts you to hear it. Mere commendation will not bring the improvement you need.

his fellow men. It might be a surprise to many so-called men of "learning" to know that they come nowhere near qualification as men of "education." It might also be a great surprise to many who believe they suffer from lack of "learning" to know that they are well "educated."

The successful lawyer is not necessarily the one who memorizes the greatest number of principles of law. On the contrary, the successful lawyer is the one who knows where to find a principle of law, plus a variety of opinions supporting that principle which fit the immediate needs of a given case.

In other words, the successful lawyer is he who knows where to find the law he wants when he needs it.

This principle applies, with equal force, to the affairs of industry and business.

Henry Ford had but little elementary schooling, yet he is one of the best "educated" men in the world because he has acquired the ability so to combine natural and economic laws, to say nothing of the minds of men, that he has the power to get anything of a material nature he wants.

Some years ago during the world war Mr. Ford brought suit against the Chicago Tribune, charging that newspaper with libelous publication of statements concerning him, one of which was the statement that Ford was an "ignoramus," an ignorant pacifist, etc.

When the suit came up for trial the attorneys for the Tribune undertook to prove, by Ford himself, that their statement was true; that he was ignorant, and with this object in view they catechized and cross-examined him on all manner of subjects.

One question they asked was:

"How many soldiers did the British send over to subdue the rebellion in the Colonies in 1776?"

With a dry grin on his face Ford nonchalantly replied:

"I do not know just how many, but I have heard that it was a lot more than ever went back."

Loud laughter from Court, jury, court-room spectators, and even from the frustrated lawyer who had asked the question.

This line of interrogation was continued for an hour or more, Ford keeping perfectly calm the meanwhile. Finally, however, he had permitted the "smart Aleck" lawyers to play with him until he was tired of it, and in reply to a question which was particularly obnoxious and insulting, Ford straightened himself up, pointed his finger at the questioning lawyer and replied:

"If I should really wish to answer the foolish question you have just asked, or any of the others you have been asking, let me remind you that I have a row of electric push-buttons hanging over my desk and by placing my finger on the right button I could call in men who could give me the correct answer to all the questions you have asked and to many that you have not the intelligence either to ask or answer. Now, will you kindly tell me why I should bother about filling my mind with a lot of useless details in order to answer every fool question that anyone may ask, when I have able men all about me who can supply me with all the facts I want when I call for them?"

This answer is quoted from memory, but it substantially relates Ford's answer.

There was silence in the court-room. The questioning attorney's under jaw dropped down, his eyes opened widely; the judge leaned forward from the bench and gazed in Mr. Ford's direction; many of the jury awoke and looked around as if they had heard an explosion (which they actually had).

A prominent clergyman who was present in the court-room at the time said, later, that the scene reminded him of that which must have existed when Jesus Christ was on trial before Pontius Pilate, just after He had given His famous reply to Pilate's question, "What is truth?"

In the vernacular of the day, Ford's reply knocked the questioner cold.

Up to the time of that reply the lawyer had been enjoying considerable fun at what he believed to be Ford's expense, by adroitly displaying his (the lawyer's) sample case of general knowledge and comparing it with what he inferred to be Ford's ignorance as to many events and subjects.

But that answer spoiled the lawyer's fun!

It also proved once more (to all who had the intelligence to accept the proof) that true education means mind development; not merely the gathering and classifying of knowledge.

Ford could not, in all probability, have named the capitals of all the States of the United States, but he could have and in fact had gathered the "capital" with which to "turn many wheels" within every State in the Union.

Education—let us not forget this—consists of the power with which to get everything one needs when he needs it, without violating the rights of his fellow men. Ford comes well within that definition, and for the reason which the author has here tried to make plain, by relating the foregoing incident connected with the simple Ford philosophy.

There are many men of "learning" who could easily entangle Ford, theoretically, with a maze of questions none of which he, personally, could answer. But Ford could turn right around and wage a battle in industry or finance that would exterminate those same men, with all of their knowledge and all of their wisdom.

Ford could not go into his chemical laboratory and separate water into its component atoms of hydrogen and oxygen and then re-combine these atoms in their former order, but he knows how to surround himself with chemists who can do this for him if he wants it done. The man who can intelligently use the knowledge possessed by another is as much or more a man of education as the person who merely has the knowledge but does not know what to do with it.

The president of a well known college inherited a large tract of very poor land. This land had no timber of commercial value, no minerals or other valuable appurtenances, therefore it was nothing but a source of expense to him, for he had to pay taxes on it. The State built a highway through the land. An "uneducated" man who was driving his automobile over this road observed that this poor land was on top of a mountain which commanded a wonderful view for many miles in all directions. He (the ignorant one) also observed that the land was covered with a growth of small pines and other saplings. He bought fifty acres of the land for $10.00 an acre. Near the public highway he built a unique log house to which he attached a large dining room. Near the house he put in a gasoline filling station. He built a dozen single-room log houses along the road, these he rented out to tourists at $3.00 a night, each. The dining room, gasoline filling station and log houses brought him a net income of $15,000.00 the first year. The next year he extended his plan by adding fifty more log houses, of three rooms each, which he now rents out as summer country homes to people in a near-by city, at a rental of $150.00 each for the season.

The building material cost him nothing, for it grew on his land in abundance (that same land which the college president believed to be worthless).

Moreover, the unique and unusual appearance of the log bungalows served as an advertisement of the plan, whereas many would have considered it a real calamity had they been compelled to build out of such crude materials.

Less than five miles from the location of these log houses this same man purchased an old worked-out farm of 150 acres, for $25.00 an acre, a price which the seller believed to be extremely high.

By building a dam, one hundred feet in length, the purchaser of this old farm turned a stream of water into a lake that covered fifteen acres of the land, stocked the lake with fish, then sold the farm off in building lots to people who wanted summering places around the lake. The total profit realized from this simple transaction was more than $25,000.00, and the time required for its consummation was one summer.

Yet this man of vision and imagination was not "educated" in the orthodox meaning of that term.

Let us keep in mind the fact that it is through these

WHEN you lose your sense of humor, get a job running an elevator, because your life will be a series of UPS and DOWNS, anyway.

simple illustrations of the use of organized knowledge that one may become educated and powerful.

In speaking of the transaction here related, the college president who sold the fifty acres of worthless (?) land for $500.00 said:

"Just think of it! That man, whom most of us might call ignorant, mixed his ignorance with fifty acres of worthless land and made the combination yield more yearly than I earn from five years of application of so-called education."

.   .   .   .

There is an opportunity, if not scores of them, in every State in America, to make use of the idea here described. From now on make it your business to study the lay of all land you see that is similar to that described in this lesson, and you may find a suitable place for developing a similar money-making enterprise. The idea is particularly adaptable in localities where bathing beaches are few, as people naturally like such conveniences.

The automobile has caused a great system of public highways to be built throughout the United States. On practically every one of these highways there is a suitable spot for a "Cabin City" for tourists which can be turned into a regular money-making mint by the man with the IMAGINATION and SELF-CONFI-DENCE to do it.

There are opportunities to make money all around you. This course was designed to help you "see" these opportunities, and to inform you how to make the most of them after you discover them.

WHO CAN PROFIT MOST BY THE LAW OF SUCCESS PHILOSOPHY?

RAILROAD OFFICIALS who want a better spirit of co-operation between their trainmen and the public they serve.

SALARIED PEOPLE who wish to increase their earning power and market their services to better advantage.

SALESPEOPLE who wish to become masters in their chosen field. The Law of Success philosophy covers every known law of selling, and includes many features not included in any other course.

INDUSTRIAL PLANT MANAGERS who understand the value of greater harmony among their employees.

RAILROAD EMPLOYEES who wish to establish records of efficiency which will lead to more responsible positions, with greater pay.

MERCHANTS who wish to extend their business by adding new customers. The Law of Success philosophy will help any merchant increase his business by teaching him how to make a walking advertisement of every customer who comes into his store.

AUTOMOBILE AGENTS who wish to increase the selling power of their salesmen. A large part of the Law of Success course was developed from the life-work and experience of the greatest automobile salesman living, and it is therefore of unusual help to the Sales Manager who is directing the efforts of Automobile Salesmen.

LIFE INSURANCE AGENTS who wish to add new

policy-holders and increase the insurance on present policy-holders. One Life Insurance Salesman, in Ohio, sold a Fifty Thousand Dollar policy to one of the officials of the Central Steel Company, as the result of but one reading of the lesson on "Profiting by Failures." This same salesman has become one of the star men of the New York Life Insurance Company's staff, as the result of his training in the Fifteen Laws of Success.

SCHOOL TEACHERS who wish to advance to the top in their present occupation, or who are looking for an opportunity to enter the more profitable field of business as a life-work.

STUDENTS, both College and High School, who are undecided as to what field of endeavor they wish to enter as a life-work. The Law of Success course covers a complete Personal Analysis service which helps the student of the philosophy to determine the work for which he or she is best fitted.

BANKERS who wish to extend their business through better and more courteous methods of serving their clients.

BANK CLERKS who are ambitious to prepare themselves for executive positions in the field of banking, or in some commercial or industrial field.

PHYSICIANS and DENTISTS who wish to extend their practice without violating the ethics of their profession by direct advertising. A prominent physician has said that the Law of Success course is worth $1,000.00 to any professional man or woman whose professional ethics prevent direct advertising.

PROMOTERS who wish to develop new and heretofore unworked combinations in business or industry.

The principle described in this Introductory Lesson is said to have made a small fortune for a man who used it as the basis of a real estate promotion.

REAL ESTATE MEN who wish new methods for promoting sales. This Introductory Lesson contains a description of an entirely new real-estate promotion plan which is sure to make fortunes for many who will put it to use. This plan may be put into operation in practically every State. Moreover, it may be employed by men who never promoted an enterprise.

FARMERS who wish to discover new methods of marketing their products so as to give them greater net returns, and those who own lands suitable for subdivision promotion under the plan referred to at the end of this Introductory Lesson. Thousands of farmers have "gold mines" in the land they own which is not suitable for cultivation, which could be used for recreation and resort purposes, on a highly profitable basis.

STENOGRAPHERS and BOOKKEEPERS who are looking for a practical plan to promote themselves into higher and better paying positions. The Law of Success course is said to be the best course ever written on the subject of marketing personal services.

PRINTERS who want a larger volume of business and more efficient production as the result of better co-operation among their own employees.

DAY LABORERS who have the ambition to advance into more responsible positions, in work that has greater responsibilities and consequently offers more pay.

LAWYERS who wish to extend their clientele through dignified, ethical methods which will bring them to the attention, in a favorable way, of a greater number of people who need legal services.

BUSINESS EXECUTIVES who wish to expand their present business, or who wish to handle their present volume with less expense, as the result of greater co-operation between their employees.

LAUNDRY OWNERS who wish to extend their business by teaching their drivers how to serve more courteously and efficiently.

LIFE INSURANCE GENERAL AGENTS who wish bigger and more efficient sales organizations.

CHAIN STORE MANAGERS who want a greater volume of business as the result of more efficient individual sales efforts.

MARRIED PEOPLE who are unhappy, and therefore unsuccessful, because of lack of harmony and co-operation in the home.

To all described in the foregoing classification the Law of Success philosophy offers both DEFINITE and SPEEDY aid.

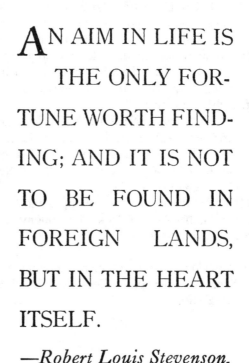

AN AIM IN LIFE IS
THE ONLY FOR-
TUNE WORTH FIND-
ING; AND IT IS NOT
TO BE FOUND IN
FOREIGN LANDS,
BUT IN THE HEART
ITSELF.

—*Robert Louis Stevenson.*

SUMMARY OF INTRODUCTORY LESSON

The purpose of this summary is to aid the student in mastering the central idea around which the lesson has been developed. This idea is represented by the term "Master Mind" which has been described in great detail throughout the lesson.

All new ideas, and especially those of an abstract nature, find lodgment in the human mind only after much repetition, a well known truth which accounts for the re-statement, in this summary, of the principle known as the "Master Mind."

A "Master Mind" may be developed by a friendly alliance, in a spirit of harmony of purpose, between two or more minds.

This is an appropriate place at which to explain that out of every alliance of minds, whether in a spirit of harmony or not, there is developed another mind which affects all participating in the alliance. No two or more minds ever met without creating, out of the contact, another mind, but not always is this invisible creation a "Master Mind."

There may be, and altogether too often there is, developed out of the meeting of two or more minds a negative power which is just the opposite to a "Master Mind."

There are certain minds which, as has already been stated throughout this lesson, cannot be made to blend in a spirit of harmony. This principle has its comparable analogy in chemistry, reference to which may enable the student to grasp more clearly the principle here referred to.

For example, the chemical formula H_2O (meaning the combining of two atoms of hydrogen with one atom of oxygen) changes these two elements into water. One atom of hydrogen and one atom of oxygen will not produce water; moreover, they cannot be made to associate themselves in harmony!

There are many known elements which, when combined, are immediately transformed from harmless into deadly poisonous substances. Stated differently, many well known poisonous elements are neutralized and rendered harmless when combined with certain other elements.

Just as the combining of certain elements changes their entire nature, the combining of certain minds changes the nature of those minds, producing either a certain degree of what has been called a "Master Mind," or its opposite, which is highly destructive.

Any man who has found his mother-in-law to be incompatible has experienced the negative application of the principle known as a "Master Mind." For some reason as yet unknown to investigators in the field of mind behavior, the majority of mothers-in-law appear to affect their daughters' husbands in a highly negative manner, the meeting of their minds with those of their sons-in-law creating a highly antagonistic influence instead of a "Master Mind."

This fact is too well known as a truth to make extended comment necessary.

Some minds will not be harmonized and cannot be blended into a "Master Mind," a fact which all leaders of men will do well to remember. It is the leader's responsibility so to group his men that those who have been placed at the most strategic points in his organization are made up of individuals whose minds CAN and WILL BE blended in a spirit of friendliness and harmony.

Ability so to group men is the chief outstanding quality of leadership. In Lesson Two of this course the student will discover that this ability was the main source of both the power and fortune accumulated by the late Andrew Carnegie.

Knowing nothing whatsoever of the technical end of the steel business, Carnegie so combined and grouped the men of which his "Master Mind" was composed that he built the most successful steel industry known to the world during his life-time.

Henry Ford's gigantic success may be traced to the successful application of this selfsame principle. With all the self-reliance a man could have, Ford, nevertheless, did not depend upon himself for the knowledge necessary in the successful development of his industries.

Like Carnegie, he surrounded himself with men who supplied the knowledge which he, himself, did not and could not possess.

Moreover, Ford picked men who could and did harmonize in group effort.

The most effective alliances, which have resulted in the creation of the principle known as the "Master Mind," have been those developed out of the blending of the minds of men and women. The reason for this is the fact that the minds of male and female will more readily blend in harmony than will the minds of males. Also, the added stimulus of sexual contact often enters into the development of a "Master Mind" between a man and a woman.

It is a well known fact that the male of the species is keener and more alert for "the chase," let the goal or object of the chase be what it may, when inspired and urged on by a female.

This human trait begins to manifest itself in the male at the age of puberty, and continues throughout his life. The first evidence of it may be observed in athletics, where boys are playing before an audience made up of females.

Remove the women from the audience and the game known as football would soon become a very tame affair. A boy will throw himself into a football game with almost superhuman effort when he knows that the girl of his choice is observing him from the grandstand.

And that same boy will throw himself into the game of accumulating money with the same enthusiasm when inspired and urged on by the woman of his choice; especially if that woman knows how to stimulate his mind with her own, through the law of the "Master Mind."

On the other hand, that same woman may, through a negative application of the law of the "Master Mind" (nagging, jealousy, selfishness, greed, vanity), drag this man down to sure defeat!

The late Elbert Hubbard understood the principle here described so well that when he discovered that the incompatibility between himself and his first wife was dragging him down to sure defeat he ran the gamut of public opinion by divorcing her and marrying the woman who is said to have been the main source of his inspiration.

Not every man would have had the courage to defy

public opinion, as Hubbard did, but who is wise enough to say that his action was not for the best interest of all concerned?

A man's chief business in life is to succeed!

The road to success may be, and generally is, obstructed by many influences which must be removed before the goal can be reached. One of the most detrimental of these obstacles is that of unfortunate alliance with minds which do not harmonize. In such cases the alliance must be broken or the end is sure to be defeat and failure.

The man who has mastered the six basic fears, one of which is the Fear of Criticism, will have no hesitancy in taking what may seem to the more convention-bound type of mind to be drastic action when he finds himself circumscribed and bound down by antagonistic alliances, no matter of what nature or with whom they may be.

It is a million times better to meet and face criticism than to be dragged down to failure and oblivion on account of alliances which are not harmonious, whether the alliances be of a business or social nature.

To be perfectly frank, the author is here justifying divorce, when the conditions surrounding marriage are such that harmony cannot prevail. This is not intended to convey the belief that lack of harmony may not be removed through other methods than that of divorce; for there are instances where the cause of antagonism may be removed and harmony established without taking the extreme step of divorce.

While it is true that some minds will not blend in a spirit of harmony, and cannot be forced or induced to do so, because of the chemical nature of the in-

IF you cannot do great things yourself, remember that you may do small things in a great way.

dividuals' brains, DO NOT BE TOO READY TO CHARGE THE OTHER PARTY TO YOUR ALLIANCE WITH ALL THE RESPONSIBILITY OF LACK OF HARMONY—REMEMBER, *THE TROUBLE MAY BE WITH YOUR OWN BRAIN!*

Remember, also, that a mind which cannot and will not harmonize with one person or persons may harmonize perfectly with other types of minds. Discovery of this truth has resulted in radical changes in methods of employing men. It is no longer customary to discharge a man because he does not fit in the position for which he was originally hired. The discriminating leader endeavors to place such a man in some other position, where, it has been proved more than once, misfits may become valuable men.

The student of this course should be sure that the principle described as the "Master Mind" is thoroughly understood before proceeding with the remaining lessons of the course. The reason for this is the fact that practically the entire course is closely associated with this law of mind operation.

If you are not sure that you understand this law, communicate with the author of the course and secure further explanation by asking such questions as you may wish concerning points in connection with which you believe you need further information.

You cannot spend too much time in serious thought and contemplation in connection with the law of the "Master Mind," for the reason that when you have mastered this law and have learned how to apply it new worlds of opportunity will open to you.

This Introductory Lesson, while not really intended as a separate lesson of the Law of Success course, contains sufficient data to enable the student who has an aptitude for selling to become a Master Salesman.

Any sales organization may make effective use of the law of the "Master Mind" by grouping the salesmen in groups of two or more people who will ally themselves in a spirit of friendly co-operation and apply this law as suggested in this lesson.

An agent for a well known make of automobile, who employs twelve salesmen, has grouped his organization in six groups of two men each, with the object of applying the law of the "Master Mind," with the result that all the salesmen have established new high sales records.

This same organization has created what it calls the "One-A-Week Club," meaning that each man belonging to the Club has averaged the sale of one car a week since the Club was organized.

The results of this effort have been surprising to all!

Each man belonging to the Club was provided with a list of 100 prospective purchasers of automobiles. Each salesman sends one postal card a week to each of his 100 prospective purchasers, and makes personal calls on at least ten of these each day.

Each postal card is confined to the description of but one advantage of the automobile the salesman is selling, and asks for a personal interview.

Interviews have increased rapidly, as have, also, sales!

The agent who employs these salesmen has offered an extra cash bonus to each salesman who earns the right to membership in the "One-A-Week Club" by averaging one car a week.

The plan has injected new vitality into the entire organization. Moreover, the results of the plan are showing in the weekly sales record of each salesman.

A similar plan could be adopted very effectively by Life Insurance Agencies. Any enterprising General Agent might easily double or even triple the volume of his business, with the same number of salesmen, through the use of this plan.

Practically no changes whatsoever would need to be made in the method of use of the plan. The Club might be called the "Policy-A-Week Club," meaning that each member pledged himself to sell at least one policy, of an agreed minimum amount, each week.

The student of this course who has mastered the second lesson, and understands how to apply the fundamentals of that lesson (A Definite Chief Aim) will be able to make much more effective use of the plan here described.

It is not suggested or intended that any student shall undertake to apply the principles of this lesson, which is merely an Introductory Lesson, until he has mastered at least the next five lessons of the Law of Success course.

The main purpose of this Introductory Lesson is to state some of the principles upon which the course is founded. These principles are more accurately described, and the student is taught in a very definite manner how to apply them, in the individual lessons of the course.

The automobile sales organization referred to in this summary meets at luncheon once a week. One hour and a half is devoted to luncheon and to the discussion of ways and means of applying the principles of this course. This gives each man an opportunity to profit by the ideas of all the other members of the organization.

Two tables are set for the luncheon.

At one table all who have earned the right to membership in the One-A-Week Club are seated. At the other table, which is serviced with tinware instead of china, all who did not earn the right to membership in the Club are seated. These, needless to say, become the object of considerable good-natured chiding from the more fortunate members seated at the other table.

It is possible to make an almost endless variety of adaptations of this plan, both in the field of automobile salesmanship and in other fields of selling.

The justification for its use is that it pays!

It pays not only the leader or manager of the organization, but every member of the sales force as well.

This plan has been briefly described for the purpose of showing the student of this course how to make practical application of the principles outlined in this course.

The final acid test of any theory or rule or principle is that it will ACTUALLY WORK! The law of the "Master Mind" has been proved sound because it WORKS.

If you understand this law you are now ready to proceed with Lesson Two, in which you will be further and much more deeply initiated in the application of the principles described in this Introductory Lesson.

A WINNER NEVER
QUITS, AND A
QUITTER NEVER
WINS!

NOTICE

Study this chart carefully and compare the ratings of these ten men before grading yourself, in the two columns at the right.

THE FIFTEEN LAWS OF SUCCESS	HENRY FORD	BENJAMIN FRANKLIN	GEORGE WASHINGTON	THEODORE ROOSEVELT
I. Definite Chief Aim —	100	100	100	100
II. Self-Confidence - - - - ,	100	80	90	100
III. Habit of Saving - - - -	100	100	75	50
IV. Initiative & Leadership	100	60	100	100
V. Imagination - - - - - -	90	90	80	80
VI. Enthusiasm - - - - - - -	75	80	90	100
VII. Self-Control - - - - - -	100	90	50	75
VIII. Habit of Doing More Than Paid For -	100	100	100	100
IX. Pleasing Personality - -	50	90	80	80
X. Accurate Thinking - - -	90	80	75	60
XI. Concentration - - - -	100	100	100	100
XII. Cooperation - - - - -	75	100	100	50
XIII. Profiting by Failure - -	100	90	75	60
XIV. Tolerance - - - - - - -	90	100	80	75
XV. Practising Golden Rule -	100	100	100	100
GENERAL AVERAGE - - - -	91	90	86	82

The ten men who have been analyzed, in the above chart, are well known throughout the world. Eight of these are known to be successful, while two are generally considered to have been failures. The failures are Jesse James and Napoleon Bonaparte. They have been analyzed for comparison. Carefully observe where these two men have been graded zero and you will see why they failed. *A grading of zero on any one of the Fifteen Laws of Success is sufficient to cause failure,* even though all other grades are high.

Abraham Lincoln	Woodrow Wilson	William H. Taft	Napoleon Bonaparte	Calvin Coolidge	Jesse James	Grade yourself in these two columns, before and after completing the Law of Success course.	
						BEFORE	AFTER
100	100	100	100	100	0		
75	80	50	100	60	75		
20	40	30	40	100	0		
60	90	20	100	25	90		
70	80	65	90	50	60		
60	90	50	80	50	80		
95	75	80	40	100	50		
100	100	100	100	100	0		
80	75	90	100	40	50		
90	80	80	90	70	20		
100	100	100	100	100	75		
90	40	100	50	60	50		
60	60	60	40	40	0		
100	70	100	10	75	0		
100	100	100	0	100	0		
81	79	75	70	71	37		

Notice that all the successful men grade 100% on a Definite Chief Aim. This is a prerequisite to success, in all cases, without exception. If you wish to conduct an interesting experiment replace the above ten names with the names of ten people whom you know, five of whom are successful and five of whom are failures, and grade each of them. When you are through, GRADE YOURSELF, taking care to see that you really know what are your weaknesses.

YOUR SIX MOST DANGEROUS ENEMIES

An After-the-Lesson Visit With the Author

The Six Specters are labeled: Fear of Poverty, Fear of Death, Fear of Ill-Health, Fear of the Loss of Love, Fear of Old Age, Fear of Criticism.

Every person on earth is afraid of something. Most fears are inherited. In this essay you may study the six basic fears which do the most damage. Your fears must be mastered before you can win in any worth-while undertaking in life. Find out how many of the six fears are bothering you, but more important than this, determine, also how to conquer these fears.

I N this picture you have the opportunity to study your six worst enemies.

These enemies are not beautiful. The artist who drew this picture did not paint the six characters as ugly as they really are. If he had, no one would have believed him.

As you read about these ugly characters analyze yourself and find out which of them does YOU the most damage!

. . . .

The purpose of this essay is to help the readers of this course throw off these deadly enemies. Observe that the six characters are at your back, where you cannot conveniently see them.

Every human being on this earth is bound down to some extent by one or more of these unseen FEARS. The first step to be taken in killing off these enemies is to find out where and how you acquired them.

They got their grip upon you through two forms of heredity. One is known as physical heredity, to which Darwin devoted so much study. The other is known as social heredity, through which the fears, superstitions and beliefs of men who lived during the dark ages have been passed on from one generation to another.

Let us study, first, the part that physical heredity has played in creating these six BASIC FEARS. Starting at the beginning, we find that Nature has been a cruel builder. From the lowest form of life to the highest, Nature has permitted the stronger to prey upon the weaker forms of animal life.

The fish prey upon the worms and insects, eating them bodily. Birds prey upon the fish. Higher forms of animal life prey upon the birds, and upon one another, all the way up the line to man. And, man preys upon all the other lower forms of animal life, and upon MAN!

The whole story of evolution is one unbroken chain of evidence of cruelty and destruction of the weaker by the stronger. No wonder the weaker forms of animal life have learned to FEAR the stronger. The Fear consciousness is born in every living animal.

.   .   .   .

So much for the FEAR instinct that came to us through physical heredity. Now let us examine social heredity, and find out what part it has played in our make-up. The term "social heredity" has reference to everything that we are taught, everything we learn or gather from observation and experience with other living beings.

Lay aside any prejudices and fixed opinions you may have formed, at least temporarily, and you may know the truth about your Six Worst Enemies, starting with:

THE FEAR OF POVERTY! It requires courage to tell the truth about the history of this enemy of mankind, and still greater courage to hear the truth after it has been told. The Fear of Poverty grows out of man's habit of preying upon his fellow men, economically. The animals which have instinct, but no power to THINK, prey upon one another physically. Man, with his superior sense of intuition, and his more powerful weapon of THOUGHT, does not eat his fellow man bodily; he gets more pleasure from eating him FINANCIALLY.

So great an offender is man, in this respect, that nearly every state and nation has been obliged to pass laws, scores of laws, to protect the weak from the strong. Every blue-sky law is indisputable evidence of man's nature to prey upon his weaker brother economically.

The second of the Six Basic Fears with which man is bound down is:

THE FEAR OF OLD AGE! This Fear grows out of two major causes. First, the thought that Old Age may bring with it POVERTY. Secondly, from false and cruel sectarian teachings which have been so well mixed with fire and brimstone that every human being learned to Fear Old Age because it meant the approach of another and, perhaps, a more horrible world than this.

The third of the Six Basic Fears is:

THE FEAR OF ILL HEALTH: This Fear is born of both physical and social heredity. From birth until death there is eternal warfare within every physical body; warfare between groups of cells, one group being known as the friendly builders of the body, and the other as the destroyers, or "disease germs." The seed of Fear is born in the physical body, to begin with, as the result of Nature's cruel plan of permitting the stronger forms of cell life to prey upon the weaker. Social heredity has played its part through lack of cleanliness and knowledge of sanitation. Also, through the law of suggestion cleverly manipulated by those who profited by ILL HEALTH.

The fourth of the Six Basic Fears is:

THE FEAR OF LOSS OF LOVE OF SOMEONE: This Fear fills the asylums with the insanely jealous, for jealousy is nothing but a form of insanity. It also fills the divorce courts and causes murders and other forms of cruel punishment. It is a holdover, handed down through social heredity, from the stone age when man preyed upon his fellow man by stealing his mate by physical force. The method, but not the practice, has now changed to some extent. Instead of physical force man now steals his fellow man's mate with pretty colorful ribbons and fast motor cars and bootleg whisky, and sparkling rocks and stately mansions.

Man is improving. He now "entices" where once he "drove."

The fifth of the Six Basic Fears is:

THE FEAR OF CRITICISM: Just how and where man got this Fear is difficult to determine, but it is certain that he has it. But for this Fear men would not become bald-headed. Bald heads come from tightly fitting hat-bands, which cut off the circulation from the roots of the hair. Women seldom are bald because they wear loose fitting hats. But for Fear of Criticism man would lay aside his hat and keep his hair.

The makers of clothing have not been slow to capitalize this Basic Fear of mankind. Every season the styles change, because the clothes makers know that few people have the courage to wear a garment that is one season out of step with what "They are all wearing." If you doubt this (you gentlemen) start down the street with last year's narrow-brimmed straw hat on, when this year's style calls for the broad brim. Or (you ladies), take a walk down the street on Easter morning with last year's hat on. Observe how uncomfortable you are, thanks to your unseen enemy, the FEAR OF CRITICISM.

The sixth, and last of the Six Basic Fears is the most dreaded of them all. It is called:

THE FEAR OF DEATH! For tens of thousands

of years man has been asking the still unanswered questions—"WHENCE?" and "WHITHER?" The more crafty of the race have not been slow to offer the answer to this eternal question, "Where did I come from and where am I going after Death?" "Come into my tent," says one leader, "and you may go to Heaven after Death." Heaven was then pictured as a wonderful city whose streets were lined with gold and studded with precious stones. "Remain out of my tent and you may go straight to hell." Hell was then pictured as a blazing furnace where the poor victim might have the misery of burning forever in brimstone.

No wonder mankind FEARS DEATH!

.   .   .   .

Take another look at the picture at the beginning of this essay and determine, if you can, which of the Six Basic Fears is doing you the greatest damage. An enemy discovered is an enemy half whipped.

Thanks to the schools and colleges man is slowly discovering these Six Enemies. The most effective tool with which to fight them is ORGANIZED KNOWLEDGE. Ignorance and Fear are twin sisters. They are generally found together.

But for IGNORANCE and SUPERSTITION the Six Basic Fears would disappear from man's nature in one generation. In every public library may be found the remedy for these six enemies of mankind, providing you know what books to read.

Begin by reading The Science of Power, by Benjamin Kidd, and you will have broken the strangle hold of most of your Six Basic Fears. Follow this by reading Emerson's essay on Compensation. Then select some good book on auto-suggestion (self-suggestion) and inform yourself on the principle through which your beliefs of today become the realities of tomorrow. Mind In the Making, by Robinson, will give you a good start toward understanding your own mind.

.   .   .   .

Through the principle of social heredity the IGNORANCE and SUPERSTITION of the dark ages have been passed on to you. But, you are living in a modern age. On every hand you may see evidence that every EFFECT has a natural CAUSE. Begin, now, to study effects by their causes and soon you will emancipate your mind from the burden of the Six Basic Fears.

Begin by studying men who have accumulated great wealth, and find out the CAUSE of their achievements. Henry Ford is a good subject to start with. Within the short period of twenty-five years he has whipped POVERTY and made himself the most powerful man on earth. There was no luck or chance or accident back of his achievement. It grew out of his careful observation of certain principles which are as available to you as they were to him.

Henry Ford is not bound down by the Six Basic Fears; make no mistake about this.

If you feel that you are too far away from Ford to study him accurately, then begin by selecting two people whom you know close at hand; one representing your idea of FAILURE and the other corresponding to your idea of SUCCESS. Find out what made one a failure and the other a success. Get the real FACTS. In the process of gathering these facts you will have taught yourself a great lesson on CAUSE and EFFECT.

Nothing ever just "happens." Everything, from the lowest animal form that creeps on the earth or swims in the seas, on up to man, is the EFFECT of Nature's evolutionary process. Evolution is "orderly change." No "miracles" are connected with this orderly change.

Not only do the physical shapes and colors of animals undergo slow, orderly change from one generation to another, but the mind of man is also undergoing constant change. Herein lies your hope for improvement. You have the power to force your mind through a process of rather quick change. In a single month of properly directed self-suggestion you may place your foot upon the neck of every one of your Six Basic Fears. In twelve months of persistent effort you may drive the entire herd into the corner where it will never again do you any serious injury.

You will resemble, tomorrow, the DOMINATING THOUGHTS that you keep alive in your mind today! Plant in your mind the seed of DETERMINATION to whip your Six Basic Fears and the battle will have been half won then and there. Keep this intention in your mind and it will slowly push your Six Worst Enemies out of sight, as they exist nowhere except in your own mind.

The man who is powerful FEARS nothing; not even God. The POWERFUL man loves God, but FEARS Him never! Enduring power never grows out of FEAR. Any power that is built upon FEAR is bound

to crumble and disintegrate. Understand this great
truth and you will never be so unfortunate as to try
to raise yourself to power through the FEARS of
other people who may owe you temporary allegiance.

Man is of soul and body formed for deeds
Of high resolve; on fancy's boldest wing
To soar unwearied, fearlessly to turn
The keenest pangs to peacefulness, and taste
The joys which mingled sense and spirit yield;

Or he is formed for abjectness and woe,
To grovel on the dunghill of his fears,
To shrink at every sound, to quench the flame
Of natural love in sensualism, to know
That hour as blest when on his worthless days
The frozen hand of death shall set its seal,
Yet fear the cure, though hating the disease.

The one is man that shall hereafter be,
The other, man as vice has made him now.

—SHELLEY.

ONE of the most destructive evils is slanderous talk. It breaks human hearts and ruins reputations with a ruthlessness unknown in connection with all other evils.

A Personal Invitation from the Publisher, Melvin Powers...

I would like to introduce you to a wonderful, unique book guaranteed to captivate your imagination as it helps you discover the secret of what is most important in life. It is *The Knight in Rusty Armor,* a delightful tale of a desperate knight in search of his true self.

Since first publishing this book we have received an unprecedented number of calls and letters from readers praising its powerful insights and entertaining style. Readers say that this memorable story, rich in wit and humor, has changed their lives in important ways. *The Knight* is one of our most popular titles. It has been published in numerous languages and has become a well-known favorite in many countries. I feel so strongly about this book that I am personally inviting you to read it.

The Knight in Rusty Armor

Join the knight as he faces a life-changing dilemma upon discovering that he is trapped in his armor, just as *we* may be trapped in *our* armor—an invisible one that we use to protect ourselves from others and from various aspects of life.

As the knight searches for a way to free himself, he receives guidance from the wise sage Merlin the Magician, who encourages him to embark on the most difficult crusade of his life. The knight takes up the challenge and travels the Path of Truth, where he meets his real self for the first time and confronts the Universal Truths that govern his life—and ours.

The knight's journey reflects our own, filled with hope and despair, belief and disillusionment, laughter and tears. His insights become our insights as we follow along on his intriguing adventure of self-discovery. Anyone who has ever struggled with the meaning of life and love will discover profound wisdom and truth as this unique fantasy unfolds. *The Knight in Rusty Armor* is an experience that will expand your mind, touch your heart, and nourish your soul.

Available at all bookstores. Or send $5.00 (CA res. $5.41) plus $2.00 S/H to Wilshire Book Company, 12015 Sherman Road, No. Hollywood, CA 91605.

For our complete catalog, visit our Web site at www.mpowers.com.

WILSHIRE SELF-IMPROVEMENT LIBRARY

RECOVERY

___DRAGON SLAYER WITH A HEAVY HEART Marcia Powers	12.00
___KNIGHT IN RUSTY ARMOR Robert Fisher	5.00
___KNIGHTS WITHOUT ARMOR (Hardcover) Aaron R. Kipnis, Ph.D.	10.00
___PRINCESS WHO BELIEVED IN FAIRY TALES Marcia Grad	12.00
___SECRET OF OVERCOMING VERBAL ABUSE Dr. Albert Ellis & Marcia Grad Powers	12.00

SELF-HELP & INSPIRATIONAL

___CHANGE YOUR VOICE, CHANGE YOUR LIFE Morton Cooper, Ph.D.	10.00
___CHARISMA—HOW TO GET "THAT SPECIAL MAGIC" Marcia Grad	10.00
___DAILY POWER FOR JOYFUL LIVING Dr. Donald Curtis	7.00
___DRAGON SLAYER WITH A HEAVY HEART Marcia Powers	12.00
___DYNAMIC THINKING Melvin Powers	7.00
___GREATEST POWER IN THE UNIVERSE U.S. Andersen	10.00
___GROW RICH WHILE YOU SLEEP Ben Sweetland	10.00
___GROW RICH WITH YOUR MILLION DOLLAR MIND Brian Adams	10.00
___GROWTH THROUGH REASON Albert Ellis, Ph.D.	10.00
___GUIDE TO PERSONAL HAPPINESS Albert Ellis, Ph.D. & Irving Becker, Ed.D.	10.00
___GUIDE TO RATIONAL LIVING Albert Ellis, Ph.D. & R. Harper, Ph.D.	15.00
___HANDWRITING ANALYSIS MADE EASY John Marley	10.00
___HANDWRITING TELLS Nadya Olyanova	10.00
___HOW TO ATTRACT GOOD LUCK A.H.Z. Carr	10.00
___HOW TO DEVELOP A WINNING PERSONALITY Martin Panzer	10.00
___HOW TO DEVELOP AN EXCEPTIONAL MEMORY Young & Gibson	10.00
___HOW TO LIVE WITH A NEUROTIC Albert Ellis, Ph.D.	10.00
___HOW TO SUCCEED Brian Adams	10.00
___I CAN Ben Sweetland	10.00
___I WILL Ben Sweetland	10.00
___KNIGHT IN RUSTY ARMOR Robert Fisher	5.00
___LAW OF SUCCESS IN SIXTEEN LESSONS Napoleon Hill (Two-Volume Set)	30.00
___MAGIC IN YOUR MIND U.S. Andersen	15.00
___MAGIC OF THINKING SUCCESS Dr. David J. Schwartz	10.00
___MAGIC POWER OF YOUR MIND Walter M. Germain	10.00
___NEVER UNDERESTIMATE THE SELLING POWER OF A WOMAN Dottie Walters	7.00
___PRINCESS WHO BELIEVED IN FAIRY TALES Marcia Grad	12.00
___PSYCHO-CYBERNETICS Maxwell Maltz, M.D.	10.00
___PSYCHOLOGY OF HANDWRITING Nadya Olyanova	10.00
___SALES CYBERNETICS Brian Adams	10.00
___SECRET OF OVERCOMING VERBAL ABUSE Dr. Albert Ellis & Marcia Grad Powers	12.00
___SECRET OF SECRETS U.S. Andersen	10.00
___SECRET POWER OF THE PYRAMIDS U.S. Andersen	7.00
___SELF-THERAPY FOR THE STUTTERER Malcolm Frazer	10.00
___STOP COMMITTING VOICE SUICIDE Morton Cooper, Ph.D.	10.00
___SUCCESS CYBERNETICS U.S. Andersen	10.00
___10 DAYS TO A GREAT NEW LIFE William E. Edwards	3.00
___THINK AND GROW RICH Napoleon Hill	12.00
___THINK LIKE A WINNER Walter Doyle Staples, Ph.D.	15.00
___THREE MAGIC WORDS U.S. Andersen	15.00
___TREASURY OF COMFORT Edited by Rabbi Sidney Greenberg	15.00
___TREASURY OF THE ART OF LIVING Edited by Rabbi Sidney Greenberg	10.00
___WHAT YOUR HANDWRITING REVEALS Albert E. Hughes	4.00
___WINNING WITH YOUR VOICE Morton Cooper, Ph.D.	10.00
___YOUR SUBCONSCIOUS POWER Charles M. Simmons	7.00

Available wherever books are sold or from the publisher.
Please add $2.00 S/H for each book ordered.

Wilshire Book Company
12015 Sherman Road, No. Hollywood, California 91605
For our complete catalog, visit our Web site at www.mpowers.com.

THE
LAW OF
SUCCESS

IN SIXTEEN LESSONS

Teaching, for the First Time in the History of the World, the True Philosophy upon which all Personal Success is Built.

BY

NAPOLEON HILL

1928

PUBLISHED BY

The RALSTON UNIVERSITY PRESS

MERIDEN, CONN.

Lesson Two

A DEFINITE CHIEF AIM

The best rose bush, after all, is not that which has the fewest thorns, but that which bears the finest roses.

—*Henry van Dyke.*

"You Can Do It if You Believe You Can!"

OU are at the beginning of a course of philosophy which, for the first time in the history of the world, has been organized from the known factors which have been used and must always be used by successful people.

Literary style has been completely subordinated for the sake of stating the principles and laws included in this course in such a manner that they may be quickly and easily assimilated by people in every walk of life.

Some of the principles described in the course are familiar to all who will read the course. Others are here stated for the first time. It should be kept in mind, from the first lesson to the last, that the value of the philosophy lies entirely in the thought stimuli it will produce in the mind of the student, and not merely in the lessons themselves.

Stated in another way, this course is intended as a mind stimulant that will cause the student to organize and direct to a DEFINITE end the forces of his or her mind, thus harnessing the stupendous power which most people waste in spasmodic, purposeless thought.

Singleness of purpose is essential for success, no matter what may be one's idea of the definition of success. Yet singleness of purpose is a quality which may, and generally does, call for thought on many allied subjects.

This author traveled a long distance to watch Jack Dempsey train for an oncoming battle. It was observed that he did not rely entirely upon one form of exercise, but resorted to many forms. The punching bag helped him develop one set of muscles, and also trained his eye to be quick. The dumb-bells trained still another set of muscles. Running developed the muscles of his legs and hips. A well balanced food ration supplied the materials needed for building muscle without fat. Proper sleep, relaxation and rest habits provided still other qualities which he must have in order to win.

The student of this course is, or should be, engaged in the business of training for success in the battle of life. To win there are many factors which must have attention. A well organized, alert and energetic mind is produced by various and sundry stimuli, all of which are plainly described in these lessons.

It should be remembered, however, that the mind requires, for its development, a variety of exercise, just as the physical body, to be properly developed, calls for many forms of systematic exercise.

Horses are trained to certain gaits by trainers who hurdle-jump them over handicaps which cause them to develop the desired steps, through habit and repetition. The human mind must be trained in a similar manner, by a variety of thought-inspiring stimuli.

You will observe, before you have gone very far into this philosophy, that the reading of these lessons will superinduce a flow of thoughts covering a wide range of subjects. For this reason the student should read the course with a note-book and pencil at hand, and follow the practice of recording these thoughts or "ideas" as they come into the mind.

By following this suggestion the student will have a collection of ideas, by the time the course has been read two or three times, sufficient to transform his or her entire life-plan.

By following this practice it will be noticed, very soon, that the mind has become like a magnet in that it will attract useful ideas right out of the "thin air," to use the words of a noted scientist who has experimented with this principle for a great number of years.

You will do yourself a great injustice if you undertake this course with even a remote feeling that you do not stand in need of more knowledge than you now possess. In truth, no man knows enough about any worth-while subject to entitle him to feel that he has the last word on that subject.

In the long, hard task of trying to wipe out some of my own ignorance and make way for some of the useful truths of life, I have often seen, in my imagination, the Great Marker who stands at the gateway entrance of life and writes "Poor Fool" on the brow of those who believe they are wise, and "Poor Sinner" on the brow of those who believe they are saints.

Which, translated into workaday language, means that none of us know very much, and by the very nature of our being can never know as much as we need to know in order to live sanely and enjoy life while we live.

Humility is a forerunner of success!

Until we become humble in our own hearts we are not apt to profit greatly by the experiences and thoughts of others.

Sounds like a preachment on morality? Well, what if it does?

Even "preachments," as dry and lacking in interest as they generally are, may be beneficial if they serve to reflect the shadow of our real selves so we may get an approximate idea of our smallness and superficiality.

Success in life is largely predicated upon our knowing men!

The best place to study the man-animal is in your own mind, by taking as accurate an inventory as possible of YOURSELF. When you know yourself thoroughly (if you ever do) you will also know much about others.

To know others, not as they seem to be, but as they really are, study them through:

1—The posture of the body, and the way they walk.

2—The tone of the voice, its quality, pitch, volume.

3—The eyes, whether shifty or direct.

4—The use of words, their trend, nature and quality.

Through these open windows you may literally "walk right into a man's soul" and take a look at the REAL MAN!

Going a step further, if you would know men study them:

When angry

When in love

When money is involved

When eating (alone, and unobserved, as they believe)

When writing

When in trouble

When joyful and triumphant

When downcast and defeated

When facing catastrophe of a hazardous nature

When trying to make a "good impression" on others

When informed of another's misfortune

When informed of another's good fortune

When losing in any sort of a game of sport

When winning at sport

When alone, in a meditative mood.

Before you can know any man, as he really is, you must observe him in all the foregoing moods, and perhaps more, which is practically the equivalent of saying that you have no right to judge others at sight.

Appearances count, there can be no doubt of that, but appearances are often deceiving.

This course has been so designed that the student who masters it may take inventory of himself and of others by other than "snap-judgment" methods. The student who masters this philosophy will be able to look through the outer crust of personal adornment, clothes, so-called culture and the like, and down deep into the heart of all about him.

This is a very broad promise!

It would not have been made if the author of this philosophy had not known, from years of experimentation and analysis, that the promise can be met.

Some who have examined the manuscripts of this

NO person is "Edu-cated" who has not at least a "Speaking Ac-quaintance" with t h e Law of Compensation, as it is described by Emer-son.

course have asked why it was not called a course in Master Salesmanship. The answer is that the word "salesmanship" is commonly associated with the marketing of goods or services, and it would, therefore, narrow down and circumscribe the real nature of the course. It is true that this is a course in Master Salesmanship, providing one takes a deeper-than-the-average view of the meaning of salesmanship.

This philosophy is intended to enable those who master it to "sell" their way through life successfully, with the minimum amount of resistance and friction. Such a course, therefore, must help the student organize and make use of much truth which is overlooked by the majority of people who go through life as mediocres.

Not all people are so constituted that they wish to know the truth about all matters vitally affecting life. One of the great surprises the author of this course has met with, in connection with his research activities, is that so few people are willing to hear the truth when it shows up their own weaknesses.

We prefer illusions to realities!

New truths, if accepted at all, are taken with the proverbial grain of salt. Some of us demand more than a mere pinch of salt; we demand enough to pickle new ideas so they become useless.

For these reasons the Introductory Lesson of this course, and this lesson as well, cover subjects intended to pave the way for new ideas so those ideas will not be too severe a shock to the mind of the student.

The thought the author wishes to "get across" has been quite plainly stated by the editor of the American

Magazine, in an editorial which appeared in a recent issue, in the following words:

"On a recent rainy night, Carl Lomen, the reindeer king of Alaska, told me a true story. It has stuck in my crop ever since. And now I am going to pass it along.

" 'A certain Greenland Eskimo,' said Lomen, 'was taken on one of the American North Polar expeditions a number of years ago. Later, as a reward for faithful service, he was brought to New York City for a short visit. At all the miracles of sight and sound he was filled with a most amazed wonder. When he returned to his native village he told stories of buildings that rose into the very face of the sky; of street cars, which he described as houses that moved along the trail, with people living in them as they moved; of mammoth bridges, artificial lights, and all the other dazzling concomitants of the metropolis.

" 'His people looked at him coldly and walked away. And forthwith throughout the whole village he was dubbed "Sagdluk," meaning "the Liar," and this name he carried in shame to his grave. Long before his death his original name was entirely forgotten.

" 'When Knud Rasmussen made his trip from Greenland to Alaska he was accompanied by a Greenland Eskimo named Mitek (Eider Duck). Mitek visited Copenhagen and New York, where he saw many things for the first time and was greatly impressed. Later, upon his return to Greenland, he recalled the tragedy of Sagdluk, and decided that it would not be wise to tell the truth. Instead, he would narrate stories that his people could grasp, and thus save his reputation.

" 'So he told them how he and Doctor Rasmussen maintained a kayak on the banks of a great river, the Hudson, and how, each morning, they paddled out for their hunting. Ducks, geese and seals were to be had a-plenty, and they enjoyed the visit immensely.

" 'Mitek, in the eyes of his countrymen, is a very honest man. His neighbors treat him with rare respect.'

"The road of the truth-teller has always been rocky. Socrates sipping the hemlock, Christ crucified, Stephen stoned, Bruno burned at the stake, Galileo terrified into retraction of his starry truths— forever could one follow that bloodly trail through the pages of history.

"Something in human nature makes us resent the impact of new ideas."

We hate to be disturbed in the beliefs and prejudices that have been handed down with the family furniture. At maturity too many of us go into hibernation, and live off the fat of ancient fetishes. If a new idea invades our den we rise up snarling from our winter sleep.

The Eskimos, at least, had some excuse. They were unable to visualize the startling pictures drawn by Sagdluk. Their simple lives had been too long circumscribed by the brooding arctic night.

But there is no adequate reason why the average man should ever close his mind to fresh "slants" on life. He does, just the same. Nothing is more tragic —or more common—than mental inertia. For every ten men who are physically lazy there are ten thousand with stagnant minds. And stagnant minds are the breeding places of fear.

An old farmer up in Vermont always used to wind up his prayers with this plea: "Oh, God, give me an open mind!" If more people followed his example they might escape being hamstrung by prejudices. And what a pleasant place to live in the world would be.

.   .   .   .

Every person should make it his business to gather new ideas from sources other than the environment in which he daily lives and works.

The mind becomes withered, stagnant, narrow and closed unless it searches for new ideas. The farmer should come to the city quite often, and walk among the strange faces and the tall buildings. He will go back to his farm, his mind refreshed, with more courage and greater enthusiasm.

The city man should take a trip to the country every so often and freshen his mind with sights new and different from those associated with his daily labors.

Everyone needs a change of mental environment at regular periods, the same as a change and variety of food are essential. The mind becomes more alert, more elastic and more ready to work with speed and accuracy after it has been bathed in new ideas, outside of one's own field of daily labor.

As a student of this course you will temporarily lay aside the set of ideas with which you perform your daily labors, and enter a field of entirely new (and in some instances, heretofore unheard-of) ideas.

Splendid! You will come out, at the other end of this course, with a new stock of ideas which will make you more efficient, more enthusiastic and more courageous, *no matter in what sort of work you may be engaged.*

Do not be afraid of new ideas! They may mean to you the difference between success and failure.

Some of the ideas introduced in this course will require no further explanation or proof of their soundness because they are familiar to practically everyone. Other ideas here introduced are new, and for that very reason many students of this philosophy may hesitate to accept them as sound.

Every principle described in this course has been thoroughly tested by the author, and the majority of the principles covered have been tested by scores of scientists and others who were quite capable of distinguishing between the merely theoretic and the practical.

For these reasons all principles here covered are known to be workable in the exact manner claimed for them. However, no student of this course is asked to accept any statement made in these lessons without having first satisfied himself or herself, by tests, experiments and analysis, that the statement is sound.

The major evil the student is requested to avoid is that of forming opinions without definite FACTS as the basis, which brings to mind Herbert Spencer's famous admonition, in these words:

"There is a principle which is a bar against all information; which is proof against all argument; and which cannot fail to keep a man in everlasting ignorance. This principle is contempt prior to examination."

It may be well to bear this principle in mind when you come to study the Law of the Master Mind de-

B^Y and Large, there is no such thing as "Something for Nothing." In the long run you get exactly that for which you pay, whether you are buying an automobile or a loaf of bread.

scribed in these lessons. This law embodies an entirely new principle of mind operation, and, for this reason alone, it will be difficult for many students to accept it as sound until after they have experimented with it.

When the fact is considered, however, that the Law of the Master Mind is believed to be the real basis of most of the achievements of those who are considered geniuses, this Law takes on an aspect which calls for more than "snap-judgment" opinions.

It is believed by many scientific men whose opinions on the subject have been given the author of this philosophy, that the Law of the Master Mind is the basis of practically all of the more important achievements resulting from group or co-operative effort.

The late Dr. Alexander Graham Bell said he believed the Law of the Master Mind, as it has been described in this philosophy, was not only sound, but that all the higher institutions of learning would soon be teaching that Law as a part of their courses in psychology.

Charles P. Steinmetz said he had experimented with the Law and had arrived at the same conclusion as that stated in these lessons, long before he talked to the author of the Law of Success philosophy about the subject.

Luther Burbank and John Burroughs made similar statements!

Edison was never interrogated on the subject, but other statements of his indicate that he would endorse the Law as being a possibility, if not in fact a reality.

Dr. Elmer Gates endorsed the Law, in a conversation with this author more than fifteen years ago. Dr. Gates is a scientist of the highest order, ranking along with Steinmetz, Edison and Bell.

The author of this philosophy has talked to scores of intelligent business men who, while they were not scientists, admitted they believed in the soundness of the Law of the Master Mind. It is hardly excusable, therefore, for men of less ability to judge such matters, to form opinions as to this Law, without serious, systematic investigation.

.   .   .   .

Let me lay before you a brief outline of what this lesson is and what it is intended to do for *you!*

Having prepared myself for the practice of law I will offer this introduction as a "statement of my case." The evidence with which to back up my case will be presented in the sixteen lessons of which the course is composed.

The facts out of which this course has been prepared have been gathered through more than twenty-five years of business and professional experience, and my only explanation of the rather free use of the personal pronoun throughout the course is that I am writing from *first-hand experience.*

Before this Reading Course on the Law of Success was published the manuscripts were submitted to two prominent universities with the request that they be read by competent professors with the object of eliminating or correcting any statements that appeared to be unsound, from an economic viewpoint.

This request was complied with and the manuscripts were carefully examined, with the result that not a single change was made with the exception of one or two slight changes in wording.

One of the professors who examined the manuscripts expressed himself, in part, as follows: "It is a tragedy that every boy and girl who enters high school is not efficiently drilled on the fifteen major parts of your Reading Course on the Law of Success. It is regrettable that the great university with which I am connected, and every other university, does not include your course as a part of its curriculum."

Inasmuch as this Reading Course is intended as a map or blueprint that will guide you in the attainment of that coveted goal called "Success," may it not be well here to define success?

Success is the development of the power with which to get whatever one wants in life without interfering with the rights of others.

I would lay particular stress upon the word "power" because it is inseparably related to success. We are living in a world and during an age of intense competition, and the law of the survival of the fittest is everywhere in evidence. Because of these facts all who would enjoy enduring success must go about its attainment through the use of power.

And what is *power?*

Power is *organized* energy or effort. This course is properly called the Law of Success for the reason that it teaches how one may organize *facts* and *knowledge* and the faculties of one's mind into a unit of power.

This course brings you a definite promise, namely:

That through its mastery and application you can get whatever you want, with but two qualifying words —"within reason."

This qualification takes into consideration your education, your wisdom or your lack of it, your physical endurance, your temperament, and all of the other qualities mentioned in the sixteen lessons of this course as being the factors most essential in the attainment of success.

Without a single exception those who have attained unusual success have done so, either consciously or unconsciously, through the aid of all or a portion of the fifteen major factors of which this course is compiled. If you doubt this statement, then master these sixteen lessons so you can go about the analysis with reasonable accuracy and analyze such men as Carnegie, Rockefeller, Hill, Harriman, Ford and others of this type who have accumulated great fortunes of material wealth, and you will see that they understood and applied the principle of *organized effort* which runs, like a golden cord of indisputable evidence, throughout this course.

Nearly twenty years ago I interviewed Mr. Carnegie for the purpose of writing a story about him. During the interview I asked him to what he attributed his *success*. With a merry little twinkle in his eyes he said:

"Young man, before I answer your question will you please define your term 'success'?"

After waiting until he saw that I was somewhat embarrassed by his request he continued: "By success you have reference to my money, have you not?" I assured him that money was the term by which most people measured success, and he then said: "Oh, well —if you wish to know how I got my money—*if that is what you call success*—I will answer your question by saying that we have a master mind here in our business, and that mind is made up of more than a score of men who constitute my personal staff of superintendents and managers and accountants and chemists and other necessary types. No one person in this group is the master mind of which I speak, but the sum total of the minds in the group, co-ordinated, organized and directed to a *definite* end in a spirit of harmonious co-operation is the power that got my money for me. No two minds in the group are exactly alike, but each man in the group does the thing that he is supposed to do and he does it better than any other person in the world could do it."

Then and there the seed out of which this course has been developed was sown in my mind, but that seed did not take root or germinate until later. This interview marked the beginning of years of research which led, finally, to the discovery of the principle of psychology described in the Introductory Lesson as the "Master Mind."

I heard all that Mr. Carnegie said, but it took the knowledge gained from many years of subsequent contact with the business world to enable me to assimilate that which he said and clearly grasp and understand the principle back of it, which was nothing more nor less than the principle of *organized effort* upon which this course on the Law of Success is founded.

Carnegie's group of men constituted a "Master Mind" and that mind was so well organized, so well co-ordinated, so powerful, that it could have accumulated millions of dollars for Mr. Carnegie in practically any sort of endeavor of a commercial or industrial nature. The steel business in which that mind was engaged was but an incident in connection with the accumulation of the Carnegie wealth. The same wealth could have been accumulated had the "Master

IF you can run a losing r a c e without blaming your loss on someone else, you have bright prospects of success further down the road in life.

Mind" been directed in the coal business or the banking business or the grocery business, for the reason that back of the mind was *power*—that sort of power which *you* may have when you shall have organized the faculties of your own mind and allied yourself with other well organized minds for the attainment of a *definite chief aim* in life.

A careful check-up with several of Mr. Carnegie's former business associates, which was made after this course was begun, proves conclusively not only that there is such a law as that which has been called the "Master Mind," but that this law was the chief source of Mr. Carnegie's success.

Perhaps no man was ever associated with Mr. Carnegie who knew him better than did Mr. C. M. Schwab. In the following words Mr. Schwab has very accurately described that "subtle something" in Mr. Carnegie's personality which enabled him to rise to such stupendous heights.

"I never knew a man with so much imagination, lively intelligence and instinctive comprehension. You sensed that he probed your thoughts and took stock of everything that you had ever done or might do. He seemed to catch at your next word before it was spoken. The play of his mind was dazzling and his habit of close observation gave him a store of knowledge about innumerable matters.

"But his outstanding quality, from so rich an endowment, was the power of inspiring other men. Confidence radiated from him. You might be doubtful about something and discuss the matter with Mr. Carnegie. In a flash he would make you see that it was right and then absolutely believe it; or he might settle your doubts by pointing out its weakness. This quality of attracting others, then spurring them on, arose from his own strength.

"The results of his leadership were remarkable. Never before in history of industry, I imagine, was there a man who, without understanding his business in its working details, making no pretense of technical knowledge concerning steel or engineering, was yet able to build up such an enterprise.

"Mr. Carnegie's ability to inspire men rested on something deeper than any faculty of judgment."

In the last sentence Mr. Schwab has conveyed a thought which corroborates the theory of the "Master Mind" to which the author of this course has attributed the chief source of Mr. Carnegie's power.

Mr. Schwab has also confirmed the statement that Mr. Carnegie could have succeeded as well in any other business as he did in the steel business. It is obvious that his success was due to his understanding of his own mind and the minds of other men, and not to mere knowledge of the steel business itself.

This thought is most consoling to those who have not yet attained outstanding success, for it shows that success is solely a matter of correctly applying laws and principles which are available to all; and these laws, let us not forget, are fully described in the Sixteen Lessons of this course.

Mr. Carnegie learned how to apply the law of the "Master Mind." This enabled him to organize the faculties of his own mind and the faculties of other men's minds, and co-ordinate the whole behind a DEFINITE CHIEF AIM.

Every strategist, whether in business or war or industry or other callings, understands the value of *organized,* co-ordinated effort. Every military strategist understands the value of sowing seeds of dissension in the ranks of the opposing forces, because this breaks up the power of co-ordination back of the opposition. During the late world war much was heard about the effects of propaganda, and it seems not an exaggeration to say that the disorganizing forces of propaganda were much more destructive than were all the guns and explosives used in the war.

One of the most important turning-points of the world war came when the allied armies were placed under the direction of the French General, Foch. There are well informed military men who claim that this was the move which spelled doom for the opposing armies.

Any modern railroad bridge is an excellent example of the value of *organized effort,* because it demonstrates quite simply and clearly how thousands of tons of weight may be borne by a comparatively small group of steel bars and beams so arranged that the weight is spread over the entire group.

There was a man who had seven sons who were always quarreling among themselves. One day he called them together and informed them that he wished to demonstrate just what their lack of co-operative effort meant. He had prepared a bundle of seven sticks which he had carefully tied together. One by one he asked his sons to take the bundle and break it. Each son tried, but in vain. Then he cut the strings and handed one of the sticks to each of his sons and asked him to break it over his knee. After the sticks had all been broken, with ease, he said:

"When you boys work together in a spirit of harmony you resemble the bundle of sticks, and no one can defeat you; but when you quarrel among yourselves anyone can defeat you one at a time."

There is a worth-while lesson in this story of the man and his seven quarrelsome sons, and it may be applied to the people of a community, the employees and employers in a given place of employment, or to the state and nation in which we live.

Organized effort may be made a power, but it may also be a dangerous power unless guided with intelligence, which is the chief reason why the sixteenth lesson of this course is devoted largely to describing how to direct the power of organized effort so that it will lead to *success;* that sort of success which is founded upon truth and justice and fairness that lead to ultimate *happiness.*

One of the outstanding tragedies of this age of struggle and money-madness is the fact that so few people are engaged in the effort which they like best. One of the objects of this course is to help each student find his or her particular niche in the world's work, where both material prosperity and *happiness* in abundance may be found. For this purpose a Character Analysis Chart accompanies the sixteenth lesson. This chart is designed to help the student take inventory of himself and find out what latent ability and hidden forces lie sleeping within him.

This entire course is intended as a stimulus with which to enable you to see yourself and your hidden forces as they are, and to awaken in you the ambition and the vision and the determination to cause you to go forth and claim that which is rightfully yours.

Less than thirty years ago a man was working in the same shop with Henry Ford, doing practically the same sort of work that he was doing. It has been said that this man was really a more competent workman, in that particular sort of work, than Ford. To-day this man is still engaged in the same sort of work, at wages of less than a hundred dollars a week, while Mr. Ford is the world's richest man.

What outstanding difference is there between these two men which has so widely separated them in terms of material wealth? Just this—Ford understood and applied the principle of *organized effort* while the other man did not.

In the little city of Shelby, Ohio, as these lines are being written, for the first time in the history of the world this principle of *organized effort* is being applied for the purpose of bringing about a closer alliance between the churches and the business houses of a community.

The clergymen and business men have formed an alliance, with the result that practically every church in the city is squarely back of every business man, and every business man is squarely back of every church. The effect has been the strengthening of the churches and the business houses to such an extent that it has been said that it would be practically impossible for any individual member of either class to fail in his calling. The others who belong to the alliance will permit no such failures.

Here is an example of what may happen when groups of men form an alliance for the purpose of placing the combined power of the group back of each individual unit. The alliance has brought both ma-

A GOOD Encyclopæ-
dia contains most of the
known facts of the world,
but they are as useless as
Sand Dunes until organ-
ized and expressed in
terms of action.

terial and moral advantages to the city of Shelby such as are enjoyed by but few other cities of its size in America. The plan has worked so effectively and so satisfactorily that a movement is now under way to extend it into other cities throughout America.

That you may gain a still more concrete vision of just how this principle of *organized effort* can be made powerful, stop for a moment and allow your imagination to draw a picture of what would likely be the result if every church and every newspaper and every Rotary Club and every Kiwanis Club and every Advertising Club and every Woman's Club and every other civic organization of a similar nature, in your city, or in any other city in the United States, should form an alliance for the purpose of pooling their power and using it for the benefit of all members of these organizations.

The results which might easily be attained by such an alliance stagger the imagination!

There are three outstanding powers in the world of *organized effort*. They are: The churches, the schools and the newspapers. Think what might easily happen if these three great powers and molders of public opinion should ally themselves together for the purpose of bringing about any needed change in human conduct. They could, in a single generation, so modify the present standard of business ethics, for example, that it would practically be business suicide for anyone to try to transact business under any standard except that of the Golden Rule. Such an alliance could be made to produce sufficient influence to change, in a single generation, the business, social and moral tendencies of the entire civilized world. Such an alliance would have sufficient power to *force* upon the minds of the oncoming generations any ideals desired.

Power is *organized effort,* as has already been stated! Success is based upon power!

That you may have a clear conception of what is meant by the term "organized effort" I have made use of the foregoing illustrations, and for the sake of further emphasis I am going to repeat the statement that the accumulation of great wealth and the attainment of any high station in life such as constitute what we ordinarily call *success,* are based upon the vision to comprehend and the ability to assimilate and apply the major principles of the sixteen lessons of this course.

This course is in complete harmony with the principles of economics and the principles of Applied Psychology. You will observe that those lessons, which depend, for their practical application, upon knowledge of psychology, have been supplemented with sufficient explanation of the psychological principles involved to render the lessons easily understood.

Before the manuscripts for this course went to the publisher they were submitted to some of the foremost bankers and business men of America, that they might be examined, analyzed and criticized by the most practical type of mind. One of the best known bankers in New York City returned the manuscripts with the following comment:

"I hold a master's degree from Yale, but I would willingly exchange all that this degree has brought me in return for what your course on the Law of Success would have brought me had I been afforded the privilege of making it a part of my training while I was studying at Yale.

"My wife and daughter have also read the manuscripts, and my wife has named your course 'the master key-board of life' because she believes that all who understand how to apply it may play a perfect symphony in their respective callings, just as a pianist may play any tune when once the key-board of the piano and the fundamentals of music have been mastered."

No two people on earth are exactly alike, and for this reason no two people would be expected to attain from this course the same viewpoint. Each student should read the course, understand it and then appropriate from its contents whatever he or she needs to develop a well rounded personality.

Before this appropriation can be properly made it will be necessary for the student to analyze himself, through the use of the questionnaire that comes with the sixteenth lesson of the course, for the purpose of finding out what his deficiencies may be. This questionnaire should not be filled out until the student thoroughly masters the contents of the entire course, for he will then be in position to answer the questions with more accuracy and understanding of himself. Through the aid of this questionnaire an experienced character analyst can take inventory of one's faculties as easily and as accurately as a merchant can inventory the goods on his shelves.

This course has been compiled for the purpose of helping the student find out what are his or her natural talents, and for the purpose of helping organize, coordinate and put into use the knowledge gained from experience. For more than twenty years I have been gathering, classifying and organizing the material that has gone into the course. During the past fourteen years I have analyzed more than 16,000 men and women, and all of the vital facts gathered from these analyses have been carefully organized and woven into this course. These analyses brought out many interesting facts which have helped to make this course practical and usable. For example, it was discovered that ninety-five per cent of all who were analyzed were failures, and but five per cent were successes. (By the term "failure" is meant that they had failed to find happiness and the ordinary necessities of life without struggle that was almost unbearable.) Perhaps this is about the proportion of successes and failures that might be found if all the people of the world were accurately analyzed. The struggle for a mere existence is terrific among people who have not learned how to organize and direct their natural talents, while the attainment of those necessities, as well as the acquiring of many of the luxuries, is comparatively simple among those who have mastered the principle of *organized effort.*

One of the most startling facts brought to light by those 16,000 analyses was the discovery that the ninety-five per cent who were classed as failures were in that class *because they had no definite chief aim in life,* while the five per cent constituting the successful ones not only had purposes that were *definite,* but they had, also, *definite plans* for the attainment of their purposes.

Another important fact disclosed by these analyses was that the ninety-five per cent constituting the failures were engaged in work which they did not like, while the five per cent constituting the successful ones were doing that which they liked best. It is doubtful whether a person could be a failure while engaged in work which he liked best. Another vital fact learned from the analyses was that all of the five per cent who were succeeding had formed the habit of systematic saving of money, while the ninety-five per cent who were failures saved nothing. This is worthy of serious thought.

One of the chief objects of this course is to aid the student in performing his or her chosen work in such a manner that it will yield the greatest returns in both money and happiness.

NO POSITION IN LIFE CAN BE SE-
CURE, AND NO
ACHIEVEMENT
CAN BE PERMA-
NENT UNLESS
BUILT UPON TRUTH
AND JUSTICE.

A Definite Chief Aim

The key-note of this entire lesson may be found in the word "definite."

It is most appalling to know that ninety-five per cent of the people of the world are drifting aimlessly through life, without the slightest conception of the work for which they are best fitted, and with no conception whatsoever of even the need of such a thing as a *definite* objective toward which to strive.

There is a psychological as well as an economic reason for the selection of a *definite chief aim* in life. Let us devote our attention to the psychological side of the question first. It is a well established principle of psychology that a person's acts are always in harmony with the dominating thoughts of his or her mind.

Any *definite chief aim* that is deliberately fixed in the mind and held there, with the determination to realize it, finally saturates the entire subconscious mind until it automatically influences the physical action of the body toward the attainment of that purpose.

Your *definite chief aim* in life should be selected with deliberate care, and after it has been selected it should be written out and placed where you will see it at least once a day, the psychological effect of which is to impress this purpose upon your subconscious mind so strongly that it accepts that purpose as a pattern or blueprint that will eventually dominate your activities in life and lead you, step by step, toward the attainment of the object back of that purpose.

The principle of psychology through which you can impress your *definite chief aim* upon your subconscious mind is called Auto-suggestion, or suggestion which you repeatedly make to yourself. It is a degree of self-hypnotism, but do not be afraid of it on that account, for it was this same principle through the aid of which Napoleon lifted himself from the lowly station of poverty-stricken Corsican to the dictatorship of France. It was through the aid of this same principle that Thomas A. Edison has risen from the lowly beginning of a news butcher to where he is accepted as the leading inventor of the world. It was through the aid of this same principle that Lincoln bridged the mighty chasm between his lowly birth, in a log cabin in the mountains of Kentucky, and the presidency of the greatest nation on earth. It was through the aid of this same principle that Theodore Roosevelt became one of the most aggressive leaders that ever reached the presidency of the United States.

You need have no fear of the principle of Auto-suggestion as long as you are sure that the objective for which you are striving is one that will bring you happiness of an enduring nature. Be sure that your *definite purpose* is constructive; that its attainment will bring hardship and misery to no one; that it will bring you peace and prosperity, then apply, to the limit of your understanding, the principle of self-suggestion for the speedy attainment of this purpose.

On the street corner, just opposite the room in which I am writing, I see a man who stands there all day long and sells peanuts. He is busy every minute. When not actually engaged in making a sale he is roasting and packing the peanuts in little bags. He is one of that great army constituting the ninety-five per cent who have no *definite purpose* in life. He is selling peanuts, not because he likes that work better than anything else he might do, but because he never sat down and thought out a *definite purpose* that would bring him greater returns for his labor. He is selling peanuts because he is a drifter on the sea of life, and one of the tragedies of his work is the fact that the same amount of effort that he puts into it, if directed along other lines, would bring him much greater returns.

Another one of the tragedies of this man's work is the fact that he is unconsciously making use of the principle of self-suggestion, but he is doing it to his own disadvantage. No doubt, if a picture could be made of his thoughts, there would be nothing in that picture except a peanut roaster, some little paper bags and a crowd of people buying peanuts. This man could get out of the peanut business if he had the vision and the ambition first to imagine himself in a more profitable calling, and the perseverance to hold that picture before his mind until it influenced him to take the necessary steps to enter a more profitable calling. He puts sufficient labor into his work to bring him a substantial return if that labor were directed toward the attainment of a *definite purpose* that offered bigger returns.

One of my closest personal friends is one of the best known writers and public speakers of this country. About ten years ago he caught sight of the possibilities of this principle of self-suggestion and began, immediately, to harness it and put it to work. He worked out a plan for its application that proved to be very effective. At that time he was neither a writer nor a speaker.

Each night, just before going to sleep, he would shut his eyes and see, *in his imagination,* a long council table at which he placed (in his imagination) certain well known men whose characteristics he wished to absorb into his own personality. At the end of the table he placed Lincoln, and on either side of the table he placed Napoleon, Washington, Emerson and Elbert Hubbard. He then proceeded to talk to these imaginary figures that he had seated at his imaginary council table, something after this manner:

Mr. Lincoln: I desire to build in my own character those qualities of patience and fairness toward all mankind and the keen sense of humor which were your outstanding characteristics. I need these qualities and I shall not be contented until I have developed them.

Mr. Washington: I desire to build in my own character those qualities of patriotism and self-sacrifice and leadership which were your outstanding characteristics.

Mr. Emerson: I desire to build in my own character those qualities of vision and the ability to interpret the laws of Nature as written in the rocks of prison walls and growing trees and flowing brooks and growing flowers and the faces of little children, which were your outstanding characteristics.

Napoleon: I desire to build in my own character those qualities of self-reliance and the strategic ability to master obstacles and profit by mistakes and develop strength out of defeat, which were your outstanding characteristics.

Mr. Hubbard: I desire to develop the ability to equal and even to excel the ability that you possessed with which to express yourself in clear, concise and forceful language.

Night after night, for many months, this man saw these men seated around that imaginary council table until finally he had imprinted their outstanding characteristics upon his own subconscious mind so clearly that he began to develop a personality which was a composite of their personalities.

The subconscious mind may be likened to a magnet, and when it has been vitalized and thoroughly saturated with any *definite purpose* it has a decided tendency to attract all that is necessary for the fulfillment of that purpose. Like attracts like, and you may see evidence of this law in every blade of grass and every growing tree. The acorn attracts from the soil and the air the necessary materials out of which to grow an oak tree. It never grows a tree that is part oak and part poplar. Every grain of wheat that is planted in the soil attracts the materials out of which to grow a stalk of wheat.

It never makes a mistake and grows both oats and wheat on the same stalk.

And men are subject, also, to this same Law of Attraction. Go into any cheap boarding house district in any city and there you will find people of the same general trend of mind associated together. On the other hand, go into any prosperous community and there you will find people of the same general tendencies associated together. Men who are successful always seek the company of others who are successful, while men who are on the ragged side of life always

DO NOT "TELL"

THE WORLD

WHAT YOU CAN

DO—

"SHOW" IT!

seek the company of those who are in similar circumstances. "Misery loves company."

Water seeks its level with no finer certainty than man seeks the company of those who occupy his own general status financially and mentally. A professor of Yale University and an illiterate hobo have nothing in common. They would be miserable if thrown together for any great length of time. Oil and water will mix as readily as will men who have nothing in common.

All of which leads up to this statement:

That you will attract to you people who harmonize with your own philosophy of life, whether you wish it or not. This being true, can you not see the importance of vitalizing your mind with a *definite chief aim* that will attract to you people who will be of help to you and not a hindrance? Suppose your *definite chief aim* is far above your present station in life. What of it? It is your privilege—nay, your *DUTY*, to aim high in life. You owe it to yourself and to the community in which you live to set a high standard for yourself.

There is much evidence to justify the belief that nothing *within reason* is beyond the possibility of attainment by the man whose *definite chief aim* has been well developed. Some years ago Louis Victor Eytinge was given a life sentence in the Arizona penitentiary. At the time of his imprisonment he was an all-around "bad man," according to his own admissions. In addition to this it was believed that he would die of tuberculosis within a year.

Eytinge had reason to feel discouraged, if anyone ever had. Public feeling against him was intense and he did not have a single friend in the world who came forth and offered him encouragement or help. Then something happened in his own mind that gave him back his health, put the dreaded "white plague" to rout and finally unlocked the prison gates and gave him his freedom.

What was that "something"?

Just this: He made up his mind to whip the white plague and regain his health. That was a very *definite chief aim*. In less than a year from the time the decision was made he had won. Then he extended that *definite chief aim* by making up his mind to gain his freedom. Soon the prison walls melted from around him.

No undesirable environment is strong enough to hold the man or woman who understands how to apply the principle of Auto-suggestion in the creation of a *definite chief aim*. Such a person can throw off the shackles of poverty; destroy the most deadly disease germs; rise from a lowly station in life to power and plenty.

All great leaders base their leadership upon a *definite chief aim*. Followers are willing followers when they know that their leader is a person with a *definite chief aim* who has the courage to back up that purpose with action. Even a balky horse knows when a driver with a *definite chief aim* takes hold of the reins; and yields to that driver. When a man with a *definite chief aim* starts through a crowd everybody stands aside and makes a way for him, but let a man hesitate and show by his actions that he is not sure which way he wants to go and the crowd will step all over his toes and refuse to budge an inch out of his way.

Nowhere is the lack of a *definite chief aim* more noticeable or more detrimental than it is in the relationship between parent and child. Children sense very quickly the wavering attitude of their parents and take advantage of that attitude quite freely. It is the same all through life—men with a *definite chief aim* command respect and attention at all times.

So much for the psychological viewpoint of a *definite purpose.* Let us now turn to the economic side of the question.

If a steamship lost its rudder, in mid-ocean, and began circling around, it would soon exhaust its fuel supply without reaching shore, despite the fact that it would use up enough energy to carry it to shore and back several times.

The man who labors without a *definite purpose* that is backed up by a definite plan for its attainment, resembles the ship that has lost its rudder. Hard labor and good intentions are not sufficient to carry a man through to success, for how may a man be sure that he has attained success unless he has established in his mind some definite object that he wishes?

Every well built house started in the form of a *definite purpose* plus a definite plan in the nature of a set of blueprints. Imagine what would happen if one tried to build a house by the haphazard method, without plans. Workmen would be in each other's way, building material would be piled all over the lot before the foundation was completed, and everybody on the job would have a different notion as to how the house ought to be built. Result, chaos and misunderstandings and cost that would be prohibitive.

Yet had you ever stopped to think that most people

finish school, take up employment or enter a trade or profession without the slightest conception of anything that even remotely resembles a *definite purpose* or a definite plan? In view of the fact that science has provided reasonably accurate ways and means of analyzing character and determining the life-work for which people are best fitted, does it not seem a modern tragedy that ninety-five per cent of the adult population of the world is made up of men and women who are failures because they have not found their proper niches in the world's work?

If *success* depends upon power, and if power is *organized effort,* and if the first step in the direction of organization is a *definite purpose,* then one may easily see why such a purpose is essential.

Until a man selects a *definite purpose* in life he dissipates his energies and spreads his thoughts over so many subjects and in so many different directions that they lead not to power, but to indecision and weakness.

With the aid of a small reading glass you can teach yourself a great lesson on the value of *organized effort.* Through the use of such a glass you can focus the sun-rays on a *definite* spot so strongly that they will burn a hole through a plank. Remove the glass (which represents the *definite purpose*) and the same rays of sun may shine on that same plank for a million years without burning it.

A thousand electric dry batteries, when properly organized and connected together with wires, will produce enough power to run a good sized piece of machinery for several hours, but take those same cells singly, disconnected, and not one of them would exert enough energy to turn the machinery over once. The faculties of your mind might properly be likened to those dry cells. When you organize your faculties, according to the plan laid down in the sixteen lessons of this Reading Course on the Law of Success, and direct them toward the attainment of a *definite purpose* in life, you then take advantage of the co-operative or accumulative principle out of which *power* is developed, which is called Organized Effort.

Andrew Carnegie's advice was this: "Place all your eggs in one basket and then watch the basket to see that no one kicks it over." By that advice he meant, of course, that we should not dissipate any of our energies by engaging in side lines. Carnegie was a sound economist and he knew that most men would do well if they so harnessed and directed their energies that some one thing would be done well.

When the plan back of this Reading Course was first born I remember taking the first manuscript to a professor of the University of Texas, and in a spirit of enthusiasm I suggested to him that I had discovered a principle that would be of aid to me in every public speech I delivered thereafter, because I would be better prepared to organize and marshal my thoughts.

He looked at the outline of the fifteen points for a few minutes, then turned to me and said:

"Yes, your discovery is going to help you make better speeches, but that is not all it will do. It will help you become a more effective writer, for I have noticed in your previous writings a tendency to scatter your thoughts. For instance, if you started to describe a beautiful mountain yonder in the distance you would be apt to sidetrack your description by calling atten-

THE BEST COM-

PENSATION

FOR DOING THINGS

IS THE ABILITY TO

DO MORE.

tion to a beautiful bed of wild flowers, or a running brook, or a singing bird, detouring here and there, zig-zag fashion, before finally arriving at the proper point from which to view the mountain. In the future you are going to find it much less difficult to describe an object, whether you are speaking or writing, because *your fifteen points represent the very foundation of organization.*"

A man who had no legs once met a man who was blind. To prove conclusively that the lame man was a *man of vision* he proposed to the blind man that they form an alliance that would be of great benefit to both. "You let me climb upon your back," said he to the blind man, "then I will use your legs and you may use my eyes. Between the two of us we will get along more rapidly."

Out of allied effort comes greater power. This is a point that is worthy of much repetition, *because it forms one of the most important parts of the foundation of this Reading Course.* The great fortunes of the world have been accumulated through the use of this principle of allied effort. That which one man can accomplish single handed, during an entire life-time, is but meagre at best, no matter how well organized that man may be, but that which one man may accomplish through the principle of alliance with other men is practically without limitation.

That "master mind" to which Carnegie referred during my interview with him was made up of more than a score of minds. In that group were men of practically every temperament and inclination. Each man was there to play a certain part and he did nothing else. There was perfect understanding and team-work between these men. It was Carnegie's business to keep harmony among them.

And he did it wonderfully well.

If you are familiar with the game of football you know, of course, that the winning team is the one that best co-ordinates the efforts of its players. Team-work is the thing that wins. It is the same in the great game of life.

In your struggle for *success* you should keep constantly in mind the necessity of knowing what it is that you want—of knowing precisely what is your *definite purpose*—and the value of the principle of *organized effort* in the attainment of that which constitutes your *definite purpose*.

In a vague sort of way nearly everyone has a definite purpose—namely, the desire for *money!* But this is not a *definite purpose* within the meaning of the term as it is used in this lesson. Before your purpose could be considered *definite,* even though that purpose were the accumulation of money, you would have to reach a decision as to the precise method through which you intend to accumulate that money. It would be insufficient for you to say that you would make money by going into some sort of business. You would have to decide just what line of business. You would also have to decide just where you would locate. You would also have to decide the business policies under which you would conduct your business.

In answering the question, "What Is Your Definite Purpose In Life," that appears in the questionnaire which I have used for the analysis of more than 16,000 people, many answered about as follows:

"My definite purpose in life is to be of as much

service to the world as possible and earn a good living."

That answer is about as *definite* as a frog's conception of the size of the universe is accurate!

The object of this lesson is not to inform you as to what your life-work should be, for indeed this could be done with accuracy only after you had been completely analyzed, but it is intended as a means of impressing upon your mind a clear conception of the value of a *definite purpose* of some nature, and of the value of understanding the principle of *organized effort* as a means of attaining the necessary power with which to materialize your *definite purpose*.

Careful observation of the business philosophy of more than one hundred men and women who have attained outstanding success in their respective callings, disclosed the fact that each was a person of prompt and definite decision.

The habit of working with a *definite chief aim* will breed in you the habit of prompt decision, and this habit will come to your aid in all that you do.

Moreover, the habit of working with a *definite chief aim* will help you to concentrate all your attention on any given task until you have mastered it.

Concentration of effort and the habit of working with a *definite chief aim* are two of the essential factors in success which are always found together. One leads to the other.

The best known successful business men were all men of prompt decision who worked always with one main, outstanding purpose as their chief aim.

Some notable examples are as follows:

Woolworth chose, as his *definite chief aim,* the belting of America with a chain of Five and Ten Cent Stores, and concentrated his mind upon this one task until he "made it and it made him."

Wrigley concentrated his mind on the production and sale of a five-cent package of chewing gum and turned this one idea into millions of dollars.

Edison concentrated upon the work of harmonizing natural laws and made his efforts uncover more useful inventions than any other man who ever lived.

Henry L. Doherty concentrated upon the building and operation of public utility plants and made himself a multimillionaire.

Ingersoll concentrated on a dollar watch and girdled the earth with "tickers" and made this one idea yield him a fortune.

Statler concentrated on "homelike hotel-service" and made himself wealthy as well as useful to millions of people who use his service.

Edwin C. Barnes concentrated on the sale of Edison Dictating Machines, and retired, while still a young man, with more money than he needs.

Woodrow Wilson concentrated his mind on the White House for twenty-five years, and became its chief tenant, thanks to his knowledge of the value of sticking to a *definite chief aim.*

Lincoln concentrated his mind on freeing the slaves and became our greatest American President while doing it.

Martin W. Littleton heard a speech which filled him with the desire to become a great lawyer, concentrated his mind on that one aim, and is now said to be the most successful lawyer in America, whose fees for a single case seldom fall below $50,000.00.

Rockefeller concentrated on oil and became the richest man of his generation.

Ford concentrated on "flivvers" and made himself the richest and most powerful man who ever lived.

Carnegie concentrated on steel and made his efforts build a great fortune and plastered his name on public libraries throughout America.

Gillette concentrated on a safety razor, gave the entire world a "close shave" and made himself a multi-millionaire.

George Eastman concentrated on the kodak and made the idea yield him a fortune while bringing much pleasure to millions of people.

Russell Conwell concentrated on one simple lecture, "Acres of Diamonds," and made the idea yield more than $6,000,000.

Hearst concentrated on sensational newspapers and made the idea worth millions of dollars.

Helen Keller concentrated on learning to speak, and, despite the fact that she was deaf, dumb and blind, realized her *definite chief aim.*

John H. Patterson concentrated on cash registers and made himself rich and others "careful."

The late Kaiser of Germany concentrated on war and got a big dose of it, let us not forget the fact!

Fleischmann concentrated on the humble little cake of yeast and made things hump themselves all over the world.

Marshall Field concentrated on the world's greatest retail store and lo! it rose before him, a reality.

Philip Armour concentrated on the butchering business and established a great industry, as well as a big fortune.

ANYONE CAN
"START," BUT
ONLY THE
THOROUGH-
BRED WILL
"FINISH!"

Millions of people are concentrating, daily, on POVERTY and FAILURE and getting both in over-abundance.

Wright Brothers concentrated on the airplane and mastered the air.

Pullman concentrated on the sleeping car and the idea made him rich and millions of people comfortable in travel.

The Anti-Saloon League concentrated on the Prohibition Amendment and (whether for better or worse) made it a reality.

Thus it will be seen that all who succeed work with some definite, outstanding aim as the object of their labors.

There is some one thing that you can do better than anyone else in the world could do it. Search until you find out what this particular line of endeavor is, make it the object of your *definite chief aim* and then organize all of your forces and attack it with the belief that you are going to win. In your search for the work for which you are best fitted, it will be well if you bear in mind the fact that you will most likely attain the greatest success by finding out what work you like best, for it is a well known fact that a man generally best succeeds in the particular line of endeavor into which he can throw his whole heart and soul.

Let us go back, for the sake of clarity and emphasis, to the psychological principles upon which this lesson is founded, because it will mean a loss that you can ill afford if you fail to grasp the real reason for establishing a *definite chief aim* in your mind. These principles are as follows:

First: Every voluntary movement of the human body is caused, controlled and directed by *thought,* through the operation of the mind.

Second: The presence of any thought or idea in your consciousness tends to produce an associated feeling and to urge you to transform that feeling into appropriate muscular action that is in perfect harmony with the nature of the thought.

For example, if you think of winking your eyelid and there are no counter influences or thoughts in your mind at the time to arrest action, the motor nerve will carry your thought from the seat of government, in your brain, and appropriate or corresponding muscular action takes place immediately.

Stating this principle from another angle: You choose, for example, a *definite purpose* as your life-work and make up your mind that you will carry out that purpose. *From the very moment that you make this choice, this purpose becomes the dominating thought in your consciousness, and you are constantly on the alert for facts, information and knowledge with which to achieve that purpose.* From the time that you plant a *definite purpose* in your mind, your mind begins, both consciously and unconsciously, to gather and store away the material with which you are to accomplish that purpose.

Desire is the factor which determines what your *definite purpose* in life shall be. No one can select your dominating *desire* for you, but once you select it yourself it becomes your *definite chief aim* and occupies the spotlight of your mind until it is satisfied by transformation into reality, unless you permit it to be pushed aside by conflicting desires.

To emphasize the principle that I am here trying to make clear, I believe it not unreasonable to suggest that to be sure of successful achievement, one's *definite chief aim* in life should be backed up with a *burning desire* for its achievement. I have noticed that boys and girls who enter college and pay their way through by working seem to get more out of their schooling than do those whose expenses are paid for them. The secret of this may be found in the fact that those who are willing to work their way through are blessed with a *burning desire* for education, and such a desire, if the object of the desire is within reason, is practically sure of realization.

Science has established, beyond the slightest room for doubt, that through the principle of Auto-suggestion any deeply rooted *desire* saturates the entire body and mind with the nature of the desire and literally transforms the mind into a powerful magnet that will attract the object of the desire, if it be within reason. For the enlightenment of those who might not properly interpret the meaning of this statement I will endeavor to state this principle in another way. For example, merely desiring an automobile will not cause that automobile to come rolling in, but, if there is a *burning desire* for an automobile, that desire will lead to the appropriate action through which an automobile may be paid for.

Merely desiring freedom would never release a man who was confined in prison if it were not sufficiently strong to cause him to do something to entitle himself to freedom.

These are the steps leading from *desire* to fulfillment: First the *burning desire*, then the crystallization of that desire into a *definite purpose,* then sufficient appropriate *action* to achieve that purpose. *Remember that these three steps are always necessary to insure success.*

I once knew a very poor girl who had a *burning desire* for a wealthy husband, and she finally got him, but not without having transformed that desire into the development of a very attractive personality which, in turn, attracted the desired husband.

I once had a *burning desire* to be able to analyze character accurately and that desire was so persistent and so deeply seated that it practically drove me into ten years of research and study of men and women.

George S. Parker makes one of the best fountain pens in the world, and despite the fact that his business is conducted from the little city of Janesville, Wisconsin, he has spread his product all the way around the globe and he has his pen on sale in every civilized country in the world. More than twenty years ago, Mr. Parker's *definite purpose* was established in his mind, and that purpose was to produce the best fountain pen that money could buy. He backed that purpose with a *burning desire* for its realization and if you carry a fountain pen the chances are that you have evidence in your own possession that it has brought him abundant success.

You are a contractor and builder, and, like men who build houses out of mere wood and brick and steel, you must draw up a set of plans after which to shape your *success building.* You are living in a wonderful age, when the materials that go into *success* are plentiful and cheap. You have at your disposal, in the archives of the public libraries, the carefully compiled results of two thousand years of research covering practically every possible line of endeavor in which one would wish to engage. If you would become a preacher you have at hand the entire history of what has been learned by men who have preceded you in this field. If you would become a mechanic you have at hand the entire history of the inventions of machines and the discovery and usages of metals and things metallic in nature. If you would become a lawyer you have at your disposal the entire history of law procedure. Through the Department of Agriculture, at Washington, you have at your disposal all that has been learned about farming and agriculture, where you may use it should you wish to find your life-work in this field.

The world was never so resplendent with *opportunity* as it is today. On every hand there is an ever-increasing demand for the services of the man or the woman who makes a better mouse-trap or performs better stenographic service or preaches a better sermon or digs a better ditch or runs a more accommodating bank.

This lesson will not be completed until you shall have made your choice as to what your *definite chief aim* in life is to be and then recorded a description of that purpose in writing and placed it where you may see it every morning when you arise and every night when you retire.

Procrastination is—but why preach about it? You know that *you* are the hewer of your own wood and the drawer of your own water and the shaper of your own *definite chief aim* in life; therefore, why dwell upon that which you already know?

A definite purpose is something that you must create

Every line a man writes, and every act in which he indulges, and every word he utters serves as unescapable evidence of the nature of that which is deeply imbedded in his own heart, a confession that he cannot disavow.

for yourself. No one else will create it for you and it will not create itself. What are you going to do about it? and when? and how?

Start now to analyze your desires and find out what it is that you wish, then make up your mind to get it. Lesson Three will point out to you the next step and show you how to proceed. Nothing is left to chance, in this Reading Course. Every step is marked plainly. Your part is to follow the directions until you arrive at your destination, which is represented by your *definite chief aim.* Make that aim clear and back it up with persistence which does not recognize the word "impossible."

When you come to select your *definite chief aim* just keep in mind the fact that you cannot *aim* too high.

Also keep in mind the never-varying truth that you'll get nowhere if you start nowhere. If your aim in life is vague your achievements will also be vague, and it might well be added, very *meager. Know what you want, when you want it, why you want it and HOW you intend to get it.* This is known to teachers and students of psychology as the WWWH formula— "what, when, why and how."

Read this lesson four times, at intervals of one week apart.

You will see much in the lesson the fourth time you read it that you did not see the first time.

Your success in mastering this course and in making it bring you success will depend very largely, if not entirely, upon how well you follow ALL the instructions it contains.

Do not set up your own rules of study. Follow those laid down in the Course, as they are the result of years of thought and experimentation. If you wish to experiment wait until you master this course in the manner suggested by its author. You will then be in position to experiment more safely. For the present content yourself by being the student. You will, let us hope, become the teacher as well as the student after you have followed the Course until you have mastered it.

If you follow the instructions laid down in this Course for the guidance of its students, you can no more fail than water can run uphill above the level of its source.

INSTRUCTIONS FOR APPLYING THE PRINCIPLES OF THIS LESSON

Through the Introductory Lesson of this course you became familiar with the principle of psychology known as the "Master Mind."

You are now ready to begin use of this principle as a means of transforming your *definite chief aim* into reality. It must have occurred to you that one might as well have no *definite chief aim* unless one has, also, a very definite and practical plan for making that aim become a reality.

Your first step is to decide what your major aim in life shall be. Your next step is to write out a clear, concise statement of this aim. This should be followed by a statement, in writing, of the plan or plans through which you intend to attain the object of your aim.

Your next and final step will be the forming of an alliance with some person or persons who will co-operate with you in carrying out these plans and transforming your *definite chief aim* into reality.

The purpose of this friendly alliance is to employ the law of the "Master Mind" in support of your plans. The alliance should be made between yourself and those who have your highest and best interests at heart. If you are a married man your wife should be one of the members of this alliance, providing there exists between you a normal state of confidence and sympathy. Other members of this alliance may be your mother, father, brothers or sisters, or some close friend or friends.

If you are a single person your sweetheart, if you have one, should become a member of your alliance. This is no joke—you are now studying one of the most powerful laws of the human mind, and you will serve your own best interests by seriously and earnestly following the rules laid down in this lesson, even though you may not be sure where they will lead you.

Those who join with you in the formation of a friendly alliance for the purpose of aiding you in the creation of a "Master Mind" should sign, with you, your statement of the object of your *definite chief aim*. Every member of your alliance must be fully acquainted with the nature of your object in forming the alliance. Moreover, every member must be in hearty accord with this object, and in full sympathy with you. Each member of your alliance must be supplied with a written copy of your statement of your *definite chief aim*. With this exception, however, *you are explicitly instructed to keep the object of your chief aim to yourself*. The world is full of "Doubting Thomases" and it will do your cause no good to have these rattle-brained people scoffing at you and your ambitions. Remember, what you need is friendly encouragement and help, not derision and doubt.

If you believe in prayer you are instructed to make your *definite chief aim* the object of your prayer at least once every twenty-four hours, and more often if convenient. If you believe there is a God who can and will aid those who are earnestly striving to be of constructive service in the world, surely you feel that you have a right to petition Him for aid in the attainment of what should be the most important thing in life to you.

If those who have been invited to join your friendly alliance believe in prayer, ask them, also, to include the object of this alliance as a part of their daily prayer.

Comes, now, one of the most essential rules which you *must follow*. Arrange with one or all of the members of your friendly alliance to state to you, in the most positive and definite terms at their command, that THEY KNOW YOU CAN AND WILL REALIZE THE OBJECT OF YOUR DEFINITE CHIEF AIM. This affirmation or statement should be made to you at least once a day; more often if possible.

These steps must be followed persistently, with full faith that they will lead you where you wish to go! It will not suffice to carry out these plans for a few days or a few weeks and then discontinue them. YOU MUST FOLLOW THE DESCRIBED PROCEDURE UNTIL YOU ATTAIN THE OBJECT OF YOUR DEFINITE CHIEF AIM, REGARDLESS OF THE TIME REQUIRED.

From time to time it may become necessary to change the plans you have adopted for the achievement of the object of your *definite chief aim*. Make these changes without hesitation. No human being has sufficient foresight to build plans which need no alteration or change.

If any member of your friendly alliance loses faith in the law known as the "Master Mind," immediately remove that member and replace him or her with some other person.

Andrew Carnegie stated to the author of this course that he had found it necessary to replace some of the members of his "Master Mind." In fact he stated

"Yes, he succeeded—but—he almost failed!" So did Robert Fulton and Abraham Lincoln and nearly all the others whom we call successful. No man ever achieved worth-while success who did not, at one time or other, find himself with at least one foot hanging well over the brink of failure.

that practically every member of whom his alliance was originally composed had, in time, been removed and replaced with some other person who could adapt himself more loyally and enthusiastically to the spirit and object of the alliance.

You cannot succeed when surrounded by disloyal and unfriendly associates, no matter what may be the object of your *definite chief aim*. Success is built upon loyalty, faith, sincerity, co-operation and the other positive forces with which one must surcharge his environment.

Many of the students of this course will want to form friendly alliances with those with whom they are associated professionally or in business, with the object of achieving success in their business or profession. In such cases the same rules of procedure which have been here described should be followed. The object of your *definite chief aim* may be one that will benefit you individually, or it may be one that will benefit the business or profession with which you are connected. The law of the "Master Mind" will work the same in either case. If you fail, either temporarily or permanently, in the application of this law *it will be for the reason that some member of your alliance did not enter into the spirit of the alliance with faith, loyalty and sincerity of purpose.*

The last sentence is worthy of a second reading!

The object of your *definite chief aim* should become your "hobby." You should ride this "hobby" continuously; you should sleep with it, eat with it, play with it, work with it, live with it and THINK with it.

Whatever you want you may get if you want it with sufficient intensity, and keep on wanting it, providing the object wanted is one within reason, and you ACTUALLY BELIEVE YOU WILL GET IT! There is a difference, however, between merely "wishing" for something and ACTUALLY BELIEVING you will get it. Lack of understanding of this difference has meant failure to millions of people. The "doers" are the "believers" in all walks of life. Those who BE-LIEVE they can achieve the object of their *definite chief aim* do not recognize the word impossible. Neither do they acknowledge temporary defeat. They KNOW they are going to succeed, and if one plan fails they quickly replace it with another plan.

Every noteworthy achievement met with some sort of temporary setback before success came. Edison made more than ten thousand experiments before he succeeded in making the first talking machine record the words, "Mary had a little lamb."

If there is one word which should stand out in your mind in connection with this lesson, it is the word PERSISTENCE!

You now have within your possession the pass-key to achievement. You have but to unlock the door to the Temple of Knowledge and walk in. But you must go to the Temple; it will not come to you. If these laws are new to you the "going" will not be easy at first. You will stumble many times, but keep moving! Very soon you will come to the brow of the mountain you have been climbing, and you will behold, in the valleys below, the rich estate of KNOWLEDGE which shall be your reward for your faith and efforts.

Everything has a price. There is no such possibility as "something for nothing." In your experiments with the Law of the Master Mind you are jockeying with Nature, in her highest and noblest form. Nature cannot be tricked or cheated. She will give up to you the object of your struggles only after you have paid her price, which is CONTINUOUS, UNYIELDING, PERSISTENT EFFORT!

What more could be said on this subject?

You have been shown *what to do, when to do it, how to do it* and *why you should do it.* If you will master the next lesson, on Self-confidence, you will then have the faith in yourself to enable you to carry out the instructions laid down for your guidance in this lesson.

Master of human destinies am I!
Fame, love, and fortune on my footsteps wait.
Cities and fields I walk; I penetrate
Deserts and seas remote, and passing by
Hovel and mart and palace—soon or late
I knock, unbidden, once at every gate!
If sleeping, wake—if feasting, rise before
I turn away. It is the hour of fate,
And they who follow me reach every state
Mortals desire, and conquer every foe
Save death; but those who doubt or hesitate,
Condemned to failure, penury, and woe,
Seek me in vain and uselessly implore.
I answer not, and I return no more!

—INGALLS.

NEGLECTING TO
BROADEN
THEIR VIEW HAS
KEPT SOME MEN
DOING ONE THING
ALL THEIR LIVES.

Lesson Three

SELF-CONFIDENCE

A MIDST all the mysteries by which we are surrounded, nothing is more certain than that we are in the presence of an Infinite and Eternal Energy from which all things proceed.

—*Herbert Spencer.*

"You Can Do It if You Believe You Can!"

EFORE approaching the fundamental principles upon which this lesson is founded it will be of benefit to you to keep in mind the fact that it is practical—that it brings you the discoveries of more than twenty-five years of research—that it has the approval of the leading scientific men and women of the world who have tested every principle involved.

Skepticism is the deadly enemy of progress and self-development. You might as well lay this book aside and stop right here as to approach this lesson with the feeling that it was written by some long-haired theorist who had never tested the principles upon which the lesson is based.

Surely this is no age for the skeptic, because it is an age in which we have seen more of Nature's laws uncovered and harnessed than had been discovered in all past history of the human race. Within three decades we have witnessed the mastery of the air; we have explored the ocean; we have all but annihilated distances on the earth; we have harnessed the lightning and made it turn the wheels of industry; we have made seven blades of grass grow where but one grew before; we have instantaneous communication between the nations of the world. Truly, this is an age of illumination and unfoldment, but we have as yet barely scratched the surface of knowledge. However, when we shall have unlocked the gate that leads to the secret power which is stored up within us it will bring us knowledge that will make all past discoveries pale into oblivion by comparison.

Thought is the most highly organized form of energy known to man, and this is an age of experimentation and research that is sure to bring us into greater understanding of that mysterious force called thought, which reposes within us. We have already found out enough about the human mind to know that a man may throw off the accumulated effects of a thousand generations of *fear,* through the aid of the principle of *Auto-suggestion.* We have already discovered the fact that *fear* is the chief reason for poverty and failure and misery that takes on a thousand different forms. We have already discovered the fact that the man who masters *fear* may march on to successful achievement in practically any undertaking, despite all efforts to defeat him.

The development of *self-confidence* starts with the elimination of this demon called *fear,* which sits upon a man's shoulder and whispers into his ear, *"You can't do it—you are afraid to try—you are afraid of public opinion—you are afraid that you will fail—you are afraid you have not the ability."*

This *fear* demon is getting into close quarters.

Science has found a deadly weapon with which to put it to flight, and this lesson on *self-confidence* has brought you this weapon for use in your battle with the world-old enemy of progress, *fear*.

THE SIX BASIC FEARS OF MANKIND: Every person falls heir to the influence of six basic fears. Under these six fears may be listed the lesser fears. The six basic or major fears are here enumerated and the sources from which they are believed to have grown are described.

The six basic fears are:

a The fear of Poverty
b The fear of Old Age
c The fear of Criticism
d The fear of Loss of Love of Someone.
e The fear of Ill Health
f The fear of Death.

Study the list, then take inventory of your own fears and ascertain under which of the six headings you can classify them.

Every human being who has reached the age of understanding is bound down, to some extent, by one or more of these six basic fears. As the first step in the elimination of these six evils let us examine the sources from whence we inherited them.

PHYSICAL AND SOCIAL HEREDITY

All that man is, both physically and mentally, he came by through two forms of heredity. One is known as physical heredity and the other is called social heredity.

Through the law of physical heredity man has slowly

evolved from the amœba (a single-cell animal form), through stages of development corresponding to all the known animal forms now on this earth, including those which are known to have existed but which are now extinct.

Every generation through which man has passed has added to his nature something of the traits, habits and physical appearance of that generation. Man's physical inheritance, therefore, is a heterogeneous collection of many habits and physical forms.

There seems little, if any, doubt that while the six basic fears of man could not have been inherited through physical heredity (these six basic fears being mental states of mind and therefore not capable of transmission through physical heredity), it is obvious that through physical heredity a most favorable lodging place for these six fears has been provided.

For example, it is a well known fact that the whole process of physical evolution is based upon death, destruction, pain and cruelty; that the elements of the soil of the earth find transportation, in their upward climb through evolution, based upon the death of one form of life in order that another and higher form may subsist. All vegetation lives by "eating" the elements of the soil and the elements of the air. All forms of animal life live by "eating" some other and weaker form, or some form of vegetation.

The cells of all vegetation have a very high order of intelligence. The cells of all animal life likewise have a very high order of intelligence.

Undoubtedly the animal cells of a fish have learned, out of bitter experience, that the group of animal cells known as a fish hawk are to be greatly feared.

By reason of the fact that many animal forms (including that of most men) live by eating the smaller and weaker animals, the "cell intelligence" of these animals which enter into and become a part of man brings with it the FEAR growing out of their experience in having been eaten alive.

This theory may seem to be far-fetched, and in fact it may not be true, but it is at least a logical theory if it is nothing more. The author makes no particular point of this theory, nor does he insist that it accounts for any of the six basic fears. There is another, and a much better explanation of the source of these fears, which we will proceed to examine, beginning with a description of social heredity.

By far the most important part of man's make-up comes to him through the law of social heredity, this term having reference to the methods by which one generation imposes upon the minds of the generation under its immediate control the superstitions, beliefs, legends and ideas which it, in turn, inherited from the generation preceding.

The term "social heredity" should be understood to mean any and all sources through which a person acquires knowledge, such as schooling of religious and all other natures; reading, word of mouth conversation, story telling and all manner of thought inspiration coming from what is generally accepted as one's "personal experiences."

Through the operation of the law of social heredity anyone having control of the mind of a child may, through intense teaching, plant in that child's mind any idea, whether false or true, in such a manner that the child accepts it as true and it becomes as much a

REMEMBER that when you make an appointment with another person you assume the responsibility of punctuality, and that you have not the right to be a single minute late.

part of the child's personality as any cell or organ of its physical body (and just as hard to change in its nature).

It is through the law of social heredity that the religionist plants in the child mind dogmas and creeds and religious ceremonies too numerous to describe, holding those ideas before that mind until the mind accepts them and forever seals them as a part of its irrevocable belief.

The mind of a child which has not come into the age of general understanding, during an average period covering, let us say, the first two years of its life, is plastic, open, clean and free. Any idea planted in such a mind by one in whom the child has confidence takes root and grows, so to speak, in such a manner that it never can be eradicated or wiped out, no matter how opposed to logic or reason that idea may be.

Many religionists claim that they can so deeply implant the tenets of their religion in the mind of a child that there never can be room in that mind for any other religion, either in whole or in part. The claims are not greatly overdrawn.

With this explanation of the manner in which the law of social heredity operates the student will be ready to examine the sources from which man inherits the six basic fears. Moreover, any student (except those who have not yet grown big enough to examine truth that steps upon the "pet corns" of their own superstitions) may check the soundness of the principle of social heredity as it is here applied to the six basic fears, without going outside of his or her own personal experiences.

Fortunately, practically the entire mass of evidence

submitted in this lesson is of such a nature that all who sincerely seek the truth may ascertain, for themselves, whether the evidence is sound or not.

For the moment at least, lay aside your prejudices and preconceived ideas (you may always go back and pick them up again, you know) while we study the origin and nature of man's Six Worst Enemies, the six basic fears, beginning with:

THE FEAR OF POVERTY: It requires courage to tell the truth about the origin of this fear, and still greater courage, perhaps, to accept the truth after it has been told. The fear of poverty grew out of man's inherited tendency to prey upon his fellow man economically. Nearly all forms of lower animals have instinct but appear not to have the power to reason and think; therefore, they prey upon one another physically. Man, with his superior sense of intuition, thought and reason, does not eat his fellow men bodily; he gets more satisfaction out of eating them FINANCIALLY!

Of all the ages of the world of which we know anything, the age in which we live seems to be the age of money worship. A man is considered less than the dust of the earth unless he can display a fat bank account. Nothing brings man so much suffering and humiliation as does POVERTY. No wonder man FEARS poverty. Through a long line of inherited experiences with the man-animal man has learned, for certain, that this animal cannot always be trusted where matters of money and other evidences of earthly possessions are concerned.

Many marriages have their beginning (and oftentimes their ending) solely on the basis of the wealth possessed by one or both of the contracting parties. It is no wonder that the divorce courts are busy!

"Society" could quite properly be spelled "$ociety," because it is inseparably associated with the dollar mark. So eager is man to possess wealth that he will acquire it in whatever manner he can; through legal methods, if possible, through other methods if necessary.

The fear of poverty is a terrible thing!

A man may commit murder, engage in robbery, rape and all other manner of violation of the rights of others and still regain a high station in the minds of his fellow men, PROVIDING always that he does not lose his wealth. Poverty, therefore, is a crime—an unforgivable sin, as it were.

No wonder man fears it!

Every statute book in the world bears evidence that the fear of poverty is one of the six basic fears of mankind, for in every such book of laws may be found various and sundry laws intended to protect the weak from the strong. To spend time trying to prove either that the fear of poverty is one of man's inherited fears, or that this fear has its origin in man's nature to cheat his fellow man, would be similar to trying to prove that three times two are six. Obviously no man would ever fear poverty if he had any grounds for trusting his fellow men, for there is food and shelter and raiment and luxury of every nature sufficient for the needs of every person on earth, and all these blessings would be enjoyed by every person except for the swinish habit that man has of trying to push all the other "swine" out of the trough, even after he has all and more than he needs.

The second of the six basic fears with which man is bound is:

THE FEAR OF OLD AGE: In the main this fear grows out of two sources. First, the thought that Old Age may bring with it POVERTY. Secondly, and by far the most common source of origin, from false and cruel sectarian teachings which have been so well mixed with "fire and brimstone" and with "purgatories" and other bogies that human beings have learned to fear Old Age because it meant the approach of another, and possibly a much more HORRIBLE, world than this one which is known to be bad enough.

In the basic fear of Old Age man has two very sound reasons for his apprehension: the one growing out of distrust of his fellow men who may seize whatever worldly goods he may possess, and the other arising from the terrible pictures of the world to come which were deeply planted in his mind, through the law of social heredity, long before he came into possession of that mind.

Is it any wonder that man fears the approach of Old Age?

The third of the six basic fears is:

THE FEAR OF CRITICISM: Just how man acquired this basic fear it would be hard, if not impossible, definitely to determine, but one thing is certain, he has it in well developed form.

Some believe that this fear made its appearance in the mind of man about the time that politics came into existence. Others believe its source can be traced no further than the first meeting of an organization of females known as a "Woman's Club." Still another school of humorists charges the origin to the contents of the Holy Bible, whose pages abound with some very vitriolic and violent forms of criticism. If the latter claim is correct, and those who believe literally all they find in the Bible are not mistaken, then God is responsible for man's inherent fear of Criticism, because God caused the Bible to be written.

This author, being neither a humorist nor a "prophet," but just an ordinary workaday type of person, is inclined to attribute the basic fear of Criticism to that part of man's inherited nature which prompts him not only to take away his fellow man's goods and wares, but to justify his action by CRITICISM of his fellow man's character.

The fear of Criticism takes on many different forms, the majority of which are petty and trivial in nature, even to the extent of being childish in the extreme.

Bald-headed men, for example, are bald for no other reason than their fear of Criticism. Heads become bald because of the protection of hats with tight fitting bands which cut off the circulation at the roots of the hair. Men wear hats, not because they actually need them for the sake of comfort, but mainly because "everybody's doing it," and the individual falls in line and does it also, lest some other individual CRITICIZE him.

Women seldom have bald heads, or even thin hair, because they wear hats that are loose, the only purpose of which is to make an appearance.

But it must not be imagined that women are free from the fear of Criticism associated with hats. If any woman claims to be superior to man with reference to this fear, ask her to walk down the street wearing a hat that is one or two seasons out of style!

IN every soul there has been deposited t h e seed of a great future, but that seed will never germinate, much less grow to maturity, except through the rendering of useful service.

The makers of all manner of clothing have not been slow to capitalize this basic fear of Criticism with which all mankind is cursed. Every season, it will be observed, the "styles" in many articles of wearing apparel change. Who establishes the "styles"? Certainly not the purchaser of clothes, but the manufacturer of clothes. Why does he change the styles so often? Obviously this change is made so that the manufacturer can sell more clothes.

For the same reason the manufacturers of automobiles (with a few rare and very sensible exceptions) change styles every season.

The manufacturer of clothing knows how the man-animal fears to wear a garment which is one season out of step with "that which they are all wearing now."

Is this not true? Does not your own experience back it up?

We have been describing the manner in which people behave under the influence of the fear of Criticism as applied to the small and petty things of life. Let us now examine human behavior under this fear when it affects people in connection with the more important matters connected with human intercourse. Take, for example, practically any person who has reached the age of "mental maturity" (from thirty-five to forty-five years of age, as a general average), and if you could read his or her mind you would find in that mind a very decided disbelief of and rebellion against most of the fables taught by the majority of the religionists.

Powerful and mighty is the fear of CRITICISM!

The time was, and not so very long ago at that,

when the word "infidel" meant ruin to whomsoever it was applied. It is seen, therefore, that man's fear of CRITICISM is not without ample cause for its existence.

The fourth basic fear is that of:

THE FEAR OF LOSS OF LOVE OF SOMEONE: The source from which this fear originated needs but little description, for it is obvious that it grew out of man's nature to steal his fellow man's mate; or at least to take liberties with her, unknown to her rightful "lord" and master. By nature all men are polygamous, the statement of a truth which will, of course, bring denials from those who are either too old to function in a normal way sexually, or have, from some other cause, lost the contents of certain glands which are responsible for man's tendency toward the plurality of the opposite sex.

There can be but little doubt that jealousy and all other similar forms of more or less mild dementia præcox (insanity) grew out of man's inherited fear of the Loss of Love of Someone.

Of all the "sane fools" studied by this author, that represented by a man who has become jealous of some woman, or that of a woman who has become jealous of some man, is the oddest and strangest. The author, fortunately, never had but one case of personal experience with this form of insanity, but from that experience he learned enough to justify him in stating that the fear of the Loss of Love of Someone is one of the most painful, if not in fact the most painful, of all the six basic fears. And it seems reasonable to add that this fear plays more havoc with the human mind than do any of the other six basic fears, often leading to the more violent forms of permanent insanity.

The fifth basic fear is that of:

THE FEAR OF ILL HEALTH: This fear has its origin, to considerable extent also, in the same sources from which the fears of Poverty and Old Age are derived.

The fear of Ill Health must needs be closely associated with both Poverty and Old Age, because it also leads toward the border line of "terrible worlds" of which man knows not, but of which he has heard some discomforting stories.

The author strongly suspects that those engaged in the business of selling good health methods have had considerable to do with keeping the fear of Ill Health alive in the human mind.

For longer than the record of the human race can be relied upon, the world has known of various and sundry forms of therapy and health purveyors. If a man gains his living from keeping people in good health it seems but natural that he would use every means at his command for persuading people that they needed his services. Thus, in time, it might be that people would inherit a fear of Ill Health.

The sixth and last of the six basic fears is that of:

THE FEAR OF DEATH: To many this is the worst of all the six basic fears, and the reason why it is so regarded becomes obvious to even the casual student of psychology.

The terrible pangs of fear associated with DEATH may be charged directly to religious fanaticism, the source which is more responsible for it than are all other sources combined.

So-called "heathen" are not as much afraid of DEATH as are the "civilized," especially that portion of the civilized population which has come under the influence of theology.

For hundreds of millions of years man has been asking the still unanswered (and, it may be, the unanswerable) questions, "W H E N C E?" and "WHITHER?" "Where did I come from and where am I going after death?"

The more cunning and crafty, as well as the honest but credulous, of the race have not been slow to offer the answer to these questions. In fact the answering of these questions has become one of the so-called "learned" professions, despite the fact that but little learning is required to enter this profession.

Witness, now, the major source of origin of the fear of DEATH!

"Come into my tent, embrace my faith, accept my dogmas (and pay my salary) and I will give you a ticket that will admit you straightway into heaven when you die," says the leader of one form of sectarianism. "Remain out of my tent," says this same leader, "and you will go direct to hell, where you will burn throughout eternity."

While, in fact, the self-appointed leader may not be able to provide safe-conduct into heaven nor, by lack of such provision, allow the unfortunate seeker after truth to descend into hell, the possibility of the latter seems so terrible that it lays hold of the mind and creates that fear of fears, the fear of DEATH!

In truth no man knows, and no man has ever known, what heaven or hell is like, or if such places exist, and this very lack of definite knowledge opens the door of the human mind to the charlatan to enter and control that mind with his stock of legerdemain and various brands of trickery, deceit and fraud.

The truth is this—nothing less and nothing more—That NO MAN KNOWS NOR HAS ANY MAN EVER KNOWN WHERE WE COME FROM AT BIRTH OR WHERE WE GO AT DEATH. Any person claiming otherwise is either deceiving himself or he is a conscious impostor who makes it a business to live without rendering service of value, through play upon the credulity of humanity.

Be it said, in their behalf, however, the majority of those engaged in "selling tickets into heaven" actually believe not only that they know where heaven exists, but that their creeds and formulas will give safe passage to all who embrace them.

This belief may be summed up in one word—CREDULITY!

Religious leaders, generally, make the broad, sweeping claim that the present civilization owes its existence to the work done by the churches. This author, as far as he is personally concerned, is willing to grant their claims to be correct, if, at the same time he be permitted to add that even if this claim be true the theologians haven't a great deal of which to brag.

But, it is not—cannot be—true that civilization has grown out of the efforts of the organized churches and creeds, if by the term "civilization" is meant the uncovering of the natural laws and the many inventions to which the world is the present heir.

If the theologians wish to claim that part of civilization which has to do with man's conduct toward his fellow man they are perfectly welcome to it, as far

YOU are fortunate if you have learned the difference between temporary defeat and failure; more fortunate still, if you have learned the truth that the very seed of success is dormant in every defeat that you experience.

as this author is concerned; but, on the other hand, if they presume to gobble up the credit for all the scientific discovery of mankind the author begs leave to offer vigorous protest.

.   .   .   .

It is hardly sufficient to state that social heredity is the method through which man gathers all knowledge that reaches him through the five senses. It is more to the point to state HOW social heredity works, in as many different applications as will give the student a comprehensive understanding of that law.

Let us begin with some of the lower forms of animal life and examine the manner in which they are affected by the law of social heredity.

Shortly after this author began to examine the major sources from which men gather the knowledge which makes them what they are, some thirty-odd years ago, he discovered the nest of a ruffed grouse. The nest was so located that the mother bird could be seen from a considerable distance when she was on the nest. With the aid of a pair of field glasses the bird was closely watched until the young birds were hatched out. It happened that the regular daily observation was made but a few hours after the young birds came out of the shell. Desiring to know what would happen, the author approached the nest. The mother bird remained near by until the intruder was within ten or twelve feet of her, then she disarranged her feathers, stretched one wing over her leg and went hobbling away, making a pretense of being crippled. Being somewhat familiar with the tricks of mother birds, the author did not follow, but, instead, went to the nest to take a look at the little ones. Without the slightest signs of fear they turned their eyes toward him, moving their heads first one way and then another. He reached down and picked one of them up. With no signs of fear it stood in the palm of his hand. He laid the bird back in the nest and went away to a safe distance to give the mother bird a chance to return.

The wait was short. Very soon she began cautiously to edge her way back toward the nest until she was within a few feet of it, when she spread her wings and ran as fast as she could, uttering, meanwhile, a series of sounds similar to those of a hen when she has found some morsel of food and wishes to call her brood to partake of it.

She gathered the little birds around and continued to quiver in a highly excited manner, shaking her wings and ruffling her feathers. One could almost hear her words as she gave the little birds their first lesson in self-defense, through the law of SOCIAL HEREDITY:

"You silly little creatures! Do you not know that men are your enemies? Shame on you for allowing that man to pick you up in his hands. It's a wonder he didn't carry you off and eat you alive! The next time you see a man approaching make yourselves scarce. Lie down on the ground, run under leaves, go anywhere to get out of sight, and remain out of sight until the enemy is well on his way."

The little birds stood around and listened to the lecture with intense interest. After the mother bird had quieted down the author again started to approach the nest. When within twenty feet or so of the guarded household the mother bird again started to lead him in the other direction by crumpling up her wing and hobbling along as if she were crippled. He looked at the nest, but the glance was in vain. The little birds were nowhere to be found! They had learned rapidly to avoid their natural enemy, thanks to their natural instinct.

Again the author retreated, awaited until the mother bird had reassembled her household, then came out to visit them, but with similar results. When he approached the spot where he last saw the mother bird not the slightest signs of the little fellows were to be found.

.   .   .   .

When a small boy the author captured a young crow and made a pet of it. The bird became quite well satisfied with its domestic surroundings and learned to perform many tricks requiring considerable intelligence. After the bird was big enough to fly it was permitted to go wherever it pleased. Sometimes it would be gone for many hours, but it always returned home before dark.

One day some wild crows became involved in a fight with an owl in a field near the house where the pet crow lived. As soon as the pet heard the "caw, caw, caw" of its wild relatives it flew up on top of the house, and with signs of great agitation, walked from one end of the house to the other. Finally it took wing and flew in the direction of the "battle." The author followed to see what would happen. In a few minutes he came up with the pet. It was sitting on the lower branches of a tree and two wild crows were sitting on a limb just above, chattering and walking back and forth, acting very much in the same fashion that angry parents behave toward their offspring when chastising them.

As the author approached, the two wild crows flew away, one of them circling around the tree a few times, meanwhile letting out a terrible flow of most abusive language, which, no doubt, was directed at its foolish relative who hadn't enough sense to fly while the flying was good.

The pet was called, but it paid no attention. That evening it returned home, but would not come near the house. It sat on a high limb of an apple tree and talked in crow language for about ten minutes, saying, no doubt, that it had decided to go back to the wild life of its fellows, then flew away and did not return until two days later, when it came back and did some more talking in crow language, keeping at a safe distance meanwhile. It then went away and never returned.

Social heredity had robbed the author of a fine pet!

The only consolation he got from the loss of his crow was the thought that it had shown fine sportsmanship by coming back and giving notice of its intention to depart. Many farm hands had left the farm without going to the trouble of this formality.

.   .   .   .

It is a well known fact that a fox will prey upon all manner of fowl and small animals with the exception of the skunk. No reason need be stated as to why Mr. Skunk enjoys immunity. A fox may tackle a skunk once, but never twice! For this reason a skunk hide, when nailed to a chicken roost, will keep all but the very young and inexperienced foxes at a safe distance.

The odor of a skunk, once experienced, is never to be forgotten. No other smell even remotely resembles it. It is nowhere recorded that any mother fox ever taught her young how to detect and keep away from the familiar smell of a skunk, but all who are informed on "fox lore" know that foxes and skunks never seek lodgment in the same cave.

But one lesson is sufficient to teach the fox all it cares to know about skunks. Through the law of social heredity, operating via the sense of smell, one lesson serves for an entire life-time.

.   .   .   .

A bullfrog can be caught on a fish-hook by attaching a small piece of red cloth or any other small red object to the hook and dangling it in front of the frog's nose. That is, Mr. Frog may be caught in this manner, provided he is hooked the first time he snaps at the bait, but if he is poorly hooked and makes a get-away, or if he feels the point of the hook when he bites at the bait but is not caught, he will never make the same mistake again. The author spent many hours in stealthy attempt to hook a particularly desirable specimen which had snapped and missed, before learning that but one lesson in social heredity is enough to teach even a humble "croaker" that bits of red flannel are things to be let alone.

The author once owned a very fine male Airedale dog which caused no end of annoyance by his habit of coming home with a young chicken in his mouth.

IS it not strange that we fear most that which never happens? That we destroy our initiative by the fear of defeat, when, in reality, defeat is a most useful tonic and should be accepted as such.

Each time the chicken was taken away from the dog and he was soundly switched, but to no avail; he continued in his liking for fowl.

For the purpose of saving the dog, if possible, and as an experiment with social heredity, this dog was taken to the farm of a neighbor who had a hen and some newly hatched chickens. The hen was placed in the barn and the dog was turned in with her. As soon as everyone was out of sight the dog slowly edged up toward the hen, sniffed the air in her direction a time or two (to make sure she was the kind of meat for which he was looking), then made a dive toward her. Meanwhile Mrs. Hen had been doing some "surveying" on her own account, for she met Mr. Dog more than halfway; moreover, she met him with such a surprise of wings and claws as he had never before experienced. The first round was clearly the hen's. But a nice fat bird, reckoned the dog, was not to slip between his paws so easily; therefore he backed away a short distance, then charged again. This time Mrs. Hen lit upon his back, drove her claws into his skin and made effective use of her sharp bill! Mr. Dog retreated to his corner, looking for all the world as if he were listening for someone to ring the bell and call the fight off until he got his bearings. But Mrs. Hen craved no time for deliberation; she had her adversary on the run and showed that she knew the value of the offensive by keeping him on the run.

One could almost understand her words as she flogged the poor Airedale from one corner to another, keeping up a series of rapid-fire sounds which for all the world resembled the remonstrations of an angry mother who had been called upon to defend her off-spring from an attack by older boys.

The Airedale was a poor soldier! After running around the barn from corner to corner for about two minutes he spread himself on the ground as flat as he could and did his best to protect his eyes with his paws. Mrs. Hen seemed to be making a special attempt to peck out his eyes.

The owner of the hen then stepped in and retrieved her—or, more accurately stating it, he retrieved the dog—which in no way appeared to meet with the dog's disapproval.

The next day a chicken was placed in the cellar where the dog slept. As soon as he saw the bird he tucked his tail between his legs and ran for a corner! He never again attempted to catch a chicken. One lesson in social heredity, via the sense of "touch," was sufficient to teach him that while chicken-chasing may offer some enjoyment, it is also fraught with much hazard.

All these illustrations, with the exception of the first, describe the process of gathering knowledge through direct experience. Observe the marked difference between knowledge gathered by direct experience and that which is gathered through the training of the young by the old, as in the case of the ruffed grouse and her young.

The most impressive lessons are those learned by the young from the old, through highly colored or emotionalized methods of teaching. When the mother grouse spread her wings, stood her feathers on end, shook herself like a man suffering with the palsy and chattered to her young in a highly excited manner, she planted the fear of man in their hearts in a manner which they were never to forget.

The term "social heredity," as used in connection with this lesson, has particular reference to all methods through which a child is taught any idea, dogma, creed, religion or system of ethical conduct, by its parents or those who may have authority over it, before reaching the age at which it may reason and reflect upon such teaching in its own way; estimating the age of such reasoning power at, let us say, seven to twelve years.

.   .   .   .

There are myriads of forms of *fear,* but none are more deadly than the fear of poverty and old age. We drive our bodies as if they were slaves because we are so afraid of poverty that we wish to hoard money for—*what—old age!* This common form of *fear* drives us so hard that we overwork our bodies and bring on the very thing we are struggling to avoid.

What a tragedy to watch a man drive himself when he begins to arrive along about the forty-year mile post of life—the age at which he is just beginning to mature mentally. At forty a man is just entering the age in which he is able to see and understand and assimilate the handwriting of Nature, as it appears in the forests and flowing brooks and faces of men and little children, yet this devil *fear* drives him so hard that he becomes blinded and lost in the entanglement of a maze of conflicting *desires.* The principle of *organized effort* is lost sight of, and instead of laying hold of Nature's forces which are in evidence all around him, and permitting those forces to carry him to the heights of great achievement, he defies them and they become forces of destruction.

Perhaps none of these great forces of Nature are more available for man's unfoldment than is the principle of Auto-suggestion, but ignorance of this force is leading the majority of the human race to apply it so that it acts as a hindrance and not as a help.

Let us here enumerate the facts which show just how this misapplication of a great force of Nature takes place:

Here is a man who meets with some disappointment; a friend proves false, or a neighbor seems indifferent. Forthwith he decides (through self-suggestion) all men are untrustworthy and all neighbors unappreciative. These thoughts so deeply imbed themselves in his subconscious mind that they color his whole attitude toward others. Go back, now, to what was said in Lesson Two, about the dominating thoughts of a man's mind attracting people whose thoughts are similar.

Apply the Law of Attraction and you will soon see and understand why the unbeliever attracts other unbelievers.

Reverse the Principle:

Here is a man who sees nothing but the best there is in all whom he meets. If his neighbors seem indifferent he takes no notice of that fact, for he makes it *his business* to fill his mind with dominating thoughts of optimism and good cheer and faith in others. If people speak to him harshly he speaks back in tones of softness. Through the operation of this same eternal Law of Attraction he draws to himself the attention of people whose attitude toward life and whose dominating thoughts harmonize with his own.

Tracing the principle a step further:

Here is a man who has been well schooled and has the ability to render the world some needed service. Somewhere, sometime, he has heard it said that modesty is a great virtue and that to push himself to the front of the stage in the game of life savors of egotism. He quietly slips in at the back door and takes a seat at the rear while other players in the game of life boldly step to the front. He remains in the back row because he *fears* "what *they* will say." Public opinion, or that which he believes to be public opinion, has him pushed to the rear and the world hears but little of him. His schooling counts for naught because he is *afraid* to let the world know that he has had it. He is constantly *suggesting* to *himself* (thus using the great force of Auto-suggestion to his own detriment) that he should remain in the background lest he be criticized, as if criticism would do him any damage or defeat his purpose.

Here is another man who was born of poor parents. Since the first day that he can remember he has seen evidence of poverty. He has heard talk of poverty. He has felt the icy hand of poverty on his shoulders and it has so impressed him that he fixes it in his mind as a curse to which *he must submit*. Quite unconsciously he permits himself to fall victim of the belief "once poor always poor" until that belief becomes the dominating thought of his mind. He resembles a horse that has been harnessed and broken until it forgets that it has the potential power with which to throw off that harness. Auto-suggestion is rapidly relegating him to the back of the stage of life. Finally he be-

YOUR work and mine are peculiarly akin; I am helping the laws of Nature create more perfect specimens of vegetation, while you are using those same laws, through the Law of Success philosophy, to create more p e r f e c t specimens of thinkers.

—*Luther Burbank.*

comes a *quitter*. Ambition is gone. Opportunity comes his way no longer, or if it does he has not the vision to see it. *He has accepted his FATE!* It is a well established fact that the faculties of the mind, like the limbs of the body, atrophy and wither away if not used. Self-confidence is no exception. It develops when used but disappears if not used.

One of the chief disadvantages of inherited wealth is the fact that it too often leads to inaction and loss of Self-confidence. Some years ago a baby boy was born to Mrs. E. B. McLean, in the city of Washington. His inheritance was said to be around a hundred million dollars. When this baby was taken for an airing in its carriage it was surrounded by nurses and assistant nurses and detectives and other servants whose duty was to see that no harm befell it. As the years passed by this same vigilance was kept up. This child did not have to dress himself; he had servants who did that. Servants watched over him while he slept and while he was at play. He was not permitted to do anything that a servant could do for him. He had grown to the age of ten years. One day he was playing in the yard and noticed that the back gate had been left open. In all of his life he had never been outside of that gate alone, and naturally that was just the thing that he wished to do. During a moment when the servants were not looking he dashed out at the gate, and was run down and killed by an automobile before he reached the middle of the street.

He had used his servants' eyes until his own no longer served him as they might have done had he learned to rely upon them.

Twenty years ago the man whom I served as secretary sent his two sons away to school. One of them went to the University of Virginia and the other to a college in New York. Each month it was a part of my task to make out a check for $100.00 for each of these boys. This was their "pin money," to be spent as they wished. How profitably I remember the way I envied those boys as I made out those checks each month. I often wondered why the hand of fate bore me into the world in poverty. I could look ahead and see how these boys would rise to the high stations in life while I remained a humble clerk.

In due time the boys returned home with their "sheep-skins." Their father was a wealthy man who owned banks and railroads and coal mines and other property of great value. Good positions were waiting for the boys in their father's employ.

But, twenty years of time can play cruel tricks on those who have never had to struggle. Perhaps a better way to state this truth would be that *time gives those who have never had to struggle a chance to play cruel tricks on themselves!* At any rate, these two boys brought home from school other things besides their sheep-skins. They came back with well developed capacities for strong drink—*capacities which they developed because the hundred dollars which each of them received each month made it unnecessary for them to struggle.*

Theirs is a long and sad story, the details of which will not interest you, but you will be interested in their "finis." As this lesson is being written I have on my desk a copy of the newspaper published in the town where these boys lived. Their father has been bankrupted and his costly mansion, where the boys were born, has been placed on the block for sale. One of the boys died of delirium tremens and the other one is in an insane asylum.

Not all rich men's sons turn out so unfortunately, but the fact remains, nevertheless, that inaction leads to atrophy and this, in turn, leads to loss of ambition and self-confidence, and without these essential qualities a man will be carried through life on the wings of uncertainty, just as a dry leaf may be carried here and there on the bosom of the stray winds.

Far from being a disadvantage, struggle is a decided advantage, because it develops those qualities which would forever lie dormant without it. Many a man has found his place in the world because of having been forced to struggle for existence early in life. Lack of knowledge of the advantages accruing from struggle has prompted many a parent to say, "I had to work hard when I was young, *but I shall see to it that my children have an easy time!*" Poor foolish creatures. An "easy" time usually turns out to be a greater handicap than the average young man or woman can survive. There are worse things in this world than being forced to work in early life. Forced idleness is far worse than forced labor. Being forced to work, and forced to *do your best,* will breed in you temperance and self-control and strength of will and content and a hundred other virtues which the idle will never know.

Not only does lack of the necessity for struggle lead to weakness of ambition and will-power, but, what is more dangerous still, it sets up in a person's mind a state of lethargy that leads to the loss of Self-confidence. The person who has quit struggling because effort is no longer necessary is literally applying the principle of Auto-suggestion in undermining his own power of Self-confidence. Such a person will finally drift into a frame of mind in which he will actually look with more or less contempt upon the person who is forced to carry on.

The human mind, if you will pardon repetition, may be likened to an electric battery. It may be positive or it may be negative. Self-confidence is the quality with which the mind is re-charged and made positive.

Let us apply this line of reasoning to salesmanship and see what part Self-confidence plays in this great field of endeavor. One of the greatest salesmen this country has ever seen was once a clerk in a newspaper office.

It will be worth your while to analyze the method through which he gained his title as "the world's leading salesman."

He was a timid young man with a more or less retiring sort of nature. He was one of those who believe it best to slip in by the back door and take a seat at the rear of the stage of life. One evening he heard a lecture on the subject of this lesson, Self-confidence, and that lecture so impressed him that he left the lecture hall with a firm determination to pull himself out of the rut into which he had drifted.

He went to the Business Manager of the paper and asked for a position as solicitor of advertising and was put to work on a commission basis. Everyone in the office expected to see him fail, as this sort of salesmanship calls for the most positive type of sales ability. He went to his room and made out a list of a certain type of merchants on whom he intended to call. One would think that he would naturally have made up his list of the names of those whom he believed he could sell with the least effort, *but he did nothing of the sort*. He placed on his list only the names of the merchants on whom other advertising solicitors had called without making a sale. His list consisted of only twelve names. Before he made a single call he went out to the city park, took out his list of twelve names, read it over a hundred times, saying to himself as he did so, *"You will purchase advertising space from me before the end of the month."*

Then he began to make his calls. The first day he closed sales with three of the twelve "impossibilities." During the remainder of the week he made sales to two others. By the end of the month he had opened advertising accounts with all but one of the merchants that he had on the list. For the ensuing month he made no sales, for the reason that he made no calls except on this one obstinate merchant. Every morning when the store opened he was on hand to interview this merchant and every morning the merchant said *"No."* The merchant knew he was not going to buy advertising space, but this young man didn't know it. When the merchant said *No* the young man did not hear it, but kept right on coming. On the last day of the month, after having told this persistent young man *No* for thirty consecutive times, the merchant said:

"Look here, young man, you have wasted a whole month trying to sell me; now, what I would like to know is this—why have you wasted your time?"

"Wasted my time nothing," he retorted; "I have

NO man can become a great leader of men unless he has the milk of human kindness in his own heart, and leads by suggestion and kindness, rather than by force.

been going to school and you have been my teacher.
Now I know all the arguments that a merchant can
bring up for not buying, and besides that I have been
drilling myself in Self-confidence."

Then the merchant said: "I will make a little confession of my own. I, too, have been going to school,
and you have been my teacher. You have taught me
a lesson in persistence that is worth money to me, and
to show you my appreciation I am going to pay my
tuition fee by giving you an order for advertising
space."

And that was the way in which the Philadelphia
North American's best advertising account was
brought in. Likewise, it marked the beginning of a
reputation that has made that same young man a
millionaire.

He succeeded because he deliberately charged his
own mind with sufficient Self-confidence to make that
mind an irresistible force. When he sat down to make
up that list of twelve names he did something that
ninety-nine people out of a hundred would not have
done—he selected the names of those whom he believed it would be hard to sell, because he understood
that out of the resistance he would meet with in trying
to sell them would come strength and Self-confidence.
He was one of the very few people who understand
that all rivers and *some men* are crooked because of
following the line of least resistance.

. . . .

I am going to digress and here break the line of
thought for a moment while recording a word of advice to the wives of men. Remember, these lines are

intended only for wives, and husbands are not expected to read that which is here set down.

From having analyzed more than 16,000 people, the
majority of whom were married men, I have learned
something that may be of value to wives. Let me
state my thought in these words:

You have it within your power to send your husband away to his work or his business or his profession each day with a feeling of Self-confidence that
will carry him successfully over the rough spots of
the day and bring him home again, at night, smiling
and happy. One of my acquaintances of former years
married a woman who had a set of false teeth. One
day his wife dropped her teeth and broke the plate.
The husband picked up the pieces and began examining them. He showed such interest in them that his
wife said:

"You could make a set of teeth like those if you
made up your mind to do it."

This man was a farmer whose ambitions had never
carried him beyond the bounds of his little farm until
his wife made that remark. She walked over and laid
her hand on his shoulder and encouraged him to try
his hand at dentistry. She finally coaxed him to make
the start, and today he is one of the most prominent
and successful dentists in the state of Virginia. I
know him well, for he is my father!

No one can foretell the possibilities of achievement
available to the man whose wife stands at his back
and urges him on to bigger and better endeavor, for
it is a well known fact that a woman can arouse a
man so that he will perform almost superhuman feats.
It is your right and your duty to encourage your hus-

band and urge him on in worthy undertakings until he shall have found his place in the world. You can induce him to put forth greater effort than can any other person in the world. Make him believe that nothing within reason is beyond his power of achievement and you will have rendered him a service that will go a long way toward helping him win in the battle of life.

.   .   .   .

One of the most successful men in his line in America gives entire credit for his success to his wife. When they were first married she wrote a creed which he signed and placed over his desk. This is a copy of the creed:

I believe in myself. I believe in those who work with me. I believe in my employer. I believe in my friends. I believe in my family. I believe that God will lend me everything I need with which to succeed if I do my best to earn it through faithful and honest service. I believe in prayer and I will never close my eyes in sleep without praying for divine guidance to the end that I will be patient with other people and tolerant with those who do not believe as I do. I believe that success is the result of intelligent effort and does not depend upon luck or sharp practices or double-crossing friends, fellow men or my employer. I believe I will get out of life exactly what I put into it, therefore I will be careful to conduct myself toward others as I would want them to act toward me. I will not slander those whom I do not like. I will not slight

*my work no matter what I may see others doing.
I will render the best service of which I am capable
because I have pledged myself to succeed in life
and I know that success is always the result of
conscientious and efficient effort. Finally, I will
forgive those who offend me because I realize that
I shall sometimes offend others and I will need their
forgiveness.*

Signed ....

The woman who wrote this creed was a practical
psychologist of the first order. With the influence and
guidance of such a woman as a helpmate any man
could achieve noteworthy success.

Analyze this creed and you will notice how freely
the personal pronoun is used. It starts off with the
affirmation of Self-confidence, which is perfectly
proper. No man could make this creed his own without developing the positive attitude that would attract
to him people who would aid him in his struggle for
success.

This would be a splendid creed for every salesman
to adopt. It might not hurt your chances for success
if *you* adopted it. Mere adoption, however, is not
enough. You must *practice* it! Read it over and
over until you know it by heart. Then repeat it at
least once a day until you have literally transformed
it into your mental make-up. Keep a copy of it before you as a daily reminder of your pledge to practice
it. By doing so you will be making efficient use of the
principle of Auto-suggestion as a means of developing
Self-confidence. Never mind what anyone may say
about your procedure. Just remember that it is your

business to succeed, and this creed, if mastered and applied, will go a long way toward helping you.

You learned in Lesson Two that any idea you firmly fix in your subconscious mind, by repeated affirmation, automatically becomes a plan or blueprint which an unseen power uses in directing your efforts toward the attainment of the objective named in the plan.

You have also learned that the principle through which you may fix any idea you choose in your mind is called Auto-suggestion, which simply means a suggestion that you give to your own mind. It was this principle of Auto-suggestion that Emerson had in mind when he wrote:

"Nothing can bring you peace but yourself!"

You might well remember that *Nothing can bring you success but yourself.* Of course you will need the co-operation of others if you aim to attain success of a far-reaching nature, but you will never get that co-operation unless you vitalize your mind with the positive attitude of Self-confidence.

Perhaps you have wondered why a few men advance to highly paid positions while others all around them, who have as much training and who seemingly perform as much work, do not get ahead. Select any two people of these two types that you choose, and study them, and the reason why one advances and the other stands still will be quite obvious to you. You will find that the one who advances *believes in himself.* You will find that he backs this belief with such dynamic, aggressive action that he lets others know that he believes in himself. You will also notice that this Self-confidence is contagious; it is impelling; it is persuasive; it attracts others.

IF you want a thing done well, call on some busy person to do it. Busy people are generally the m o s t painstaking and thorough in all they do.

You will also find that the one who does not advance shows clearly, by the look on his face, by the posture of his body, by the lack of briskness in his step, by the uncertainty with which he speaks, that he lacks Self-confidence. No one is going to pay much attention to the person who has no confidence in himself.

He does not attract others because his mind is a negative force that repels rather than attracts.

In no other field of endeavor does Self-confidence or the lack of it play such an important part as in the field of salesmanship, and you do not need to be a character analyst to determine, the moment you meet him, whether a salesman possesses this quality of Self-confidence. If he has it the signs of its influence are written all over him. He inspires you with confidence in him and in the goods he is selling the moment he speaks.

We come, now, to the point at which you are ready to take hold of the principle of Auto-suggestion and make direct use of it in developing yourself into a positive and dynamic and self-reliant person. You are instructed to copy the following formula, sign it and commit it to memory:

SELF-CONFIDENCE FORMULA

First: I know that I have the ability to achieve the object of my *definite purpose,* therefore I *demand* of myself persistent, aggressive and continuous action toward its attainment.

Second: I realize that the dominating thoughts of my mind eventually reproduce themselves in outward, bodily action, and gradually transform themselves into physical reality, therefore I will concentrate my mind for thirty minutes daily upon the task of thinking of the person I intend to be, by creating a mental picture of this person and then transforming that picture into reality through practical service.

Third: I know that through the principle of Auto-suggestion, any desire that I persistently hold in my mind will eventually seek expression through some practical means of realizing it, therefore I shall devote ten minutes daily to demanding of myself the development of the factors named in the sixteen lessons of this Reading Course on the Law of Success.

Fourth: I have clearly mapped out and written down a description of my *definite purpose* in life, for the coming five years. I have set a price on my services for each of these five years; a price that I intend to *earn* and *receive*, through strict application of the principle of efficient, satisfactory service which I will render in advance.

Fifth: I fully realize that no wealth or position can long endure unless built upon truth and justice, therefore *I will engage in no transaction which does not benefit all whom it affects*. 1 will succeed by attracting to me the forces I wish to use, and the co-operation of other people. I will induce others to serve me because I will first serve them. I will eliminate hatred, envy, jealousy, selfishness and cynicism by developing love for all humanity, because I know that a negative attitude toward others can never bring me success. I will cause others to *believe in me* because I will believe in them and in myself.

I will sign my name to this formula, commit it to memory and repeat it aloud once a day with full *faith* that it will gradually influence my entire life so that I will become a successful and happy worker in my chosen field of endeavor.

Signed.................................

Before you sign your name to this formula make sure that you intend to carry out its instructions. Back of this formula lies a law that no man can explain. The psychologists refer to this law as Auto-suggestion and let it go at that, but you should bear in mind one point about which there is no uncertainty, and that is the fact that whatever this law is it *actually works!*

Another point to be kept in mind is the fact that, just as electricity will turn the wheels of industry and serve mankind in a million other ways, or snuff out life if wrongly applied, so will this principle of Auto-suggestion lead you up the mountain-side of peace and prosperity, or down into the valley of misery and poverty, according to the application you make of it. If you fill your mind with doubt and unbelief in your ability to achieve, then the principle of Auto-suggestion takes this spirit of unbelief and sets it up in your subconscious mind as your dominating thought and slowly but surely draws you into the whirlpool of *failure*. But, if you fill your mind with radiant Self-confidence, the principle of Auto-suggestion takes this belief and sets it up as your dominating thought and helps you master the obstacles that fall in your way until you reach the mountain-top of *success*.

THE POWER OF HABIT

Having, myself, experienced all the difficulties that stand in the road of those who lack the understanding to make practical application of this great principle of Auto-suggestion, let me take you a short way into the principle of habit, through the aid of which you may easily apply the principle of Auto-suggestion in any direction and for any purpose whatsoever.

Habit grows out of environment; out of doing the same thing or thinking the same thoughts or repeating the same words over and over again. Habit may be likened to the groove on a phonograph record, while the human mind may be likened to the needle that fits into that groove. When any habit has been well formed, through repetition of thought or action, the mind has a tendency to attach itself to and follow the course of that habit as closely as the phonograph needle follows the groove in the wax record.

Habit is created by *repeatedly* directing one or more of the five senses of seeing, hearing, smelling, tasting and feeling, in a given direction. It is through this repetition principle that the injurious drug habit is formed. It is through this same principle that the desire for intoxicating drink is formed into a habit.

After habit has been well established it will automatically control and direct our bodily activity, wherein may be found a thought that can be transformed into a powerful factor in the development of *Self-confidence*. The thought is this: *Voluntarily, and by force if necessary, direct your efforts and your thoughts along a desired line until you have formed the habit that will lay hold of you and continue, voluntarily, to direct your efforts along the same line.*

The object in writing out and repeating the Self-confidence formula is to form the habit of making *belief in yourself* the dominating thought of your mind until that thought has been thoroughly imbedded in your subconscious mind, through the principle of *habit.*

You learned to write by repeatedly directing the muscles of your arm and hand over certain outlines known as letters, until finally you formed the habit of tracing these outlines. Now you write with ease and rapidity, without tracing each letter slowly. Writing has become a *habit* with you.

The principle of habit will lay hold of the faculties of your mind just the same as it will influence the physical muscles of your body, as you can easily prove by mastering and applying this lesson on Self-confidence. Any statement that you repeatedly make to yourself, or any *desire* that you deeply plant in your mind through repeated statement, will eventually seek expression through your physical, outward bodily efforts. The principle of habit is the very foundation upon which this lesson on Self-confidence is built, and if you will understand and follow the directions laid down in this lesson you will soon know more about the law of habit, from first-hand knowledge, than could be taught you by a thousand such lessons as this.

You have but little conception of the possibilities which lie sleeping within you, awaiting but the awakening hand of vision to arouse you, and you will never have a better conception of those possibilities unless you develop sufficient Self-confidence to lift you

A HOME is some-thing that cannot be bought. You can buy a house but only a woman can make of it a home.

above the commonplace influences of your present environment.

The human mind is a marvelous, mysterious piece of machinery, a fact of which I was reminded a few months ago when I picked up Emerson's Essays and re-read his essay on Spiritual Laws. A strange thing happened. I saw in that essay, which I had read scores of times previously, much that I had never noticed before. I saw more in this essay than I had seen during previous readings because the unfoldment of my mind since the last reading had prepared me to interpret more.

The human mind is constantly unfolding, like the petals of a flower, until it reaches the maximum of development. What this maximum is, where it ends, or whether it ends at all or not, are unanswerable questions, but the degree of unfoldment seems to vary according to the nature of the individual and the degree to which he keeps his mind at work. A mind that is forced or coaxed into analytical thought every day seems to keep on unfolding and developing greater powers of interpretation.

Down in Louisville, Kentucky, lives Mr. Lee Cook, a man who has practically no legs and has to wheel himself around on a cart. In spite of the fact that Mr. Cook has been without legs since birth, he is the owner of a great industry and a millionaire through his own efforts. He has proved that a man can get along very well without legs if he has a well developed Self-confidence.

In the city of New York one may see a strong able-bodied and able-headed young man, without legs, rolling himself down Fifth Avenue every afternoon, with cap in hand, begging for a living. His head is perhaps as sound and as able to think as the average.

This young man could duplicate anything that Mr. Cook, of Louisville, has done, if *he thought of himself as Mr. Cook thinks of himself.*

Henry Ford owns more millions of dollars than he will ever need or use. Not so many years ago, he was working as a laborer in a machine shop, with but little schooling and without capital. Scores of other men, some of them with better organized brains than his, worked near him. Ford threw off the poverty consciousness, developed confidence in himself, thought of success and attained it. Those who worked around him could have done as well had they *thought* as he did.

Milo C. Jones, of Wisconsin, was stricken down with paralysis a few years ago. So bad was the stroke that he could not turn himself in bed or move a muscle of his body. His physical body was useless, but there was nothing wrong with his brain, so it began to function in earnest, probably for the first time in its existence. Lying flat on his back in bed, Mr. Jones made that brain create a *definite purpose.* That purpose was prosaic and humble enough in nature, but it was *definite* and it was a *purpose,* something that he had never known before.

His *definite purpose* was to make pork sausage. Calling his family around him he told of his plans and began directing them in carrying the plans into action. With nothing to aid him except a sound mind and plenty of *Self-confidence,* Milo C. Jones spread the name and reputation of "Little Pig Sausage" all over the United States, and accumulated a fortune besides.

All this was accomplished after paralysis had made it impossible for him to work with his hands.

Where *thought* prevails power may be found!

Henry Ford has made millions of dollars and is still making millions of dollars each year because *he believed in Henry Ford* and transformed that belief into a *definite purpose* and backed that purpose with a definite plan. The other machinists who worked along with Ford, during the early days of his career, visioned nothing but a weekly pay envelope and that was all they ever got. They demanded nothing out of the ordinary of themselves. If you want to *get more* be sure to *demand* more of yourself. Notice that this demand is to be made on *yourself!*

There comes to mind a well known poem whose author expressed a great psychological truth:

> If you think you are beaten, you are;
>   If you think you dare not, you don't;
> If you like to win, but you think you can't,
>   It is almost certain you won't.

> If you think you'll lose you've lost,
>   For out of the world we find
> Success begins with a fellow's will—
>   It's all in the state of mind.

> If you think you are outclassed, you are—
>   You've got to think high to rise.
> You've got to be sure of yourself before
>   You can ever win a prize.

> Life's battles don't always go
>   To the stronger or faster man;
> But soon or late the man who wins
>   Is the man who thinks he can.

It can do no harm if you commit this poem to memory and use it as a part of your working equipment in the development of Self-confidence.

Somewhere in your make-up there is a "subtle something" which, if it were aroused by the proper outside influence, would carry you to heights of achievement such as you have never before anticipated. Just as a master player can take hold of a violin and cause that instrument to pour forth the most beautiful and entrancing strains of music, so is there some outside influence that can lay hold of your mind and cause you to go forth into the field of your chosen endeavor and play a glorious symphony of *success*. No man knows what hidden forces lie dormant within *you*. You, yourself, do not know your capacity for achievement, and you never will know until you come in contact with that particular stimulus which arouses you to greater action and extends your vision, develops your Self-confidence and moves you with a deeper *desire* to achieve.

It is not unreasonable to expect that some statement, some idea or some stimulating word of this Reading Course on the Law of Success will serve as the needed stimulus that will re-shape your destiny and re-direct your thoughts and energies along a pathway that will lead you, finally, to your coveted goal of life. It is strange, but true, that the most important turning-points of life often come at the most unex-

pected times and in the most unexpected ways. I
have in mind a typical example of how some of the
seemingly unimportant experiences of life often turn
out to be the most important of all, and I am relating
this case because it shows, also, what a man can accomplish when he awakens to a full understanding of
the value of Self-confidence. The incident to which I
refer happened in the city of Chicago, while I was
engaged in the work of character analysis. One day a
tramp presented himself at my office and asked for an
interview. As I looked up from my work and greeted
him he said, "I have come to see the man who wrote
this little book," as he removed from his pocket a
copy of a book entitled Self-confidence, which I had
written many years previously. "It must have been
the hand of fate," he continued, "that slipped this
book into my pocket yesterday afternoon, because I
was about ready to go out there and punch a hole in
Lake Michigan. I had about come to the conclusion
that everything and everybody, including God, had it
in for me until I read this book, and it gave me a new
viewpoint and brought me the courage and the hope
that sustained me through the night. I made up my
mind that if I could see the man who wrote this book
he could help me get on my feet again. Now, I am
here and I would like to know what you can do for a
man like me."

While he was speaking I had been studying him
from head to foot, and I am frank to admit that down
deep in my heart I did not believe there was anything
I could do for him, but I did not wish to tell him so.
The glassy stare in his eyes, the lines of discouragement in his face, the posture of his body, the ten days'

THE only man who makes no mistakes is the man who never does anything. Do not be afraid of mistakes providing you do not make the same one twice.

—*Roosevelt.*

growth of beard on his face, the nervous manner about this man all conveyed to me the impression that he was hopeless, but I did not have the heart to tell him so, therefore I asked him to sit down and tell me his whole story. I asked him to be perfectly frank and tell me, as nearly as possible, just what had brought him down to the ragged edge of life. I promised him that after I had heard his entire story I would then tell him whether or not I could be of service to him. He related his story, in lengthy detail, the sum and substance of which was this: He had invested his entire fortune in a small manufacturing business. When the world war began in 1914, it was impossible for him to get the raw materials necessary in the operation of his factory, and he therefore failed. The loss of his money broke his heart and so disturbed his mind that he left his wife and children and became a tramp. He had actually brooded over his loss until he had reached the point at which he was contemplating suicide.

After he had finished his story, I said to him: "I have listened to you with a great deal of interest, and I wish that there was something which *I* could do to help you, but *there is absolutely nothing.*"

He became as pale as he will be when he is laid away in a coffin, and settled back in his chair and dropped his chin on his chest as much as to say, "That settles it." I waited for a few seconds, then said:

"While there is nothing that I can do for you, there is a man in this building to whom I will introduce you, if you wish, who can help you regain your lost fortune and put you back on your feet again." These words had barely fallen from my lips when he jumped up, grabbed me by the hands and said, "For God's sake lead me to this man."

It was encouraging to note that he had asked this "for God's sake." This indicated that there was still a spark of hope within his breast, so I took him by the arm and led him out into the laboratory where my psychological tests in character analysis were conducted, and stood with him in front of what looked to be a curtain over a door. I pulled the curtain aside and uncovered a tall looking-glass in which he saw himself from head to foot. Pointing my finger at the glass I said:

"There stands the man to whom I promised to introduce you. There is the only man in this world who can put you back on your feet again, and unless you sit down and become acquainted with that man, as you never became acquainted with him before, you might just as well go on over and 'punch a hole' in Lake Michigan, because you will be of no value to yourself or to the world until you know this man better."

He stepped over to the glass, rubbed his hands over his bearded face, studied himself from head to foot for a few moments, then stepped back, dropped his head and began to weep. I knew that the lesson had been driven home, so I led him back to the elevator and sent him away. I never expected to see him again, and I doubted that the lesson would be sufficient to help him regain his place in the world, because he seemed to be too far gone for redemption. He seemed to be not only *down*, but almost *out*.

A few days later I met this man on the street. His

transformation had been so complete that I hardly recognized him. He was walking briskly, with his head tilted back. That old, shifting, nervous posture of his body was gone. He was dressed in new clothes from head to foot. He looked prosperous and he felt prosperous. He stopped me and related what had happened to bring about his rapid transformation from a state of abject failure to one of hope and promise.

"I was just on my way to your office," he explained, "to bring you the good news. I went out the very day that I was in your office, a down-and-out tramp, and despite my appearance I sold myself at a salary of $3,000.00 a year. *Think of it, man, three thousand dollars a year!* And my employer advanced me money enough with which to buy some new clothes, as you can see for yourself. He also advanced me some money to send home to my family, and I am once more on the road to success. It seems like a dream when I think that only a few days ago I had lost hope and faith and courage, and was actually contemplating suicide.

"I was coming to tell you that one of these days, when you are least expecting me, I will pay you another visit, and when I do I will be a successful man. I will bring with me a check, signed in blank and made payable to you, and you may fill in the amount because you have saved me from *myself* by introducing me to *myself*—that self which I never knew until you stood me in front of that looking-glass and pointed out the *real* me."

As that man turned and departed in the crowded streets of Chicago I saw, for the first time in my life, what strength and power and possibility lie hidden in the mind of the man who has never discovered the value of *Self-reliance*. Then and there I made up my mind that I, too, would stand in front of that same looking-glass and point an accusing finger at myself for not having discovered the lesson which I had helped another to learn. I did stand before that same looking-glass, and as I did so I then and there fixed in my mind, as my *definite purpose* in life, the determination to help men and women discover the forces that lie sleeping within them. The book you hold in your hands is evidence that my definite purpose is being carried out.

The man whose story I have related is now the president of one of the largest and most successful concerns of its kind in America, with a business that extends from coast to coast and from Canada to Mexico.

A short while after the incident just related, a woman came to my office for personal analysis. She was then a teacher in the Chicago public schools. I gave her an analysis chart and asked her to fill it out. She had been at work on the chart but a few minutes when she came back to my desk, handed back the chart and said, "I do not believe I will fill this out." I asked her why she had decided not to fill out the chart and she replied: "To be perfectly frank with you, one of the questions in this chart put me to thinking and I now know what is wrong with me, therefore I feel it unnecessary to pay you a fee to analyze me." With that the woman went away and I did not hear from her for two years. She went to New York City, became a writer of advertising copy for one of the largest agencies in the country and her income at the time she wrote me was $10,000.00 a year.

This woman sent me a check to cover the cost of my analysis fee, because she felt that the fee had been earned, even though I did not render her the service that I usually render my clients. It is impossible for anyone to foretell what seemingly insignificant incident may lead to an important turning-point in one's career, but there is no denying the fact that these "turning-points" may be more readily recognized by those who have well-rounded-out confidence in themselves.

One of the irreparable losses to the human race lies in the lack of knowledge that there is a definite method through which Self-confidence can be developed in any person of average intelligence. What an immeasurable loss to civilization that young men and women are not taught this known method of developing Self-confidence before they complete their schooling, for no one who lacks faith in himself is really educated in the proper sense of the term.

Oh, what glory and satisfaction would be the happy heritage of the man or woman who could pull aside the curtain of *fear* that hangs over the human race and shuts out the sunlight of understanding that Self-confidence brings, wherever it is in evidence.

Where *fear* controls, noteworthy achievement becomes an impossibility, a fact which brings to mind the definition of *fear*, as stated by a great philosopher:

"Fear is the dungeon of the mind into which it runs and hides and seeks seclusion. Fear brings on superstition and superstition is the dagger with which hypocrisy assassinates the soul."

In front of the typewriter on which I am writing

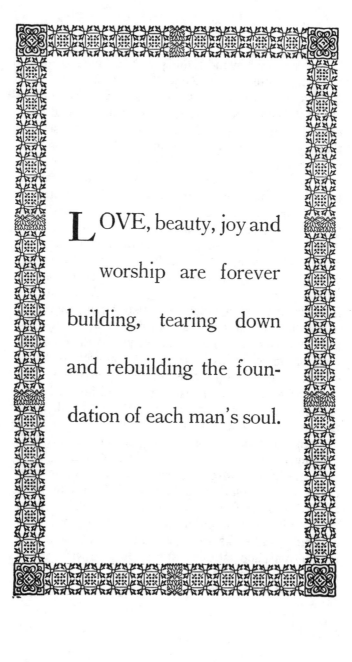

LOVE, beauty, joy and worship are forever building, tearing down and rebuilding the foundation of each man's soul.

the manuscripts for this Reading Course hangs a sign
with the following wording, in big letters:

"Day by day in every way I am becoming more
successful."

A skeptic who read that sign asked if I really believed "that stuff" and I replied, "Of course not. All
it ever did for me was to help me get out of the coal
mines, where I started as a laborer, and find a place
in the world in which I am serving upwards of
100,000 people, in whose minds I am planting the
same positive thought that this sign brings out; therefore, why should I believe in it?"

As this man started to leave he said: "Well, perhaps there is something to this sort of philosophy,
after all, for I have always been afraid that I would
be a failure, and so far my fears have been thoroughly
realized."

You are condemning yourself to poverty, misery
and failure, or you are driving yourself on toward the
heights of great achievement, solely by the thoughts
you think. If you *demand* success of yourself and
back up this demand with intelligent action you are
sure to win. Bear in mind, though, that there is a
difference between *demanding* success and just merely
wishing for it. You should find out what this difference is, and take advantage of it.

Do you remember what the Bible says (look it up,
somewhere in the book of Matthew) about those who
have faith as a grain of mustard seed? Go at the
task of developing Self-confidence with at least that
much faith if not more. Never mind "what *they* will
say" because you might as well know that *"they"* will
be of little aid to you in your climb up the mountain-

side of life toward the object of your *definite purpose*. You have within you all the power you need with which to get whatever you want or need in this world, and about the best way to avail yourself of this power is to *believe in yourself*.

"Know thyself, man; know thyself."

This has been the advice of the philosophers all down the ages. When you *really* know yourself you will know that there is nothing foolish about hanging a sign in front of you that reads like this: "Day by day in every way I am becoming more successful," with due apologies to the Frenchman who made this motto popular. I am not afraid to place this sort of suggestion in front of my desk, and, what is more to the point, I am not afraid to believe that it will influence me so that I will become a more positive and aggressive human being.

More than twenty-five years ago I learned my first lesson in Self-confidence building. One night I was sitting before an open fire-place, listening to a conversation between some older men, on the subject of Capital and Labor. Without invitation I joined in the conversation and said something about employers and employees settling their differences on the Golden Rule basis. My remarks attracted the attention of one of the men, who turned to me, with a look of surprise on his face and said:

"Why, you are a bright boy, and if you would go out and get a schooling you would make your mark in the world."

Those remarks fell on "fertile" ears, even though that was the first time anyone had ever told me that I was bright, or that I might accomplish anything worth while in life. The remark put me to thinking, and the more I allowed my mind to dwell upon that thought the more certain I became that the remark had back of it a possibility.

It might be truthfully stated that whatever service I am rendering the world and whatever good I accomplish, should be credited to that off-hand remark.

Suggestions such as this are often powerful, and none the less so when they are deliberate and self-expressed. Go back, now, to the Self-confidence formula and master it, for it will lead you into the "power-house" of your own mind, where you will tap a force that can be made to carry you to the very top of the Ladder of Success.

Others will believe in you only when you believe in yourself. They will "tune in" on your thoughts and feel toward you just as you feel toward yourself. The law of mental telepathy takes care of this. You are continuously broadcasting what you think of yourself, and if you have no faith in yourself others will pick up the vibrations of your thoughts and mistake them for their own. Once understand the law of mental telepathy and you will know why Self-confidence is the second of the Fifteen Laws of Success.

You should be cautioned, however, to learn the difference between Self-confidence, which is based upon sound knowledge of what you know and what you can do, and egotism, which is only based upon what you *wish* you knew or could do. Learn the difference between these two terms or you will make yourself boresome, ridiculous and annoying to people of culture and understanding. Self-confidence is something which should never be proclaimed or announced except through intelligent performance of constructive deeds.

If you have Self-confidence those around you will discover this fact. Let them make the discovery. They will feel proud of their alertness in having made the discovery, and you will be free from the suspicion of egotism. Opportunity never stalks the person with a highly developed state of egotism, but brick-bats and ugly remarks do. Opportunity forms affinities much more easily and quickly with Self-confidence than it does with egotism. Self-praise is never a proper measure of self-reliance. Bear this in mind and let your Self-confidence speak only through the tongue of constructive service rendered without fuss or flurry.

Self-confidence is the product of knowledge. Know yourself, know how much you know (and how little), why you know it, and how you are going to use it. "Four-flushers" come to grief, therefore, do not pretend to know more than you actually do know. There's no use of pretense, because any educated person will measure you quite accurately after hearing you speak for three minutes. What you really are will speak so loudly that what you "claim" you are will not be heard.

If you heed this warning the last four pages of this one lesson may mark one of the most important turning-points of your life.

Believe in yourself, but do not tell the world what you can do—SHOW IT!

You are now ready for Lesson Four, which will take you the next step up the Ladder of Success.

DISCONTENTMENT

An After-the-Lesson Visit With the Author

The marker stands at the Entrance Gate of Life and writes "Poor Fool" on the brow of the wise man and "Poor Sinner" on the brow of the saint.

The supreme mystery of the universe is life! We come here without our consent, from whence we know not! We go away without our consent, whither, we know not!

We are eternally trying to solve this great riddle of "LIFE," and, for what purpose and to what end?

That we are placed on this earth for a definite reason there can be no doubt by any thinker. May it not be possible that the power which placed us here will know what to do with us when we pass on beyond the Great Divide?

Would it not be a good plan to give the Creator who placed us here on earth, credit for having enough intelligence to know what to do with us after we pass on; or, should we assume the intelligence and the ability to control the future life in our own way? May it not be possible that we can co-operate with the Creator very intelligently by assuming to con-

135

trol our conduct on this earth to the end that
we may be decent to one another and do all
the good we can in all the ways we can during
this life, leaving the hereafter to one who
probably knows, better than we, what is best
for us?

THE artist has told a powerful story in the picture
at the top of this page.

From birth until death the mind is always reaching
out for that which it does not possess.

The little child, playing with its toys on the floor,
sees another child with a different sort of toy and
immediately tries to lay hands on that toy.

The female child (grown tall) believes the other
woman's clothes more becoming than her own and
sets out to duplicate them.

The male child (grown tall) sees another man with
a bigger collection of railroads or banks or merchandise and says to himself: "How fortunate! How fortunate! How can I separate him from his belongings?"

F. W. Woolworth, the Five and Ten Cent Store
king, stood on Fifth Avenue in New York City and
gazed upward at the tall Metropolitan Building and
said: "How wonderful! I will build one much
taller." The crowning achievement of his life was
measured by the Woolworth Building. That building
stands as a temporary symbol of man's nature to
excel the handiwork of other men. A MONUMENT
TO THE VANITY OF MAN, WITH BUT LITTLE
ELSE TO JUSTIFY ITS EXISTENCE!

.   .   .   .

The little ragged newsboy on the street stands, with
wide-open mouth, and envies the business man as he

alights from his automobile at the curb and starts into his office. "How happy I would be," the newsboy says to himself, "if I owned a Lizzie." And, the business man seated at his desk inside, thinks how happy he would be if he could add another million dollars to his already overswollen bank roll.

The grass is always sweeter on the other side of the fence, says the jackass, as he stretches his neck in the attempt to get to it.

Turn a crowd of boys into an apple orchard and they will pass by the nice mellow apples on the ground. The red, juicy ones hanging dangerously high in the top of the tree look much more tempting, and up the tree they will go.

The married man takes a sheepish glance at the daintily dressed ladies on the street and thinks how fortunate he would be if his wife were as pretty as they. Perhaps she is much prettier, but he misses that beauty because—well, because "the grass is always greener on the other side of the fence." Most divorce cases grow out of man's tendency to climb the fence into the other fellow's pastures.

· · · · · · ·

Happiness is always just around the bend; always in sight but just out of reach. Life is never complete, no matter what we have or how much of it we possess. One thing calls for something else to go with it.

Milady buys a pretty hat. She must have a gown to match it. That calls for new shoes and hose and gloves, and other accessories that run into a big bill far beyond her husband's means.

Man longs for a home—just a plain little house setting off in the edge of the woods. He builds it, but it is not complete; he must have shrubbery and flowers and landscaping to go with it. Still it is not complete; he must have a beautiful fence around it, with a graveled driveway.

That calls for a motor car and a garage in which to house it.

All these little touches have been added, but to no avail! The place is now too small. He must have a house with more rooms. The Ford Coupe must be replaced by a Cadillac sedan, so there will be room for company in the cross country tours.

On and on the story goes, ad infinitum!

.   .   .   .

The young man receives a salary sufficient to keep him and his family fairly comfortable. Then comes a promotion and an advance in salary of a thousand dollars a year. Does he lay the extra thousand dollars away in the savings account and continue living as before? He does nothing of the sort. Immediately he must trade the old car in for a new one. A porch must be added to the house. The wife needs a new wardrobe. The table must be set with better food and more of it. (Pity his poor, groaning stomach.) At the end of the year is he better off with the increase? He is nothing of the sort! The more he gets the more he wants, and the rule applies to the man with millions the same as to the man with but a few thousands.

The young man selects the girl of his choice, believing he cannot live without her. After he gets her he is not sure that he can live with her. If a man remains a bachelor he wonders why he is so stupid as to deprive himself of the joys of married life. If he marries he wonders how she happened to catch him off guard long enough to "harpoon" him.

And the god of Destiny cries out "O fool, O fool! You are damned if you DO and you are damned if you DON'T."

At every crossroad of Life the imps of Discontentment stand in the shadows of the back-ground, with a grin of mockery on their faces, crying out "Take the road of your own choice! We will get you in the end!"

. . . .

At last man becomes disillusioned and begins to learn that Happiness and Contentment are not of this world. Then begins the search for the pass-word that will open the door to him in some world of which he knows not. Surely there must be Happiness on the other side of the Great Divide. In desperation his tired, care-worn heart turns to religion for hope and encouragement.

But, his troubles are not over; they are just starting!

"Come into our tent and accept our creed," says one sect, "and you may go straight to heaven after death." Poor man hesitates, looks and listens. Then he hears the call of another brand of religion whose leader says:

"Stay out of the other camp or you'll go straight to hell! They only sprinkle water on your head, but we push you all the way under, thereby insuring you safe passage into the Land of Promise."

In the midst of sectarian claims and counter-claims poor man becomes undecided. Not knowing whether to turn this way or that, he wonders which brand of religion offers the safest passage-way, until Hope vanishes.

> "Myself when young
>   did eagerly frequent
> Doctor and Saint and heard
>   great argument
> About it and about; but
>   evermore
> Came out by the same door
>   where in I went."

Always seeking but never finding—thus might be described man's struggle for Happiness and Contentment. He tries one religion after another, finally joining the "Big Church" which the world has named the "Damned." His mind becomes an eternal question mark, searching hither and yon for an answer to the questions—"Whence and Whither?"

> "The worldly hope men set
>   their Hearts upon
> Turns Ashes—or it prospers;
>   and anon,
> Like Snow upon the Desert's
>   Dusty Face
> Lighting a little Hour or two—
>   is gone."

Life is an everlasting question-mark!

That which we want most is always in the embryonic distance of the future. Our power to acquire is always a decade or so behind our power to DESIRE!

And, if we catch up with the thing we want we no longer want it!

Fortunate is the young woman who learns this great truth and keeps her lover always guessing, always on the defensive lest he may lose her.

Our favorite author is a hero and a genius until we meet him in person and learn the sad truth that, after all, he is only a man. "How often must we learn this lesson? Men cease to interest us when we find their limitations. The only sin is limitation. As soon as you once come up with a man's limitations, it is all over with him."—EMERSON.

How beautiful the mountain yonder in the distance; but, the moment we draw near it we find it to be nothing but a wretched collection of rocks and dirt and trees.

Out of this truth grew the oft-repeated adage "Familiarity breeds contempt."

Beauty and Happiness and Contentment are states of mind. They can never be enjoyed except through vision of the afar. The most beautiful painting of Rembrandt becomes a mere smudge of daubed paint if we come too near it.

Destroy the Hope of unfinished dreams in man's heart and he is finished.

The moment a man ceases to cherish the vision of future achievement he is through. Nature has built man so that his greatest and only lasting Happiness is that which he feels in the pursuit of some yet unattained object. Anticipation is sweeter than realization. That which is at hand does not satisfy. The only enduring satisfaction is that which comes to the person who keeps alive in his heart the HOPE of future achievement. When that hope dies write FINIS across the human heart.

.   .   .   .

Life's greatest inconsistency is the fact that most of that which we believe is not true. Russel Conwell wrote the most popular lecture ever delivered in the English language. He called it "Acres of Diamonds." The central idea of the lecture was the statement that one need not seek opportunity in the distance; that opportunity may be found in the vicinity of one's birth. Perhaps! but, how many believe it?

Opportunity may be found wherever one really looks for it, and nowhere else! To most men the picking looks better on the other side of the fence. How futile to urge one to try out one's luck in the little home-town when it is man's nature to look for opportunity in some other locality.

Do not worry because the grass looks sweeter on the other side of the fence. Nature intended it so. Thus does she allure us and groom us for the life-long task of GROWTH THROUGH STRUGGLE.

THE highest compact

we can make with

our fellow is: Let there

be truth between us two

forevermore.

—*Emerson.*

Treat Yourself to This Fun, Inspirational Book and Discover
How to Find Happiness and Serenity . . .
No Matter What Life Dishes Out

The Dragon Slayer
With a Heavy Heart

*This new book by best-selling author Marcia Powers promises to be
one of the most important you will ever read—and one of the most
entertaining, uplifting, and memorable.*

*It brings the Serenity Prayer—which for years has been the guiding
light of 12-step programs worldwide—to everyone . . . and teaches
both new and longtime devotees how to apply it most effectively to
their lives.*

Sometimes things happen we wish hadn't. Sometimes things *don't*
happen we wish *would.* In the course of living, problems arise, both
big and small. We might wish our past had been different or that *we*
could be different. We struggle through disappointments and
frustrations, losses and other painful experiences.

As hard as we may try to be strong, to have a good attitude, not to
let things get us down, we don't always succeed. We get upset. We
worry. We feel stressed. We get depressed. We get angry. We do the
best we can and wait for things to *get* better so we can *feel* better. In
the meantime, our hearts may grow heavy . . . perhaps very heavy.

That's what happened to Duke the Dragon Slayer. In fact, *his*
heart grew *so* heavy with all that was wrong, with all that was not the
way it should be, with all that was unfair, that he became desperate to
lighten it—and set forth on the Path of Serenity to find out how.

Accompany Duke on this life-changing adventure. His guides will
be your guides. His answers will be your answers. His tools will be
your tools. His success will be your success. And by the time he is
heading home, both Duke and you will know how to take life's
inevitable lumps and bumps in stride—and find happiness and
serenity anytime . . . even when you really, REALLY wish some things
were different.

"A BEAUTIFUL, EXCEPTIONALLY WELL-WRITTEN STORY THAT CAN HELP
EVERYONE TO BE EMOTIONALLY STRONGER AND BETTER ABLE TO COPE
WITH ADVERSITY."
                                         Albert Ellis, Ph.D.
                                     President, Albert Ellis Institute
                                 Author of *A Guide to Rational Living*

THE
LAW OF
SUCCESS

IN SIXTEEN LESSONS

Teaching, for the First Time in the
History of the World, the True Philosophy upon which all Personal Success
is Built.

••◦❦◦••

BY

NAPOLEON HILL

••◦❦◦••

1928

PUBLISHED BY
The RALSTON UNIVERSITY PRESS
MERIDEN, CONN.

Lesson Four

THE HABIT OF SAVING

THE only lasting fa-
vor which the par-
ent may confer upon the
child is that of helping the
child to help itself.

"Man is a combination of flesh, bone, blood, hair and brain cells. These are the building materials out of which he shapes, through the Law of Habit, his own personality."

TO advise one to save money without describing how to save would be somewhat like drawing the picture of a horse and writing under it, "This is a horse." It is obvious to all that the saving of money is one of the essentials for success, but the big question uppermost in the minds of the majority of those who do not save is:

"How can I do it?"

The saving of money is solely a matter of *habit*. For this reason this lesson begins with a brief analysis of the Law of Habit.

It is literally true that man, through the Law of Habit, shapes his own personality. Through repetition, any act indulged in a few times becomes a habit, and the mind appears to be nothing more than a mass of motivating forces growing out of our daily habits.

When once fixed in the mind a habit voluntarily impels one to action. For example, follow a given route to your daily work, or to some other place that you frequently visit, and very soon the habit has been formed and your mind will lead you over that route without thought on your part. Moreover, if you start out with the intention of traveling in another direction, without keeping the thought of the change in routes constantly in mind, you will find yourself following the old route.

Public speakers have found that the telling over and over again of a story, which may be based upon pure fiction, brings into play the Law of Habit, and very soon they forget whether the story is true or not.

WALLS OF LIMITATION BUILT THROUGH HABIT

Millions of people go through life in poverty and want because they have made destructive use of the Law of Habit. Not understanding either the Law of Habit or the Law of Attraction through which "like attracts like," those who remain in poverty seldom realize that they are where they are as the result of their own acts.

Fix in your mind the thought that your ability is limited to a given earning capacity and you will never earn more than that, because the law of habit will set up a definite limitation of the amount you can earn, your subconscious mind will accept this limitation, and very soon you will feel yourself "slipping" until finally you will become so hedged in by FEAR OF POVERTY (one of the six basic fears) that opportunity will no longer knock at your door; your doom will be sealed; your fate fixed.

Formation of the Habit of Saving does not mean that you shall limit your earning capacity; it means just the opposite—that you shall apply this law so that it not only conserves that which you earn, in a systematic manner, but it also places you in the way of greater opportunity and gives you the vision, the self-confidence, the imagination, the enthusiasm, the initiative and leadership actually to increase your earning capacity.

Stating this great law in another way, when you thoroughly understand the Law of Habit you may insure yourself success in the great game of money-making by "playing both ends of that game against the middle."

You proceed in this manner:

First, through the law of Definite Chief Aim you set up, in your mind, an accurate, definite description of that which you want, including the amount of money you intend to earn. Your subconscious mind takes over this picture which you have created and uses it as a blueprint, chart or map by which to mold your thoughts and actions into practical plans for attaining the object of your Chief Aim, or purpose. Through the Law of Habit you keep the object of your Definite Chief Aim fixed in your mind (in the manner described in Lesson Two until it becomes firmly and permanently implanted there. This practice will destroy the poverty consciousness and set up, in its place, a prosperity consciousness. You will actually begin to DEMAND prosperity, you will begin to expect it, you will begin to prepare yourself to receive it and to use it wisely, thus paving the way or setting the stage for the development of the Habit of Saving.

Second, having in this manner increased your earning power you will make further use of the Law of Habit by provision, in your written statement of your Definite Chief Aim, for saving a definite proportion of all the money you earn.

Therefore, as your earnings increase, your savings will, likewise, increase in proportion.

By ever urging yourself on and demanding of yourself increased earning power, on the one hand, and by systematically laying aside a definite amount of all your earnings, on the other hand, you will soon reach the point at which you have removed all imaginary limitations from your own mind and you will then be well started on the road toward financial independence.

Nothing could be more practical or more easily accomplished than this!

Reverse the operation of the Law of Habit, by setting up in your mind the Fear of Poverty, and very soon this fear will reduce your earning capacity until you will be barely able to earn sufficient money to take care of your actual necessities.

The publishers of newspapers could create a panic in a week's time by filling their columns with news items concerning the actual business failures of the country, despite the fact that but few businesses, compared to the total number in existence, actually fail.

The so-called "crime waves" are very largely the products of sensational journalism. A single murder case, when exploited by the newspapers of the country, through scare headlines, is sufficient to start a regular "wave" of similar crimes in various localities. Following the repetition in the daily papers of the Hickman murder story, similar cases began to be reported from other parts of the country.

We are the victims of our habits, no matter who we are or what may be our life-calling. Any idea that is deliberately fixed in the mind, or any idea that is permitted to set itself up in the mind, as the result of suggestion, environment, the influence of associates, etc., is sure to cause us to indulge in acts which conform to the nature of the idea.

Form the habit of thinking and talking of prosperity and abundance, and very soon material evidence of these will begin to manifest itself in the nature of wider opportunity and new and unexpected opportunity.

Like attracts like! If you are in business and have formed the habit of talking and thinking about "business being bad" business will be bad. One pessimist, providing he is permitted to continue his destructive influence long enough, can destroy the work of half a dozen competent men, and he will do it by setting adrift in the minds of his associates the thought of poverty and failure.

Don't be this type of man or woman.

One of the most successful bankers in the state of Illinois has this sign hanging in his private office:

YOU are a human magnet and you are constantly attracting to you people whose characters harmonize with your own.

"WE TALK AND THINK ONLY OF ABUN-
DANCE HERE.   IF YOU HAVE A TALE OF WOE
PLEASE KEEP IT, AS WE DO NOT WANT IT."

No business firm wants the services of a pessimist,
and those who understand the Law of Attraction and
the Law of Habit will no more tolerate the pessimist
than they would permit a burglar to roam around their
place of business, for the reason that one such person
will destroy the usefulness of those around him.

In tens of thousands of homes the general topic of
conversation is poverty and want, and that is just
what they are getting.   They think of poverty, they
talk of poverty, they accept poverty as their lot in
life.   They reason that because their ancestors were
poor before them they, also, must remain poor.

The poverty consciousness is formed as the result
of the habit of thinking of and fearing poverty.
"Lo! the thing I had feared has come upon me."

THE SLAVERY OF DEBT

Debt is a merciless master, a fatal enemy of the
savings habit.

Poverty, alone, is sufficient to kill off ambition,
destroy self-confidence and destroy hope, but add to it
the burden of debt and all who are victims of these
two cruel task-masters are practically doomed to
failure.

No man can do his best work, no man can express
himself in terms that command respect, no man can
either create or carry out a definite purpose in life,
with heavy debt hanging over his head.   The man
who is bound in the slavery of debt is just as helpless

as the slave who is bound by ignorance, or by actual chains.

The author has a very close friend whose income is $1,000 a month. His wife loves "society" and tries to make a $20,000 showing on a $12,000 income, with the result that this poor fellow is usually about $8,000 in debt. Every member of his family has the "spending habit," having acquired this from the mother. The children, two girls and one boy, are now of the age when they are thinking of going to college, but this is impossible because of the father's debts. The result is dissension between the father and his children which makes the entire family unhappy and miserable.

It is a terrible thing even to think of going through life like a prisoner in chains, bound down and owned by somebody else on account of debts. The accumulation of debts is a habit. It starts in a small way and grows to enormous proportions slowly, step by step, until finally it takes charge of one's very soul.

Thousands of young men start their married lives with unnecessary debts hanging over their heads and never manage to get out from under the load. After the novelty of marriage begins to wear off (as it usually does) the married couple begin to feel the embarrassment of want, and this feeling grows until it leads, oftentimes, to open dissatisfaction with one another, and eventually to the divorce court.

A man who is bound by the slavery of debt has no time or inclination to set up or work out ideals, with the result that he drifts downward with time until he eventually begins to set up limitations in his own mind, and by these he hedges himself behind prison walls of FEAR and doubt from which he never escapes.

No sacrifice is too great to avoid the misery of debt!

"Think of what you owe yourself and those who are dependent upon you and resolve to be no man's debtor," is the advice of one very successful man whose early chances were destroyed by debt. This man came to himself soon enough to throw off the habit of buying that which he did not need and eventually worked his way out of slavery.

Most men who develop the habit of debt will not be so fortunate as to come to their senses in time to save themselves, because debt is something like quicksand in that it has a tendency to draw its victim deeper and deeper into the mire.

The Fear of Poverty is one of the most destructive of the six basic fears described in Lesson Three. The man who becomes hopelessly in debt is seized with this poverty fear, his ambition and self-confidence become paralyzed, and he sinks gradually into oblivion.

There are two classes of debts, and these are so different in nature that they deserve to be here described, as follows:

1. There are debts incurred for luxuries which become a dead loss.

2. There are debts incurred in the course of professional or business trading which represent service or merchandise that can be converted back into assets.

The first class of debts is the one to be avoided. The second class may be indulged in, providing the one incurring the debts uses judgment and does not go beyond the bounds of reasonable limitation. The moment one buys beyond his limitations he enters the realm of speculation, and speculation swallows more of its victims than it enriches.

Practically all people who live beyond their means are tempted to speculate with the hope that they may recoup, at a single turn of the wheel of fortune, so to speak, their entire indebtedness. The wheel generally stops at the wrong place and, far from finding themselves out of debt, such people as indulge in speculation are bound more closely as slaves of debt.

The Fear of Poverty breaks down the will-power of its victims, and they then find themselves unable to restore their lost fortunes, and, what is still more sad, they lose all ambition to extricate themselves from the slavery of debt.

Hardly a day passes that one may not see an account in the newspapers of at least one suicide as the result of worry over debts. The slavery of debt causes more suicides every year than all other causes combined, which is a slight indication of the cruelty of the poverty fear.

During the war millions of men faced the front-line trenches without flinching, knowing that death might overtake them any moment. Those same men, when facing the Fear of Poverty, often cringe and out of sheer desperation, which paralyzes their reason, sometimes commit suicide.

The person who is free from debt may whip poverty and achieve outstanding financial success, but, if he is bound by debt, such achievement is but a remote possibility, and never a probability.

Fear of Poverty is a negative, destructive state of

mind. Moreover, one negative state of mind has a tendency to attract other similar states of mind. For example, the Fear of Poverty may attract the fear of Ill Health, and these two may attract the Fear of Old Age, so that the victim finds himself poverty-stricken, in ill health and actually growing old long before the time when he should begin to show the signs of old age.

Millions of untimely, nameless graves have been filled by this cruel state of mind known as the Fear of Poverty!

Less than a dozen years ago a young man held a responsible position with the City National Bank, of New York City. Through living beyond his income he contracted a large amount of debts which caused him to worry until this destructive habit began to show up in his work and he was dismissed from the bank's service.

He secured another position, at less money, but his creditors embarrassed him so that he decided to resign and go away into another city, where he hoped to escape them until he had accumulated enough money to pay off his indebtedness. Creditors have a way of tracing debtors, so very soon they were close on the heels of this young man, whose employer found out about his indebtedness and dismissed him from his position.

He then searched in vain for employment for two months. One cold night he went to the top of one of the tall buildings on Broadway and jumped off. Debt had claimed another victim.

WHO told you it couldn't be done? and, what great achievement has he to his credit that entitles him to use the word "impossible" so freely?

HOW TO MASTER THE FEAR OF POVERTY

To whip the Fear of Poverty one must take two very definite steps, providing one is in debt. First, quit the habit of buying on credit, and follow this by gradually paying off the debts that you have already incurred.

Being free from the worry of indebtedness you are ready to revamp the habits of your mind and re-direct your course toward prosperity. Adopt, as a part of your Definite Chief Aim, the habit of saving a regular proportion of your income, even if this be no more than a penny a day. Very soon this habit will begin to lay hold of your mind and you will actually get joy out of saving.

Any habit may be discontinued by building in its place some other and more desirable habit. The "spending" habit must be replaced by the "saving" habit by all who attain financial independence.

Merely to discontinue an undesirable habit is not enough, as such habits have a tendency to reappear unless the place they formerly occupied in the mind is filled by some other habit of a different nature.

The discontinuance of a habit leaves a "hole" in the mind, and this hole must be filled up with some other form of habit or the old one will return and claim its place.

Throughout this course many psychological formulas, which the student has been requested to memorize and practice, have been described. You will find such a formula in Lesson Three, the object of which is to develop Self-confidence.

These formulas may be assimilated so they become a part of your mental machinery, through the Law of Habit, if you will follow the instructions for their use which accompany each of them.

It is assumed that you are striving to attain financial independence. The accumulation of money is not difficult after you have once mastered the Fear of Poverty and developed in its place the Habit of Saving.

The author of this course would be greatly disappointed to know that any student of the course got the impression from anything in this or any of the other lessons that Success is measured by dollars alone.

However, money does represent an important factor in success, and it must be given its proper value in any philosophy intended to help people in becoming useful, happy and prosperous.

The cold, cruel, relentless truth is that in this age of materialism a man is no more than so many grains of sand, which may be blown helter-skelter by every stray wind of circumstance, unless he is entrenched behind the power of money!

Genius may offer many rewards to those who possess it, but the fact still remains that genius without money with which to give it expression is but an empty, skeleton-like honor.

The man without money is at the mercy of the man who has it!

And this goes, regardless of the amount of ability he may possess, the training he has had or the native genius with which he was gifted by nature.

There is no escape from the fact that people will weigh you very largely in the light of bank balances, no matter who you are or what you can do. The first question that arises, in the minds of most people, when they meet a stranger, is, "How much money has he?" If he has money he is welcomed into homes and business opportunities are thrown his way. All sorts of attention are lavished upon him. He is a prince, and as such is entitled to the best of the land.

But if his shoes are run down at the heels, his clothes are not pressed, his collar is dirty, and he shows plainly the signs of impoverished finances, woe be his lot, for the passing crowd will step on his toes and blow the smoke of disrespect in his face.

These are not pretty statements, but they have one virtue—THEY ARE TRUE!

This tendency to judge people by the money they have, or their power to control money, is not confined to any one class of people. We all have a touch of it, whether we recognize the fact or not.

Thomas A. Edison is one of the best known and most respected inventors in the world, yet it is no misstatement of facts to say that he would have remained a practically unknown, obscure personage had he not followed the habit of conserving his resources and shown his ability to save money.

Henry Ford never would have got to first base with his "horseless carriage" had he not developed, quite early in life, the habit of saving. Moreover, had Mr. Ford not conserved his resources and hedged himself behind their power he would have been "swallowed up" by his competitors or those who covetously desired to take his business away from him, long, long years ago.

Many a man has gone a very long way toward success, only to stumble and fall, never again to rise, because of lack of money in times of emergency. The mortality rate in business each year, due to lack of reserve capital for emergencies, is stupendous. To this one cause are due more of the business failures than to all other causes combined!

Reserve Funds are essential in the successful operation of business!

Likewise, Savings Accounts are essential to success on the part of individuals. Without a savings fund the individual suffers in two ways: first, by inability to seize opportunities that come only to the person with some ready cash, and, second, by embarrassment due to some unexpected emergency calling for cash.

It might be said, also, that the individual suffers in still a third respect by not developing the Habit of Saving, through lack of certain other qualities essential for success which grow out of the practice of the Habit of Saving.

The nickels, dimes and pennies which the average person allows to slip through his fingers would, if systematically saved and properly put to work, eventually bring financial independence.

Through the courtesy of a prominent Building and Loan Association the following table has been compiled, showing what a monthly saving of $5.00, $10.00, $25.00 or $50.00 will amount to at the end of ten years. These figures are startling when one comes to consider the fact that the average person spends from $5.00 to $50.00 a month for useless merchandise or so-called "entertainment."

The making and saving of money is a science, yet

The Amazing Way Your Money Grows

SAVE $5 A MONTH (Only 17 cents a day)

	Amount Saved	Profit	Savings Plus Profits	Withdrawal Value
1st yr.	$ 60.00	$ 4.30	$ 64.30	$ $61.30
2nd yr.	$ 120.00	$ 16.55	$ 136.00	$ 125.00
3rd yr.	$ 180.00	$ 36.30	$ 216.30	$ 191.55
4th yr.	$ 240.00	$ 64.00	$ 304.00	$ 260.20
5th yr.	$ 300.00	$ 101.00	$ 401.00	$ 338.13
6th yr.	$ 360.00	$ 140.00*	$ 500.00*	$ 414.75*
7th yr.	$ 420.00	$ 197.10	$ 617.10	$ 495.43
8th yr.	$ 480.00	$ 257.05	$ 737.05	$ 578.32
9th yr.	$ 540.00	$ 324.95	$ 864.95	$ 687.15
10th yr.	$ 600.00	$ 400.00	$ 1000.00	$ 1000.00

SAVE $10 A MONTH (Only 33 cents a day)

	Amount Saved	Profit	Savings Plus Profits	Withdrawal Value
1st yr.	$ 120.00	$ 8.60	$ 128.60	$ 122.60
2nd yr.	$ 240.00	$ 33.11	$ 273.11	$ 250.00
3rd yr.	$ 360.00	$ 72.60	$ 432.60	$ 383.10
4th yr.	$ 480.00	$ 128.00	$ 608.00	$ 520.40
5th yr.	$ 600.00	$ 202.00	$ 802.00	$ 676.25
6th yr.	$ 720.00	$ 280.00	$ 1000.00*	$ 829.50*
7th yr.	$ 840.00	$ 394.20	$ 1234.20	$ 990.85
8th yr.	$ 960.00	$ 514.10	$ 1474.10	$ 1156.64
9th yr.	$1080.00	$ 649.90	$ 1729.90	$ 1374.30
10th yr.	$1200.00	$ 800.00	$ 2000.00	$ 2000.00

SAVE $25 A MONTH (Only 83 cents a day)

	Amount Saved	Profit	Savings Plus Profits	Withdrawal Value
1st yr.	$ 300.00	$ 21.50	$ 321.50	$ 306.50
2nd yr.	$ 600.00	$ 82.75	$ 682.75	$ 625.00
3rd yr.	$ 900.00	$ 181.50	$ 1081.50	$ 957.75
4th yr.	$1200.00	$ 320.00	$ 1520.00	$ 1301.00
5th yr.	$1500.00	$ 505.00	$ 2005.00	$ 1690.63
6th yr.	$1800.00	$ 700.00	$ 2500.00*	$ 2073.75*
7th yr.	$2100.00	$ 985.50	$ 3085.50	$ 2477.13
8th yr.	$2400.00	$1285.25	$ 3685.25	$ 2891.60
9th yr.	$2700.00	$1624.75	$ 4324.75	$ 3435.75
10th yr.	$3000.00	$2000.00	$ 5000.00	$ 5000.00

SAVE $50 A MONTH (Only $1.66 a day)

	Amount Saved	Profit	Savings Plus Profits	Withdrawal Value
1st yr.	$ 600.00	$ 43.00	$ 643.00	$ 613.00
2nd yr.	$1200.00	$ 165.50	$ 1365.50	$ 1250.00
3rd yr.	$1800.00	$ 363.00	$ 2163.00	$ 1915.50
4th yr.	$2400.00	$ 640.00	$ 3040.00	$ 2602.00
5th yr.	$3000.00	$1010.00	$ 4010.00	$ 3381.25
6th yr.	$3600.00	$1400.00	$ 5000.00*	$ 4147.50*
7th yr.	$4200.00	$1971.00	$ 6171.00	$ 4954.25
8th yr.	$4800.00	$2570.50	$ 7370.50	$ 5783.20
9th yr.	$5400.00	$3249.50	$ 8649.50	$ 6871.50
10th yr.	$6000.00	$4000.00	$10,000.00	$10,000.00

EVERY failure, every adversity, every heartache may be a blessing in disguise providing it softens the animal portion of our nature.

the rules by which money is accumulated are so simple that anyone may follow them. The main prerequisite is a willingness to subordinate the present to the future, by eliminating unnecessary expenditures for luxuries.

A young man, who was earning only $20.00 a week as chauffeur for a prominent New York banker, was induced by his employer to keep an accurate account of every cent he spent for one week. The following is an itemized list of his expenses:

Cigarettes	$ .75
Chewing gum	.30
Soda fountain	1.80
Cigars for associates	.1.50
Moving picture show	1.00
Shaves, including tips,	1.60
Newspaper, daily and Sunday ..	.22
Shoe shines	.30
	$ 7.47
Board and room	$12.00
Money on hand	.53
	$20.00

These figures tell a tragic story which might as well apply to thousands of other people as to the young man who kept this account. His actual savings out of $20.00 were only 53 cents. He spent $7.47 for items, every one of which could have been greatly reduced, and most of which could have been eliminated entirely. In fact, by shaving himself and shining his own shoes, he could have saved every cent of the $7.47.

Now turn to the table made up by the Building and Loan Association and observe what the saving of $7.47 a week would amount to. Suppose the amount this young man actually saved had been only $25.00 a month; the saving would have increased to the snug sum of $5,000.00 by the end of the first ten years.

The young man in question was twenty-one years old at the time he kept this expense account. By the time he reached the age of thirty-one years he could have had a substantial amount in the bank, had he saved $25.00 a month, and this saving would have brought him many opportunities that would have led directly to financial independence.

Some who are short-sighted, pseudo-philosophers, are fond of pointing to the fact that no one can become rich merely by saving a few dollars a week. This may be true enough, as far as the reasoning goes (which is not very far) but the other side of the story is that the saving of even a small sum of money places one in position where, oftentimes, this small sum may enable one to take advantage of business opportunities which lead directly and quite rapidly to financial independence.

The foregoing table, showing what a saving of $5.00 a month will amount to at the end of ten years, should be copied and pasted on your mirror, where it will stare you in the face every morning when you get up and every night as you retire, providing you have not already acquired the habit of systematic saving of money. This table should be reproduced, in letters and figures an inch tall, and placed on the walls of every public school throughout the land, where it might serve as a constant reminder to all school children of the value of the savings habit.

Some years ago, before giving serious thought to the value of the savings habit, this author made up an account of the money which had slipped through his fingers. The amount was so alarming that it resulted in the writing of this lesson, and adding the Habit of Saving as one of the Fifteen Laws of Success.

Following is an itemized statement of this account:

$ 4,000.00   inherited, invested in automobile supply business with a friend who lost the entire amount in one year.

   3,600.00   extra money earned from sundry writing for magazines and newspapers, all spent uselessly.

  30,000.00   earned from training 3,000 salesmen, with the aid of the Law of Success philosophy, invested in a magazine which was not a success because there was no reserve capital back of it.

   3,400.00   extra money earned from public addresses, lectures, etc., all of which was spent as it came in.

   6,000.00   estimated amount that could have been saved during a period of ten years, out of regular earnings, at the rate of only $50 a month.

———————

$47,000.00

This amount, had it been saved and invested as received, in Building and Loan Associations, or in some other manner that would have earned compound interest, would have grown into the sum of $94,000.00 at the time this lesson is being written.

The author is not a victim of any of the usual habits of dissipation, such as gambling, drinking and excessive entertaining. It is almost unbelievable that a man whose habits of living are reasonably moderate could spend $47,000.00 within a little over ten years without having anything to show for the money, but it can be done!

A capital reserve of $94,000.00, working at compound interest, is sufficient to give any man all the financial freedom he needs.

I recall one occasion when the president of a large corporation sent me a check for $500.00 for an address I delivered at a banquet given to the employees, and I distinctly recall what went through my mind when I opened the letter and saw the check. I had wanted a new automobile and this check was exactly the amount required for the first payment. I had it spent before it had been in my hands thirty seconds.

Perhaps this is the experience of the majority of people. They think more of how they are going to SPEND what they have than they do about ways and means of SAVING. The idea of saving, and the self-control and self-sacrifice which must accompany it, is always accompanied by thoughts of an unpleasant nature, but oh, how it does thrill one to think of SPENDING.

There is a reason for this, and that reason is the fact that most of us have developed the habit of spending while neglecting the Habit of Saving, and any idea that frequents the human mind but seldom is not as welcome as that which frequents it often.

In truth, the Habit of Saving can be made as fascinating as the habit of spending, but not until it has become a regular, well grounded, systematic habit. We like to do that which is often repeated, which is but another way of stating what the scientists have discovered, that we are victims of our habits.

The habit of saving money requires more force of character than most people have developed, for the reason that saving means self-denial and sacrifice of amusements and pleasures in scores of different ways.

For this very reason one who develops the savings habit acquires, at the same time, many of the other needed habits which lead to success: especially Self-control, Self-confidence, Courage, Poise and Freedom from Fear.

HOW MUCH SHOULD ONE SAVE?

The first question that will arise is, "How Much Should One Save?" The answer cannot be given in a few words, for the amount one should save depends upon many conditions, some of which may be within one's control and some of which may not be.

Generally speaking, a man who works for a salary should apportion his income about as follows:

    Savings Account 20%
    Living—Clothes, Food and Shelter ...50%
    Education 10%
    Recreation 10%
    Life Insurance 10%
                                      ————
                                      100%

CAREFUL analysis of 178 men who are known to be successful disclosed the fact that all had failed many times before arriving.

The following, however, indicates the approximate distribution which the average man actually makes of his income:

Savings Account ....NOTHING
Living—Clothes, Food and Shelter ...60%
Education 0%
Recreation 35%
Life Insurance 5%

———
100%

Under the item of "recreation" is included, of course, many expenditures that do not really "re-create," such as money spent for alcoholic drinks, dinner parties and other similar items which may actually serve to undermine one's health and destroy character.

An experienced analyst of men has stated that he could tell very accurately, by examining a man's monthly budget, what sort of a life the man is living; moreover, that he will get most of his information from the one item of "recreation." This, then, is an item to be watched as carefully as the greenhouse keeper watches the thermometer which controls the life and death of his plants.

Those who keep budget accounts often include an item called "entertainment," which, in a majority of cases, turns out to be an evil because it depletes the income heavily and when carried to excess depletes, also, the health.

We are living, right now, in an age when the item of "entertainment" is altogether too high in most budget allowances. Tens of thousands of people who earn not more than $50.00 a week are spending as much as one third of their incomes for what they call "entertainment," which comes in a bottle, with a questionable label on it, at anywhere from $6.00 to $12.00 a quart. Not only are these unwise people wasting the money that should go into a savings fund, but, of far greater danger, they are destroying both character and health.

Nothing in this lesson is intended as a preachment on morality, or on any other subject. We are here dealing with cold facts which, to a large extent, constitute the building materials out of which SUCCESS may be created.

However, this is an appropriate place to state some FACTS which have such a direct bearing on the subject of achieving success that they cannot be omitted without weakening this entire course in general and this lesson in particular.

The author of this course is NOT a reformer! Neither is he a preacher on morals, as this field of useful endeavor is quite well covered by others who are able workers. What is here stated, therefore, is intended as a necessary part of a course of philosophy whose purpose is to mark a safe road over which one may travel to honorable achievement.

During the year 1926 the author was in partnership with the late Don R. Mellett, who was, at that time, the publisher of the Canton (Ohio) Daily News. Mr. Mellett became interested in the Law of Success philosophy because it offered, as he believed, sound counsel to young men and young women who really wish to get ahead in life. Through the pages of the Daily News Mr. Mellett was conducting a fierce battle against the underworld forces of Canton. With the aid of detectives and investigators, some of whom were supplied by the Governor of Ohio, Mr. Mellett and the author gathered accurate data concerning the way most of the people in Canton were living.

In July, 1926, Mr. Mellett was assassinated from ambush, and four men, one of them a former member of the Canton police force, are now serving life sentences in the Ohio State Penitentiary for the crime.

During the investigation into crime conditions in Canton all reports came to the author's office, and the data here described are, therefore, known to be absolutely accurate.

One of the officials of a large industrial plant whose salary was $6,000.00 a year paid a Canton bootlegger an average of $300.00 a month for the liquor (if "stuff" can be called liquor) which he used for "entertaining." His wife participated in these "entertainments" which took place in his own home.

A paying teller in a bank, whose salary was $150.00 a month, was spending an average of $75.00 a month for liquor, and in addition to this unpardonable waste of money, out of a salary which was none too great at most, he was traveling at a pace and with a crowd which meant ruin for him later on.

The superintendent of a large manufacturing plant, whose salary was $5,000.00 a year, and who should have been saving at least $125.00 a month, was actually saving nothing. His bootlegger's bill averaged $150.00 a month.

A policeman whose income was $160.00 a month was spending over $400.00 a month on dinner parties, at a near-by roadhouse. Where he got the difference between his legitimate income and his actual expenditures is a question that reflects no particular credit on the policeman.

A bank official whose income, as near as it could be estimated from his previous years' income tax reports, was about $8,000.00 a year, had a monthly bootlegger's bill of more than $500.00 during the three months that his activities were checked by the Mellett investigators.

A young man who worked in a department store, at a salary of $20.00 a week, was spending an average of $35.00 a week with one bootlegger. The assumption was that he was stealing the difference from his employer. Old Man Trouble awaited this young man, just around the corner, although it is not known by the author whether or not the two have come together as yet.

A salesman for a life insurance company, whose income was not known because he worked on a commission basis, was spending an average of $200.00 a month with one bootlegger. No record of any savings account was found, and the assumption is that he had none. This assumption was later confirmed when the company for which the young man worked had him arrested for embezzlement of its funds. No doubt he was spending the money which he should have turned in to the company. He is now serving a long sentence in the Ohio State Penitentiary.

A young lad who was attending high school was spending large sums for liquor. The actual amount was not obtainable for the reason that he paid cash as he got the liquor, and the bootlegger's records did not, therefore, disclose the actual amount. Later this boy's parents had him locked up "to save him from himself." It was found that he was stealing money from a savings fund kept by his mother, somewhere about the house. He had stolen and spent more than $300.00 of this money when discovered.

This author conducted a Lecture Bureau in forty-one high schools, where he lectured once a month during the entire school season. The principals of these high schools stated that less than two per cent of the students showed any tendency toward saving money, and an examination through the aid of a questionnaire prepared for that purpose disclosed the fact that only five per cent of the students, out of a total of 11,000, of the high-school age, believed that the savings habit was one of the essentials for success.

It is no wonder the rich are becoming richer and the poor are becoming poorer!

Call this a socialistic statement, if you please, but the facts bear out its accuracy. It is not difficult for any man to become rich, in a country of spendthrifts such as this, where millions of people spend every cent that comes into their possession.

Many years ago, before the present wave of mania for spending spread over the country, F. W. Woolworth devised a very simple method of catching the nickels and dimes that millions of people throw away for trash, and his system netted him over ONE HUNDRED MILLION DOLLLARS in a few years' time. Woolworth has died, but his system of saving nickels and dimes continues, and his estate is growing bigger and bigger.

Five and Ten Cent Stores are usually painted with a bright red front. That is an appropriate color, for red denotes danger. Every Five and Ten Cent Store

ALL salesmen will do well to remember that no one wants anything that someone else is trying to "get rid of."

is a striking monument that proves, to a nicety, that one of the cardinal faults of this generation is the SPENDING HABIT.

We are all victims of HABIT!

Unfortunately for most of us, we are reared by parents who have no conception whatsoever of the psychology of habit, and, without being aware of their fault, most parents aid and abet their offspring in the development of the spending habit by overindulgence with spending money, and by lack of training in the Habit of Saving.

The habits of early childhood cling to us all through life.

Fortunate, indeed, is the child whose parents have the foresight and the understanding of the value, as a character builder, of the Habit of Saving, to inculcate this habit in the minds of their children.

It is a training that yields rich rewards.

Give the average man $100.00 that he did not contemplate receiving, and what will he do with it? Why, he will begin to cogitate in his own mind on how he can SPEND the money. Dozens of things that he needs, or THINKS he needs, will flash into his mind, but it is a rather safe bet that it will never occur to him (unless he has acquired the savings habit) to make this $100.00 the beginning of a savings account. Before night comes he will have the $100.00 spent, or at least he will have decided in his mind how he is going to SPEND IT, thus adding more fuel to the already too bright flame of Habit of Spending.

We are ruled by our habits!

It requires force of character, determination and power of firm DECISION to open a savings account and then add to it a regular, if small, portion of all subsequent income.

There is one rule by which any man may determine, well in advance, whether or not he will ever enjoy the financial freedom and independence which is so universally desired by all men, and this rule has absolutely nothing to do with the amount of one's income.

The rule is that if a man follows the systematic habit of saving a definite proportion of all money he earns or receives in other ways, he is practically sure to place himself in a position of financial independence. If he saves nothing, he IS ABSOLUTELY SURE NEVER TO BE FINANCIALLY INDEPENDENT, no matter how much his income may be.

The one and only exception to this rule is that a man who does not save might possibly inherit such a large sum of money that he could not spend it, or he might inherit it under a trust which would protect it for him, but these eventualities are rather remote; so much so, in fact, that YOU cannot rely upon such a miracle happening to you.

This author enjoys a rather close acquaintance with many hundreds of people throughout the United States and in some foreign countries. For nearly twenty-five years he has been watching many of these acquaintances, and knows, therefore, from actual experience, how they live, why some of them have failed while others have succeeded, and the REASONS FOR BOTH FAILURE AND SUCCESS.

This list of acquaintances covers men who control hundreds of millions of dollars, and actually own many millions which they have acquired. Also men who have had millions of dollars, all of which passed through their fingers and they are now penniless.

For the purpose of showing the student of this philosophy just how the law of habit becomes a sort of pivotal point on which success or failure turns, and exactly why no man can become financially independent without developing the habit of SYSTEMATIC SAVING, the living habits of some of these many acquaintances will be described.

We will begin with a complete history, in his own words, of a man who has made a million dollars in the field of advertising, but who now has nothing to show for his efforts. This story first appeared in the American Magazine, and it is here reprinted through the courtesy of the publishers of that publication.

The story is true, in every respect, and it has been included as a part of this lesson because the author of the story, Mr. W. C. Freeman, is willing to have his mistakes made public with the hope that others may avoid them.

"I HAVE MADE A MILLION DOLLLARS BUT I HAVEN'T GOT A CENT"

While it is embarrassing, yes, humiliating, publicly to confess to an outstanding fault that has made a good deal of a mess of my life today, nevertheless I have decided to make this confession for the good it may do.

I am going to make a clean breast of how I let slip through my fingers all the money I have earned thus far in my life-time, which approximates one million dollars. This amount I made through my work in the field of advertising, except a few thousand dollars I earned up to twenty-five years of age by teaching in country schools and by writing news letters to some country weeklies and daily newspapers.

Maybe one lone million does not seem a lot of money in these days of many millions and even billions; but it is a big sum of money, just the same. If there are any who think to the contrary, let them count a million. I tried to figure out the other night how long it would take to do so. I found I could count an average of one hundred a minute. On this basis it would take me twenty days of eight hours each, plus six hours and forty minutes on the twenty-first day to do the stunt. I doubt very much if you or I were given an assignment to count one million one-dollar bills, upon the promise that all of them would be ours at the end of that time, that we could complete it. It would probably drive us mad—and a lot of use the money would be to us then, wouldn't it?

Let me say at the outset of my story that I do not regret, not for one minute, that I spent ninety per cent of the money I made. To wish any of this ninety per cent back at this time would make me feel that I would have denied much happiness to my family and to many others.

My only regret is that I spent *all* of my money, and more besides. If I had today the ten per cent I could have saved easily, I would have one hundred thousand dollars safely invested, and no debts. If I had this money I would feel really and truly that I was rich; and I mean just this, for I have never had a desire to accumulate money for money's sake.

Those school-teaching and newspaper-correspondence days of mine brought some cares and responsibilities, but they were met optimistically.

I married at the age of twenty-one, with the full approval of parents on both sides, who believed thoroughly in the doctrine preached by Henry Ward Beecher, that "early marriages are virtuous marriages."

Just one month and one day after I was married my father met a tragic death. He was suffocated by coal gas. Having been an educator all his life—and one of the best—he had not accumulated any money.

When he passed out of our family circle it was up to all of us to pull together and get along somehow, which we did.

Apart from the void left in our home by my father's death (my wife and I and my mother and only sister lived together), we had a joyful life, despite the fact that it was a tight squeeze to make ends meet.

My mother, who was exceptionally talented and resourceful (she had taught school with my father until I was born), decided to open our home to a married couple, old friends of the family. They came to live with us and their board helped to pay expenses. My mother was known far and wide for the wonderful meals she served. Later on, two well-to-do women friends of the family were taken into our home; thus increasing our revenue.

My sister helped very substantially by teaching a kindergarten class, which met in the big living-room of our home; my wife contributed her share to the household by taking charge of the sewing and mending.

Those were very happy days. Nobody in the house-

THINK well before you speak because your words may plant the seed of either success or failure in the mind of some other person.

hold was extravagant or had any extravagant tendencies except perhaps myself, for I was always inclined to be free with money. I liked to make gifts to the family and to entertain friends.

When the first baby came into our home—a boy—we all thought heaven had opened its doors to us. My wife's parents, who took the keenest and deepest interest in our affairs, and who were always ready to lend a helping hand, were equally happy over the coming of their first grandchild. My brother-in-law, much older than my wife, and a bachelor, could not understand at first the joy we all felt; but even he began to strut around like a proud peacock after a while. What a difference a baby makes in a home!

I am injecting these details into my story merely to emphasize how the early days of my life were lived. I had no opportunity to spend much money, and yet I had as much happiness in those days as I have ever had since.

The strange thing about it all is that the experience of those days did not teach me the value of money. If anybody ever had a practical lesson to guide him in his future, I certainly had it.

But let me tell you how this early experience affected me. The birth of my son inspired me to do something that would make more money than I was getting at teaching school and in writing for newspapers. I did not want my wife, mother and sister to feel that they would have to continue indefinitely to do their part in sustaining the household. Why should a fellow, big and strong and healthy as I have always been, and with a reasonable amount of ability, be content to remain a spoke in the wheel? Why shouldn't I be the whole wheel, as far as providing for the family was concerned?

Following my desire to make more money, I took on the selling of books in addition to teaching and writing for newspapers. This earned for me quite a little extra money. Finally, I gave up teaching and concentrated on selling books, and writing for newspapers.

My book-selling took me to Bridgeton, New Jersey. It was here that I got my first real start in making money. I had to be away from home a great deal to do this work, but the sacrifice was worth while. I earned enough money in a few weeks to send more money home than I had contributed to the household in any year from my school-teaching and newspaper correspondence. After combing the territory in the Bridgeton zone, I became interested in a newspaper in that city, the Morning Star. It seemed to me that the editor and publisher of this paper needed a helper. I called on him and told him so. He said, "Heavens, young man, how can I hire you? I am not earning enough money to pay for my own living!"

"That's just it," said I. "I believe together we can make the Star a success. I'll tell you what I'll do: I'll work for you for one week for one dollar a day. At the end of the week, if I have made good, I'll expect you to pay me three dollars a day for the second week; and then, if I continue to do well, I'll expect you to pay me six dollars a day for the third week, and will continue from then on until the paper makes enough money to pay me fifty dollars a week."

The owner agreed to my proposition. At the end of two months, I was being paid fifty dollars a week, which in those days was considered a big salary. I began to feel that I was well on my way toward making money—but all I wanted it for was to make my family more comfortable. Fifty dollars a week was just four times as much as I had made teaching school.

My job on the Star embraced editorial writing (not very brilliant), reporting (just ordinary), the writing and selling of advertisements (fairly successful), proof reading, bill collecting, and so forth. It kept me humping six days a week; but I could stand it, for I was strong and healthy, and, besides, the work was very interesting. I also contributed correspondence to the New York Sun, Philadelphia Record, and the Trenton (N. J.) Times, which brought me in an average of one hundred and fifty dollars a month, for this was a good news territory.

I learned a lesson on the Star which eventually shaped the course of my life. I found out that there is a great deal more money to be earned by selling advertising for newspapers than in writing for them. Advertising brings grist to the mill.

I put over one advertising stunt on the Star—a write-up of the south Jersey oyster industry, paid for by the oyster men—that brought in three thousand dollars cash, which the publisher divided with me fifty-fifty. I had never seen so much money at one time in all my life. Think of it! Fifteen hundred dollars—twenty-five per cent more than I had made in two years of school-teaching and odd tasks.

Did I save this money or any part of it? I did not. What was the use? I could do so much with it to make my wife, boy, mother and sister happy that I let it go far easier than I had made it.

But would it not have been a fine thing if I had put this money away for a rainy day?

My work in Bridegton attracted the attention of Sam Hudson, New Jersey correspondent of the Philadelphia Record, who was a shining example of that type of newspaper men whose greatest pleasure in life is doing things for others.

Sam told me that it was time for me to get located in a big city. He thought I had it in me to make good. He said he would get me a job in Philadelphia. He did, and I moved with my wife and baby to Germantown. I was given charge of the advertising department of the Germantown (Philadelphia) Gazette, a weekly newspaper.

At the start I did not make as much money as I had earned in Bridegton, because I had to give up my newspaper correspondence. The news for this section was covered by other correspondents. But very soon I was making twenty-five per cent more money. The Gazette increased its size three times to accommodate its advertising, and each time I received a very substantial increase in salary.

In addition to this, I was given a job to gather social news for the Sunday edition of the Philadelphia Press. Bradford Merrill, managing editor of that newspaper, now a very important New York newspaper executive, assigned me a big territory to cover. This kept me busy every night in the week except Saturdays. I was paid five dollars a column; but I averaged seven columns every Sunday; which made me thirty-five dollars a week extra.

It was more money for me to spend, and I spent it. I did not know anything about budgeting my expenses. I just let it go as it came. I did not have time, or thought I hadn't, to watch my step in spending.

A year later I was invited to join the advertising staff of the Philadelphia Press, a big opportunity for a young man, for I got wonderful training under the management of William L. McLean, now the owner of the Philadelphia Evening Bulletin. I still retained my job as gatherer of social news—so my income was just about the same as I had been making in Germantown.

But before long my work attracted the attention of James Elverson, Sr., publisher of the old Saturday Night and Golden Days, who had just purchased the Philadelphia Inquirer. I was offered and accepted the advertising management of this newspaper.

This meant a big increase in my income. And soon afterward there came a happy increase in my family, the birth of a daughter. Then I was able to do what I had longed to do since the birth of my son. I got the family together again under one roof—my wife and two babies, my mother and sister. At last I was able to relieve my mother of any cares or responsibilities, and never again did she have either as long as she lived. She died in her eighty-first year, twenty-five years after my father's death. I shall never forget her last words to me: "Will, you have never caused me a moment's worry since you were born, and I could not have had more than you have given me had I been the Queen of England."

I was making at this time four times more money than my father had made as superintendent of public schools in my home town of Phillipsburg, New Jersey.

I AM thankful that I was born poor—that I did not come into this world burdened by the whims of wealthy parents, with a bag of gold around my neck.

All the money, however, passed out of my pockets as easily as water flows through a sieve. Expenses increased with every increase in my income, which is the habit, I suppose, with most people. There was no sane reason, though, for letting my expenses go beyond my income, which I did. I found myself piling up debts, and from this time on I was never out of debt. I did not worry about my debts, though, for I thought I could pay them off at any time. It never occurred to me—not until fully twenty-five years later—that debt eventually would bring upon me not only great anxiety and unhappiness, but that I would lose friends and credit as well.

But I must pat myself on the back for one thing: I was giving full rein to my big fault—spending money as fast as I made it, often faster; but I never shirked my work. I was always trying to find more things to do, and I always found them. I spent very little time with my family. I would go home to dinner every night and romp with the babies until their bedtime, then I would return to the office and often work.

So the years went by. Another daughter arrived. Presently I wanted my daughters to have a pony and cart, and I wanted my son to have a riding horse. Then I thought I needed a team to take me around with the family, driving them to a closed coupé or an open trap. I got them all. Instead of one horse and a carry-all, or perhaps a team, which would have been sufficient for our needs and something we could have afforded, I had to have a stable, with all that goes with it. This outfit cost me nearly one fourth of my annual income.

Then I took up golf. This was in my forty-first year. I went at my play the same as I went at my work—put my whole heart in it. I learned to play pretty well. My son and elder daughter played with me, and they learned to play well, too.

It was necessary that my younger daughter should spend the winter in the South and summers in the Adirondacks; but instead of her mother going with her alone, I felt it would be fine if the son and other daughter went along with them. This arrangement was carried out. They went to Pinehurst, North Carolina, every winter and to expensive resorts in the Adirondacks or in New Hampshire in the summer.

All this took a great deal of money. My son and elder daughter were keen about golf and spent a lot of money on it. I also disbursed quite a little on golf courses around New York. Between the three of us we won 80 prizes, most of which are now in storage. I sat down one day and calculated what these prizes had cost me. I discovered that each trophy had cost me $250.00 or a total of $45,000.00 over a period of fifteen years, an average of $3,000.00 a year. Ridiculous, wasn't it?

I entertained lavishly at my home. Montclair folks thought I was a millionaire. I frequently invited groups of business men to have a day of golf at the club, and then to have dinner with me in the evening. They would have been satisfied with a plain home dinner, but, no, I must serve them an elaborate affair staged by a famous caterer. These dinners never cost less than ten dollars a plate, which did not include the money spent for music while they were dining. I had a negro quartet come to the house. Our dining-room comfortably seated twenty people, and it was filled to capacity many times.

It was all very lovely, and I was glad to be their host. In fact, I was very happy over it. I never stopped to think how rapidly I was piling up debts. The day came when they began to bother me a lot. I had entertained so many guests at the golf club one month, paying for luncheons, cigars, and greens fees, that my bill was four hundred and fifty dollars. This attracted the attention of the directors of the club, who were all good friends of mine and very much interested in my welfare. They made it their business to tell me that I was spending entirely too much money, and they wished for my sake that I could check my expenses.

This gave me a bit of a jolt. It made me think seriously long enough to get rid of my horses and traps—at a big sacrifice, of course. I gave up our home and moved back to the city; but I did not leave any unpaid bills in Montclair. I borrowed the money to pay them. It was always easy for me to get all the money I wanted, despite my well known financial short-comings.

Here are two sidelights on my experience during my "flaring forties."

Besides spending money foolishly and perhaps recklessly, I loaned it with equal abandon. In cleaning out my desk at home before moving to the city I looked over a package of due bills, the total of which was over forty thousand dollars. That was money handed out to just anybody who came along. I tore them all up; but I realized that if I had that money in hand I wouldn't owe a dollar.

One of the prosperous business men I had entertained many times and who in turn had entertained me, said to me: "Billy, I've got to stop going on outings with you. You spend entirely too much money for me. I can't keep up with you."

Think of that coming from a man who was making more money than I was! It should have struck home, but it didn't. I went on spending just the same, and foolishly thinking that I was having a good time, and with no thought of the future. This man is now one of the vice presidents of one of New York's greatest financial institutions, and is reported to be worth many millions of dollars.

I should have taken his advice.

In the fall of 1908, after my disastrous experience of six months in another line of business following my resignation from the Hearst organization, I resumed newspaper work as advertising manager of the New York Evening Mail. I had known Henry L. Stoddard, editor and owner, back in the Philadelphia days, when he was political correspondent for the Press.

Despite the fact that I was bothered by debts, I did the best work of my life on the Evening Mail, and made more money during the five years I was associated with it than I had ever made before. Moreover, Mr. Stoddard gave me the privilege of syndicating advertising talks, which ran in his paper for one thousand consecutive publication days, and earned for me more than fifty-five thousand dollars.

Mr. Stoddard was very generous in many other ways, and frequently paid me special sums of money for doing what he considered unusual things in the way of developing business. During this period, I was so deeply in debt that, in order to keep things moving as smoothly as possible, but without retrenching in the slightest way in my expenses, I borrowed money from Peter to pay Paul and from Paul to pay Peter. That item of fifty-five thousand dollars earned from syndicating advertising talks would have more than paid all my debts and left a nice nest egg besides. But all of it was spent as easily as though I hadn't a care in the world.

In 1915 I went on my own in the advertising business. From that time until the spring of 1922 my fees ran into very big figures. I was still making more money than I ever did, and was spending it just as fast as I made it, until finally my friends got tired of making me loans.

If I had shown the slightest inclination to curb my expenses to the extent of only ten per cent, these wonderful men would have been willing to divide fifty-fifty with me, letting me pay them five per cent of it and saving five per cent. They did not care so much about the return of the money they had loaned me, as that they wanted to see me pull myself together.

The crash in my affairs came five years ago. Two friends who had stood by me loyally became impatient, and told me frankly that I needed a drastic lesson. They gave it to me all right. I was forced into bankruptcy, which nearly broke my heart. I felt that every person I knew was pointing the finger of scorn at me. This was very foolish. While there was comment, it was not at all unfriendly. It was expressive of keen regret that a man who had attained so much prestige in his profession, and had earned so

FORTUNATE is the person who has learned that the most certain way to "get" is to first "give" through some sort of useful service.

much money, should have allowed himself to get into financial difficulties.

Proud and sensitive to the core I felt the disgrace of bankruptcy so keenly that I decided to go to Florida, where I had once done a special piece of work for a client. It seemed to me to be the coming El Dorado. I figured that maybe I could make sufficient money in a few years so that I could return to New York, not only with a competency but with enough to pay all my debts in full. For a time it looked as though I would realize this ambition; but I was caught in the big real estate collapse. So here I am back in the old town where I once had big earning power and hundreds of friends and well-wishers.

It has been a strange experience.

One thing is certain: I have learned my lesson at last. I feel sure that opportunities will come my way to redeem myself, and that my earning power will be restored to me. And when that time comes I know that I shall be able to live as well as I ever did, on *forty* per cent of my income. Then I shall divide the remaining sixty per cent into two parts, setting aside thirty per cent to pay my creditors and thirty per cent for insurance and savings.

If I allowed myself to feel depressed over my past, or filled my mind with worries, I would not be capable of carrying on the fight to redeem myself.

Besides, I would be ungrateful to my Maker for having endowed me with wonderful health all my life. Is there any greater blessing?

I would be ungrateful to the memory of my parents, whose splendid training has kept me anchored pretty safely to moral standards. Slipping from moral moorings is infinitely more serious, in the end, than slipping from the thrift standard.

I would lack appreciation of the encouragement and support I have had in generous measure from hundreds of business men and to many good friends who helped me build a fine reputation in my profession.

These memories are the sunshine of my life. And I shall use them to pave the way to my future achievement.

With abundance of health, unfaltering faith, unflagging energy, unceasing optimism, and unbounded confidence that a man can win his fight, even though he commences late in life to realize the kind of fight he must make—is there anything but death to stop him?*

. . . .

Mr. Freeman's story is the same as that which might be told by thousands of other men who save nothing, with the exception that the amounts of their incomes would vary. The manner of living, the way the money was spent, and why, as told in Mr. Freeman's narrative, show the way the spender's mind works.

. . . .

Compilation of statistics covering family incomes and expenditures of over 16,000 families of men who have been analyzed by the author disclosed some facts that will be of help to the person who wishes to budget

* Reprinted by courtesy of The American Magazine. Copyright, The Crowell Publishing Company, 1927.

his income and disbursements on a practical working basis that is sound and economical.

The average income runs all the way from $100.00 to $300.00 per month. The budget allowance covering incomes within these two amounts should be about as follows:

A family consisting of two persons, whose income is $100.00 a month, should manage to set aside at least $10 or $12 a month for the savings account. The cost of shelter, or rent, should not exceed $25 or $30 a month. Food costs should average about $25 to $30. Clothing should be kept within an expenditure of $15 to $20 a month. Recreation and incidentals should be kept down to about $8 to $10 a month.

A family whose income is $100.00 a month, should that income be increased to $125.00, ought to save at least $20 of the amount.

A family of two persons, whose income is $150.00 a month, should budget their funds about as follows: Savings $25. Shelter or rent $35 to $40. Food $35 to $40. Clothes, $20 to $30. Recreation $10 to $15.

On a salary of $200 a month the budget should be: Savings $50. Shelter or rent $40 to $50. Food $35 to $45. Clothes $30 to $35. Recreation $15 to $20.

A family of two, on a salary or income of $300.00 a month, should apportion the income about thus: Savings $55 to $65. Shelter or rent $45 to $60. Food $45 to $60. Clothes $35 to $45. Recreation and education $50 to $75.

Some might argue that a family of two, making a salary of $300.00 a month, might live just as cheaply as one making but $100 or $125. However, this is not quite correct, because one who has the ability to earn $300.00 a month must as a rule associate with people who make better appearances and more entertainment necessary.

A single man, earning $100.00, $150.00 or $300.00 a month, should save considerably more than a man with a family could save on the same amounts. As a rule, a single man, who has no dependents, and who is not in debt, should live on a budget of $50 a month for room and food, and not to exceed $30 a month for clothes and perhaps $10 for recreation. These amounts might be slightly increased by one who earned from $150.00 to $300.00 a month.

A boy who lives away from home, and whose weekly income is only $20.00 should save $5 of the amount. The remainder should cover cost of food, room and clothes.

A girl, living away from home, on the same income, would require a slightly larger allowance for clothes, as women's wearing apparel is more costly than men's, and it is generally imperative that women watch, more closely than men, their personal appearance.

A family of three will be able to save considerably less than the amounts which can be saved by a family of two. With rare exceptions, however, such as cases where the family is involved in debt which must be absorbed out of the monthly income, any family can save at least five per cent of the gross income.

It is a common practice today for families to purchase automobiles on monthly payments which involve too great an expenditure compared to their income. A man with a Ford income has no business purchasing a Studebaker car. He should curb his desires and content himself with a Ford. Many single men spend their entire incomes, and often go into debt besides, because they maintain automobiles out of keeping with their incomes. This common practice is fatal to success as far as financial independence may be considered a part of success, in thousands of instances.

The instalment plan of buying has become so common, and it is so easy to purchase practically anything one desires, that the tendency to spend out of proportion to one's income is rapidly increasing. This tendency must be curbed by the person who has made up his mind to gain financial independence.

It can be done by anyone who is willing to try.

Another evil, which is both an evil and a blessing, is the fact that this country is so very prosperous that money comes easily, and if not watched it goes still more easily. Since the beginning of the World War there has been a steady demand for practically everything manufactured in the United States, and this condition of prosperity has caused people to lapse into a state of careless, unjustified spending.

There is no virtue in "keeping up with the pace set by neighbors" when this means sacrifice of the habit of saving a regular part of one's income. It is far better, in the long run, to be considered a bit behind the times than it is to go along through youth, into the days of maturity, and finally into old age, without having formed the habit of systematic saving.

It is better to sacrifice during the age of youthfulness, than it is to be compelled to do so during the age of maturity, as all who have not developed the habit of saving generally have to do.

There is nothing quite so humiliating, that carries

I AM thankful for the adversities which have crossed my pathway, for they have taught me tolerance, sympathy, self-control, perseverance a n d some other virtues I might never have known.

such great agony and suffering, as poverty in old age, when personal services are no longer marketable, and one must turn to relatives or to charitable institutions for existence.

A budget system should be maintained by every person, both the married and the single, but no budget system will work out if the person trying to keep it lacks the courage to cut expenses on such items as those of entertainment and recreation. If you feel so weak in will-power that you think it necessary to "keep up with the Smiths" with whom you associate socially, and whose income is greater than your own, or who spend all of their income foolishly, then no budget system can be of service to you.

Forming the savings habit means that, to some extent at least, you must seclude yourself from all except a well selected group of friends who enjoy you without elaborate entertaining on your part.

To admit that you lack the courage to trim down your expenditures so that you can save money, even if only a small amount, is the equivalent of admitting at the same time a lack of the sort of character which leads to success.

It has been proved times too numerous to be mentioned, that people who have formed the habit of saving money are always given preference in positions of responsibility; therefore, the saving of money not only adds advantages in the nature of preferred employment and a larger bank account, but it also increases the actual earning capacity. Any business man will prefer to employ a person who saves money regularly, not because of the mere fact that such person saves money, but because of the characteristics possessed

by such a person which make him or her more efficient.

Many firms will not employ a man or a woman who
does not save money.

It should be a common practice for all business
houses to require all employees to save money. This
would be a blessing to thousands of people who would
not otherwise have the will-power to form the savings
habit.

Henry Ford has gone a very long way, perhaps as
far as is expedient, to induce his employees not only
to save their money, but to spend what they do spend
wisely, and to live sanely and economically. The man
who induces his employees to form the habit of saving
is a practical philanthropist.

OPPORTUNITIES THAT COME TO THOSE WHO HAVE SAVED MONEY

A few years ago a young man came to Philadelphia,
from the farming district of Pennsylvania, and went
to work in a printing plant. One of his fellow workmen owned some shares in a Building and Loan Company, and had formed the habit of saving $5.00 a
week, through this Association. This young man was
influenced by his associate to open an account with
the Building and Loan Company. At the end of three
years he had saved $900.00. The printing plant for
which he worked got into financial difficulty and was
about to fail. He came to the rescue with his $900.00
which he had saved in small amounts, and in return
was given a half interest in the business.

By inaugurating a system of close economy he

helped the business to pay off its indebtedness, and today he is drawing out of it, as his half of the profits, a little better than $25,000.00 a year.

This opportunity never would have come, or, if it had, he would not have been prepared to embrace it, had he not formed the habit of saving money.

When the Ford automobile was perfected, during the early days of its existence, Henry Ford needed capital to promote the manufacture and sale of his product. He turned to a few friends who had saved up a few thousand dollars, one of whom was Senator Couzens. These friends came to his rescue, put in a few thousand dollars with him, and later drew out millions of dollars in profits.

When Woolworth first started his Five and Ten Cent Store Plan he had no capital, but he turned to a few friends who had saved, by the closest sort of economy and great sacrifice, a few thousand dollars. These friends staked him and later they were paid back hundreds of thousands of dollars in profits.

Van Heusen (of soft-collar fame) conceived the idea of producing a semi-soft collar for men. His idea was sound, but he had not a cent to promote it. He turned to a few friends who had only a few hundred dollars, who gave him a start, and the collar made each of them wealthy.

The men who started the El Producto Cigar business had but little capital, and what they did have was money they had saved from their small earnings as cigar makers. They had a good idea, and knew how to make a good cigar, but the idea would have died "a-bornin'" had they not saved a little money. With their meager savings they launched the cigar, and a few years later they sold out their business to the American Tobacco Company for $8,000,000.00.

Back of practically every great fortune one may find, as its beginning, a well developed habit of saving money.

John D. Rockefeller was an ordinary bookkeeper. He conceived the idea of developing the oil business, which was then not even considered a business. He needed capital, and because he had developed the habit of saving, and had thereby proved that he could conserve the funds of other people, he had no difficulty in borrowing what money he needed.

It may be truthfully stated that the real basis of the Rockefeller fortune is the habit of saving money which Mr. Rockefeller developed, while working as a bookkeeper at a salary of $40.00 a month.

James J. Hill was a poor young man, working as a telegrapher, at a salary of $30.00 a month. He conceived the idea of the Great Northern Railway System, but his idea was out of proportion to his ability to finance. However, he had formed the habit of saving money, and on the meager salary of $30.00 a month had saved enough to enable him to pay his expenses on a trip to Chicago, where he interested capitalists in financing his plan. The fact that he, himself, had saved money on a small salary was considered good evidence that he would be a safe man to trust with other people's money.

Most business men will not trust another man with their money unless he has demonstrated his ability to take care of his own and use it wisely. The test, while it is often embarrassing to those who have not formed the Habit of Saving, is a very practical one.

A young man who worked in a printing plant in the city of Chicago wanted to open a small print shop and go into business for himself. He went to a printing supply house manager and made known his wants, saying he desired credit for a printing press and some type and other small equipment.

The first question asked by the manager was: "Have you saved any money of your own?"

He had! Out of his salary of $30.00 a week he had saved $15.00 a week regularly for nearly four years. He got the credit he wanted. Later on he got more credit, until today he has built up one of the most successful printing plants in the city of Chicago. His name is George B. Williams, and he is well known, as are also the facts here stated, to the author of this course.

Many years after this incident, the author of this course became acquainted with Mr. Williams, and at the end of the war, in 1918, the author went to Mr. Williams and asked for credit amounting to many thousands of dollars, for the purpose of publishing the Golden Rule Magazine. The first question asked was: "Have you formed the habit of saving money." Despite the fact that all the money I had saved was lost in the war, the mere fact that I had actually formed the savings habit was the real basis on which I got credit for upward of $30,000.00.

There are opportunities on every corner, but they exist only for those who have ready money, or who can command money because they have formed the Habit of Saving, and developed the other characteristics which go with the formation of the savings habit known by the general term of "character."

LOVE and Justice are the real arbiters of all disputes. Give them a chance and you will no longer want to defeat a brother sojourner by the wayside of life.

The late J. P. Morgan once said he would rather loan a million dollars to a man of sound character, who had formed the habit of saving money, than he would a thousand dollars to a man without character, who was a spendthrift.

Generally speaking, this is the attitude which the world takes toward all men who save money.

It often happens that a small savings account of no more than two or three hundred dollars is sufficient to start one on the highway to financial independence. A few years ago a young inventor invented a household article which was unique and practical. He was handicapped, as inventors so often are, because he did not have the money to market his invention. Moreover, not having formed the savings habit he found it impossible to borrow money through banking sources.

His room-mate was a young machinist who had saved $200.00. He came to the inventor's aid with this small sum of money, and had enough of the articles manufactured to give them a start. They went out and sold, from house to house, the first supply, then came back and had another supply made up, and so on, until they had accumulated (thanks to the thrift and savings ability of the room-mate) a capital of $1,000.00. With this, plus some credit they secured, they bought the tools for manufacturing their own product.

The young machinist sold his half interest in the business, six years later, for $250,000.00. He never would have handled this much money, during his entire life, had he not formed the habit of saving, which enabled him to come to the rescue of his inventor friend.

This case might be multiplied a thousand times, with but slight variation as to details, as it is fairly descriptive of the beginning of many great fortunes that have been made and are now in the making, in the United States.

It may seem like a sad, cruel fact, but it is a FACT none the less, that if you have no money, and have not developed the habit of saving, you are "out of luck" as far as availing yourself of the opportunity to make money is concerned.

It can do no harm to repeat—in fact it should be repeated over and over again—that the real start of nearly all fortunes, whether great or small, is the formation of the habit of saving money!

Get this basic principle firmly founded in your mind and you will be well on the road toward financial independence!

It is a sad sight to see a man, well along in years, who has sentenced himself to the wearisome treadmill of hard labor all the days of his life because he has neglected forming the habit of saving money, yet there are millions of such men living, in the United States alone, today.

The greatest thing in life is FREEDOM!

There can be no real freedom without a reasonable degree of financial independence. It is a terrible thing to be compelled to be at a certain place, at a certain task (perhaps a task which one does not like) for a certain number of hours every working day of the week, for a whole life-time. In some ways this is the same as being in prison, since one's choice of action is always limited. It is really no better than being in prison with the privilege of a "trusty," and in some ways it is even worse because the man who is imprisoned has escaped the responsibility of providing a place to sleep, something to eat and clothes to wear.

The only hope of escape from this life-long toil which curtails freedom is to form the habit of saving money, and then live up to that habit, no matter how much sacrifice it may require. There is no other way out for millions of people, and unless you are one of the rare exceptions this lesson and all these statements of fact are meant for YOU, and apply to you!

> Neither a borrower, nor a
> lender be:
> For loan oft loses both itself
> and friend,
> And borrowing dulls the edge
> of husbandry.
> This above all: to thine own
> self be true,
> And it must follow, as the
> night the day,
> Thou canst not then be false
> to any man.
>
> —SHAKESPEARE

EVERYTHING

PASSES AT PAR,

TEMPORARILY;

TRUTH ALONE

REMAINS

PERMANENTLY.

Lesson Five

INITIATIVE AND
LEADERSHIP

WHEN you do not know what to do or which way to turn, smile. This will relax your mind and let the sunshine of happiness into your soul.

"You Can Do It if You Believe You Can!"

EFORE you proceed to the mastery of this lesson your attention is directed to the fact that there is perfect co-ordination of thought running throughout this course. You will observe that the entire sixteen lessons harmonize and blend with each other so that they constitute a perfect chain that has been built, link by link, out of the factors that enter into the development of power through *organized effort.*

You will observe, also, that the same fundamental principles of Applied Psychology form the foundation of each of these sixteen lessons, although different application is made of these principles in each of the lessons.

This lesson, on *Initiative* and *Leadership,* follows the lesson on Self-confidence for the reason that no one could become an efficient leader or take the initiative in any great undertaking without belief in himself.

Initiative and *Leadership* are associated terms in

71

this lesson for the reason that *Leadership* is essential for the attainment of *Success,* and *Initiative* is the very foundation upon which this necessary quality of *Leadership* is built. *Initiative* is as essential to success as a hub is essential to a wagon wheel.

And what is *Initiative?*

It is that exceedingly rare quality that prompts— nay, impels—a person to do that which ought to be done *without being told to do it.* Elbert Hubbard expressed himself on the subject of *Initiative* in these words:

"The world bestows its big prizes, both in money and honors, for one thing, and that is *Initiative.*

"What is initiative? I'll tell you: It is doing the right thing without being told.

"But next to doing the right thing without being told is to do it when you are told once. That is to say, 'Carry the message to Garcia.' Those who can carry a message get high honors, but their pay is not always in proportion.

"Next, there are those who do the right thing only when necessity kicks them from behind, and these get indifference instead of honors, and a pittance for pay.

"This kind spend most of the time polishing a bench with a hard luck story.

"Then, still lower down in the scale than this we have the fellow who will not do the right thing even when someone goes along to show him how and stays to see that he does it; he is always out of a job, and receives the contempt he deserves, unless he has a rich pa, in which case destiny patiently waits around the corner with a stuffed club.

"To which class do *you* belong?"

Inasmuch as you will be expected to take inventory of yourself and determine which of the fifteen factors of this course you need most, after you have completed the sixteenth lesson, it may be well if you begin to get ready for this analysis by answering the question that Elbert Hubbard has asked:

To which class do you belong?

One of the peculiarities of *Leadership* is the fact that it is never found in those who have not acquired the *habit* of taking the initiative. *Leadership* is something that you must invite yourself into; it will never thrust itself upon you. If you will carefully analyze all leaders whom you know you will see that they not only exercised *Initiative,* but they went about their work with a *definite purpose* in mind. You will also see that they possessed that quality described in the third lesson of this course, *Self-confidence.*

These facts are mentioned in this lesson for the reason that it will profit you to observe that successful people make use of *all* the factors covered by the sixteen lessons of the course; and, for the more important reason that it will profit you to understand thoroughly the principle of *organized effort* which this Reading Course is intended to establish in your mind.

This seems an appropriate place to state that this course is not intended as a *short-cut* to success, nor is it intended as a mechanical formula that you may use in noteworthy achievement without effort on your part. The *real* value of the course lies in the *use* that you will make of it, and not in the course itself. The chief purpose of the course is to help you develop in yourself the fifteen qualities covered by the sixteen lessons of the course, and one of the most important of these qualities is *Initiative,* the subject of this lesson.

We will now proceed to apply the principle upon which this lesson is founded by describing, in detail, just how it served successfully to complete a business transaction which most people would call difficult.

In 1916 I needed $25,000.00 with which to create an educational institution, but I had neither this sum nor sufficient collateral with which to borrow it through the usual banking sources. Did I bemoan my fate or think of what I might accomplish if some rich relative or Good Samaritan would come to my rescue by loaning me the necessary capital?

I did nothing of the sort!

I did just what you will be advised, throughout this course, to do. First of all, I made the securing of this capital my *definite chief aim.* Second, I laid out a complete *plan* through which to transform this *aim* into reality. Backed by sufficient Self-confidence and spurred on by *Initiative,* I proceeded to put my plan into action. But, before the "action" stage of the plan had been reached, more than six weeks of constant, persistent study and effort and thought were embodied in it. If a plan is to be sound it must be built of carefully chosen material.

You will here observe the application of the principle of *organized effort,* through the operation of which it is possible for one to ally or associate several interests in such a way that *each of these interests* is greatly strengthened and each supports all the others, just as one link in a chain supports all the other links.

I wanted this $25,000.00 in capital for the purpose

of creating a school of Advertising and Salesmanship. Two things were necessary for the organization of such a school. One was the $25,000.00 capital, which I did not have, and the other was the proper course of instruction, which *I did have*. My problem was to *ally myself* with some group of men who needed that which I had, and who would supply the $25,000.00. This alliance had to be made through a plan that would benefit all concerned.

After my plan had been completed, and I was satisfied that it was equitable and sound, I laid it before the owner of a well known and reputable business college which just then was finding competition quite keen and was badly in need of a plan for meeting this competition.

My plan was presented in about these words:

Whereas, you have one of the most reputable business colleges in the city; and,

Whereas, you need some plan with which to meet the stiff competition in your field; and,

Whereas, your good reputation has provided you with all the credit you need; and,

Whereas, I have the plan that will help you meet this competition successfully.

Be it resolved, that we ally ourselves through a plan that will give you that which you need and at the same time supply me with something which I need.

Then I proceeded to unfold my plan, further, in these words:

I have written a very practical course on Advertising and Salesmanship. Having built this course out of my actual experience in training and directing salesmen and my experience in planning and directing

THE space you occupy and the authority you exercise may be measured with mathematical exactness by the service you render.

many successful advertising campaigns, I have back of it plenty of evidence of its soundness.

If you will use your credit in helping market this course I will place it in your business college, as one of the regular departments of your curriculum and take entire charge of this newly created department. No other business college in the city will be able to meet your competition, for the reason that no other college has such a course as this. The advertising that you do in marketing this course will serve, also, to stimulate the demand for your regular business course. You may charge the entire amount that you spend for this advertising, to my department, and the advertising bill will be paid out of that department, leaving you the accumulative advantage that will accrue to your other departments without cost to you.

Now, I suppose you will want to know where I profit by this transaction, and I will tell you. I want you to enter into a contract with me in which it will be agreed that when the cash receipts from my department equal the amount that you have paid out or contracted to pay out for advertising, my department and my course in Advertising and Salesmanship become my own and I may have the privilege of separating this department from your school and running it under my own name.

The plan was agreeable and the contract was closed.

(Please keep in mind that my *definite purpose* was to secure the use of $25,000.00 for which I had no security to offer.)

In a little less than a year the Business College had paid out slightly more than $25,000.00 for advertising and marketing my course and the other expenses incidental to the operation of this newly organized department, while the department had collected and turned back to the College, in tuition fees, a sum equaling the amount the College had spent, and I took the department over, as a going and self-sustaining business, according to the terms of my contract.

As a matter of fact this newly created department not only served to attract students for the other departments of the College, but at the same time the tuition fees collected through this new department were sufficient to place it on a self-sustaining basis before the end of the first year.

Now you can see that while the College did not loan me one penny of actual capital, it nevertheless supplied me with credit which served exactly the same purpose.

I said that my plan was founded upon equity; that it contemplated a benefit to all parties concerned. The benefit accruing to me was the use of the $25,000.00, which resulted in an established and self-sustaining business by the end of the first year. The benefit accruing to the college was the students secured for its regular commercial and business course as a result of the money spent in advertising my department, all advertising having been done under the name of the College.

Today that business college is one of the most successful schools of its kind, and it stands as a monument of sound evidence with which to demonstrate the value of *allied effort*.

This incident has been related, not alone because it shows the value of *initiative* and *leadership*, but for the reason that it leads up to the subject covered by the next lesson of this Reading Course on the Law of Success, which is *imagination*.

There are generally many plans through the operation of which a desired object may be achieved, and it often happens to be true that the obvious and usual methods employed are not the best. The usual method of procedure, in the case related, would have been that of borrowing from a bank. You can see that this method was impractical, in this case, for the reason that no collateral was available.

A great philosopher once said: *"Initiative is the pass-key that opens the door to opportunity."*

I do not recall who this philosopher was, but I know that he was *great* because of the soundness of his statement.

We will now proceed to outline the exact procedure that you must follow if you are to become a person of *initiative* and *leadership*.

First: You must master the habit of *procrastination* and eliminate it from your make-up. This habit of putting off until tomorrow that which you should have done last week or last year or a score of years ago is gnawing at the very vitals of your being, and you can accomplish nothing until you throw it off.

The method through which you eliminate *procrastination* is based upon a well known and scientifically tested principle of psychology which has been referred to in the two preceding lessons of this course as Autosuggestion.

Copy the following formula and place it conspicuously in your room where you will see it as you retire at night and as you arise in the morning:

INITIATIVE AND LEADERSHIP

Having chosen a *definite chief aim* as my life-work I now understand it to be my duty to transform this purpose into reality.

Therefore, I will form the habit of taking some *definite* action each day that will carry me one step nearer the attainment of my *definite chief aim*.

I know that *procrastination* is a deadly enemy of all who would become leaders in any undertaking, and I will eliminate this habit from my make-up by:

(*a*) Doing some one definite thing each day, that ought to be done, without anyone telling me to do it.

(*b*) Looking around until I find at least one thing that I can do each day, that I have not been in the habit of doing, and that will be of value to others, without expectation of pay.

(*c*) Telling at least one other person, each day, of the value of practicing this habit of doing something that ought to be done without being told to do it.

I can see that the muscles of the body become strong in proportion to the extent to which they are used, therefore I understand that the *habit of initiative* also becomes fixed in proportion to the extent that it is practiced.

I realize that the place to begin developing the *habit of initiative* is in the small, commonplace things connected with my daily work, therefore I will go at my work each day as if I were doing it solely for the purpose of developing this necessary *habit of initiative*.

I understand that by practicing this *habit* of taking

the *initiative* in connection with my daily work I will be not only developing that habit, but I will also be attracting the attention of those who will place greater value on my services as a result of this practice.

Signed...................................

Regardless of what you are now doing, every day brings you face to face with a chance to render some service, outside of the course of your regular duties, that will be of value to others. In rendering this additional service, of your own accord, you of course understand that you are not doing so with the object of receiving monetary pay. You are rendering this service because it provides you with ways and means of exercising, developing and making stronger the aggressive spirit of *initiative* which you must possess before you can ever become an outstanding figure in the affairs of your chosen field of life-work.

Those who work for *money* alone, and who receive for their pay nothing but money, are always underpaid, no matter how much they receive. Money is necessary, but the big prizes of life cannot be measured in dollars and cents.

No amount of money could possibly be made to take the place of the happiness and joy and pride that belong to the person who digs a better ditch, or builds a better chicken coop, or sweeps a cleaner floor, or cooks a better meal. Every normal person loves to create something that is better than the average. The joy of *creating* a work of art is a joy that cannot be replaced by money or any other form of material possession.

I have in my employ a young lady who opens, assorts

W HAT helped you over the great ob-stacles of life?" was asked of a highly successful man. "The other ob-stacles," he replied.

and answers much of my personal mail. She began in my employ more than three years ago. Then her duties were to take dictation when she was asked to do so. Her salary was about the same as that which others receive for similar service. One day I dictated the following motto which I asked her to typewrite for me:

Remember that your only limitation is the one that you set up in your own mind.

As she handed the typewritten page back to me she said, "Your motto has given me an idea that is going to be of value to both you and me."

I told her I was glad to have been of service to her. The incident made no particular impression on my mind, but from that day on I could see that it had made a *tremendous* impression on her mind. She began to come back to the office after supper and performed service that she was neither paid for nor expected to perform. Without anyone telling her to do it she began to bring to my desk letters that she had answered for me. She had studied my style and these letters were attended to as well as I could have done it; in some instances much better. She kept up this habit until my personal secretary resigned. When I began to look for someone to take his place, what was more natural than to turn to this young woman to fill the place. Before I had time to give her the position *she took it on her initiative.* My personal mail began to come to my desk with a new secretary's name attached, and she was that secretary. On her own time, after hours, without additional pay, she had prepared herself for the best position on my staff.

But that is not all. This young lady became so

noticeably efficient that she began to attract the attention of others who offered her attractive positions. I have increased her salary many times and she now receives a salary more than four times as large as the amount she received when she first went to work for me as an ordinary stenographer, and, to tell you the truth, I am helpless in the matter, because she has made herself so valuable to me that I cannot get along without her.

That is initiative transformed into practical, understandable terms. I would be remiss in my duties if I failed to direct your attention to an advantage, other than a greatly increased salary, that this young lady's *initiative* has brought her. It has developed in her a spirit of cheerfulness that brings her happiness which most stenographers never know. Her work is not work—it is a great interesting game at which she is playing. Even though she arrives at the office ahead of the regular stenographers and remains there long after they have watched the clock tick off *five o'clock* and *quitting time,* her hours are shorter by far than are those of the other workers. Hours of labor do not drag on the hands of those who are happy at their work.

This brings us to the next step in our description of the exact procedure that you must follow in developing *initiative* and *leadership.*

Second: You of course understand that the only way to get *happiness* is by giving it away, to others. The same applies to the development of *initiative.* You can best develop this essential quality in yourself by making it your business to interest those around you in doing the same. It is a well known fact that a man learns best that which he endeavors to teach others. If a man embraces a certain creed or religious faith, the first thing he does is to go out and try to "sell" it to others. And in exact proportion to the extent to which he impresses others does he impress *himself*.

In the field of salesmanship it is a well known fact that no salesman is successful in selling others until he has first made a good job of selling *himself*. Stated conversely, no salesman can do his best to sell others without sooner or later selling himself that which he is trying to sell to others.

Any statement that a person repeats over and over again for the purpose of inducing others to believe it, he, also, will come to believe, and this holds good whether the statement is false or true.

You can now see the advantage of making it your business to *talk initiative, think initiative, eat initiative, sleep initiative* and *practice initiative*. By so doing you are becoming a person of *initiative* and *leadership,* for it is a well known fact that people will readily, willingly and voluntarily follow the person who shows by his actions that he is a person of *initiative*.

In the place where you work or the community in which you live you come in contact with other people. Make it your business to interest every one of them who will listen to you, in the development of *initiative*. It will not be necessary for you to give your reasons for doing this, nor will it be necessary for you to announce the fact that you are doing it. *Just go ahead and do it.* In your own mind you will understand, of course, that you are doing it because this practice will

help you and will, at least, do those whom you influence in the same practice no harm.

If you wish to try an experiment that will prove
both interesting and profitable to you, pick out some
person of your acquaintance whom you know to be a
person who never does anything that he is not expected
to do, and begin selling him your idea of *initiative*.
Do not stop by merely discussing the subject once;
keep it up every time you have a convenient opportunity. Approach the subject from a different angle
each time. If you go at this experiment in a tactful
and forceful manner you will soon observe a change in
the person on whom you are trying the experiment.

And, you will observe something else of more importance still: *You will observe a change in yourself!*

Do not fail to try this experiment.

You cannot talk *initiative* to others without developing a desire to practice it yourself. Through the operation of the principle of Auto-suggestion every
statement that you make to others leaves its imprint
on your own subconscious mind, and this holds good
whether your statements are false or true.

You have often heard the saying: "He who lives by
the sword will die by the sword."

Properly interpreted, this simply means that we
are constantly attracting to ourselves and weaving into
our own characters and personalities those qualities
which our influence is helping to create in others. If
we help others develop the habit of *initiative*, we, in
turn, develop this same habit. If we sow the seeds
of hatred and envy and discouragement in others, we,
in turn, develop these qualities in ourselves. This
principle through which a man comes to resemble in

his own nature those whom he most admires is fully brought out in Hawthorne's story, The Great Stone Face, a story that every parent should have his offspring read.

We come, now, to the next step in our description of the exact procedure that you must follow in developing *initiative* and *leadership*.

Third: Before we go further let it be understood what is meant by the term "Leadership," as it is used in connection with this Reading Course on the Law of Success. There are two brands of *leadership*, and one of them is as deadly and destructive as the other is helpful and constructive. The deadly brand, which leads not to *success*, but to *absolute failure*, is the brand adopted by pseudo-leaders who *force* their leadership on unwilling followers. It will not be necessary here to describe this brand or to point out the fields of endeavor in which it is practiced, with the exception of the field of war, and in this field we will mention but one notable example, that of Napoleon.

Napoleon was a *leader;* there can be no doubt about this, but he led his followers and himself to destruction. The details are recorded in the history of France and the French people, where you may study them if you choose.

It is not Napoleon's brand of *leadership* that is recommended in this course, although I will admit that Napoleon possessed all the necessary fundamentals for great leadership, excepting one—he lacked the spirit of helpfulness to others as an objective. His desire for the power that comes through leadership was based solely upon self-aggrandizement. His desire for leadership was built upon personal ambition and not upon

CHERISH your visions and your dreams as they are the children of your soul; the blue-prints of your ultimate achievements.

the desire to lift the French people to a higher and nobler station in the affairs of nations.

The brand of *leadership* that is recommended through this course of instruction is the brand which leads to self-determination and freedom and self-development and enlightenment and justice. This is the brand that endures. For example, and as a contrast with the brand of *leadership* through which Napoleon raised himself into prominence, consider our own American commoner, Lincoln. The object of his *leadership* was to bring truth and justice and understanding to the people of the United States. Even though he died a martyr to his belief in this brand of *leadership*, his name has been engraved upon the heart of the world in terms of loving kindliness that will never bring aught but good to the world.

Both Lincoln and Napoleon led armies in warfare, but the objects of their *leadership* were as different as night is different from day. If it would give you a better understanding of the principles upon which this Reading Course is based, you could easily be cited to *leadership* of today which resembles both the brand that Napoleon employed and that which Lincoln made the foundation of his life-work, but this is not essential; your own ability to look around and analyze men who take the leading parts in all lines of endeavor is sufficient to enable you to pick out the Lincoln as well as the Napoleon types. Your own judgment will help you decide which type you prefer to emulate.

There can be no doubt in your mind as to the brand of *leadership* that is recommended in this Reading Course, and there should be no question in your mind as to which of the two brands described you will adopt as your brand.   We make no recommendations on this subject, however, for the reason that this Reading Course has been prepared as a means of laying before its students the fundamental principles upon which power is developed, and not as a preachment on ethical conduct.   We present both the constructive and the destructive possibilities of the principles outlined in this course, that you may become familiar with both, but we leave entirely to your own discretion the choice and application of these principles, believing that your own intelligence will guide you to make a wise selection.

THE PENALTY OF LEADERSHIP *

In every field of human endeavor, he that is first must perpetually live in the white light of publicity. Whether the leadership be vested in a man or in a manufactured product, emulation and envy are ever at work.

In art, in literature, in music, in industry, the reward and the punishment are always the same.   The reward is widespread recognition; the punishment, fierce denial and detraction.

When a man's work becomes a standard for the whole world, it also becomes a target for the shafts of the envious few.   If his work be merely mediocre, he will be left severely alone—if he achieve a masterpiece, it will set a million tongues a-wagging.

Jealousy does not protrude its forked tongue at the artist who produces a commonplace painting.

*(With the compliments of the Cadillac Motor Car Co.)

Whatsoever you write, or paint, or play, or sing or build, no one will strive to surpass or slander you, unless your work be stamped with the seal of a genius.

Long, long after a great work or a good work has been done, those who are disappointed or envious continue to cry out that it cannot be done.

Mean voices were raised against the author of the Law of Success before the ink was dry on the first textbooks. Poisoned pens were released against both the author and the philosophy the moment the first edition of the course was printed.

Spiteful little voices in the domain of art were raised against our own Whistler as a mountebank, long after the big world acclaimed him its greatest artistic genius.

Multitudes flocked to Beyreuth to worship at the musical shrine of Wagner, while the little group of those whom he had dethroned and displaced argued angrily that he was no musician at all.

The little world continued to protest that Fulton could never build a steamboat, while the big world flocked to the river banks to see his boat steam by.

Small, narrow voices cried out that Henry Ford would not last another year, but above and beyond the din of their childish prattle Ford went silently about his business and made himself the richest and most powerful man on earth.

The leader is assailed because he is a leader, and the effort to equal him is merely added proof of his leadership.

Failing to equal or to excel, the follower seeks to depreciate and to destroy—but only confirms the superiority of that which he strives to supplant.

There is nothing new in this.

It is as old as the world and as old as the human passions—envy, fear, greed, ambition and the desire to surpass.

And it all avails nothing.

If the leader truly leads, he remains the LEADER!

Master-poet, master-painter, master-workman, each in his turn is assailed, and each holds his laurels through the ages.

That which is good or great makes itself known, no matter how loud the clamor of denial.

A real leader cannot be slandered or damaged by lies of the envious, because all such attempts serve only to turn the spot-light on his ability, and real ability always finds a generous following.

Attempts to destroy real Leadership is love's labor lost, because that which deserves to live, lives!

.   .   .   .

We come back, now, to the discussion of the third step of the procedure that you must follow in developing *initiative* and *leadership*. This third step takes us back for a review of the principle of *organized effort,* as described in the preceding lessons of this course.

You have already learned that no man can accomplish enduring results of a far-reaching nature without the aid and co-operation of others. You have already learned that when two or more persons ally themselves in any undertaking, in a spirit of harmony and understanding, each person in the alliance thereby multiplies his own powers of achievement. Nowhere is this principle more evidenced than it is in an industry or business in which there is perfect team-work between the employer and the employees. Wherever you find this team-work you find prosperity and good-will on both sides.

Co-operation is said to be the most important word in the English language. It plays an important part in the affairs of the home, in the relationship of man and wife, parents and children. It plays an important part in the affairs of state. So important is this principle of co-operation that no leader can become powerful or last long who does not understand and apply it in his *leadership*.

Lack of Co-operation has destroyed more business enterprises than have all other causes combined. In my twenty-five years of active business experience and observation I have witnessed the destruction of all manner of business enterprises because of dissension and lack of application of this principle of Co-operation. In the practice of law I have observed the destruction of homes and divorce cases without end as a result of the lack of Co-operation between man and wife. In the study of the histories of nations it becomes alarmingly obvious that lack of Co-operative effort has been a curse to the human race all back down the ages. Turn back the pages of these histories and study them and you will learn a lesson in Co-operation that will impress itself indelibly upon your mind.

You are paying, and your children and your children's children will continue to pay, for the cost of the most expensive and destructive war the world has ever known, because nations have not yet learned that a part of the world cannot suffer without damage and suffering to the whole world.

SERVICE, Sacrifice and Self-Control are three words which must be well understood by the person who succeeds in doing something that is of help to the world.

This same rule applies, with telling effect, in the conduct of modern business and industry. When an industry becomes disorganized and torn asunder by strikes and other forms of disagreement, both the employers and employees suffer irreparable loss. But, the damage does not stop here; this loss becomes a burden to the public and takes on the form of higher prices and scarcity of the necessities of life.

The people of the United States who rent their homes are feeling the burden, at this very moment, of lack of co-operation between contractors and builders and the workers. So uncertain has the relationship between the contractors and their employees become that the contractors will not undertake a building without adding to the cost an arbitrary sum sufficient to protect them in the event of labor troubles. This additional cost increases rents and places unnecessary burdens upon the backs of millions of people. In this instance the lack of co-operation between a few men places heavy and almost unbearable burdens upon millions of people.

The same evil exists in the operation of our railroads. Lack of harmony and co-operation between the railroad management and the workers has made it necessary for the railroads to increase their freight and passenger rates, and this, in turn, has increased the cost of life's necessities to almost unbearable proportions. Here, again, lack of co-operation between a few leads to hardship for millions of people.

These facts are cited without effort or desire to place the responsibility for this lack of co-operation, since the object of this Reading Course is to help its students get at facts.

It may be truthfully stated that the high cost of living that everywhere manifests itself today has grown out of lack of application of the principle of co-operative *leadership*. Those who wish to decry present systems of government and industrial management may do so, but in the final analysis it becomes obvious to all except those who are not seeking the *truth* that the evils of government and of industry have grown out of lack of *co-operation*.

Nor can it be truthfully said that all the evils of the world are confined to the affairs of state and industry. Take a look at the churches and you will observe the damaging effects of lack of co-operation. No particular church is cited, but analyze any church or group of churches where lack of co-ordination of effort prevails and you will see evidence of disintegration that limits the service those churches could render. For example, take the average town or small city where rivalry has sprung up between the churches and notice what has happened; especially those towns in which the number of churches is far out of proportion to the population.

Through harmonized effort and through co-operation, the churches of the world could wield sufficient influence to render war an impossibility. Through this same principle of co-operative effort the churches and the leaders of business and industry could eliminate rascality and sharp practices, and all this could be brought about speedily.

These possibilities are not mentioned in a spirit of criticism, but only as a means of illustrating the power of co-operation, and to emphasize my belief in the potential power of the churches of the world. So there

will be no possibility of misinterpretation of my
meaning in the reference that I have here made to
the churches I will repeat that which I have so often
said in person; namely, that had it not been for the
influence of the churches no man would be safe in
walking down the street. Men would be at each
other's throat like wolves and civilization would still
be in the pre-historic age. My complaint is not against
the work that the churches have done, but the work
that *they could have done* through *leadership* that was
based upon the principle of co-ordinated, co-operative
effort which would have carried civilization at least a
thousand years ahead of where it is today. It is not
yet too late for such leadership.

That you may more fully grasp the fundamental
principle of co-operative effort you are urged to go to
the public library and read The Science of Power, by
Benjamin Kidd. Out of scores of volumes by some of
the soundest thinkers of the world that I have read
during the past fifteen years, no single volume has
given me such a full understanding of the possibilities
of co-operative effort as has this book. In recommending that you read this book it is not my purpose
to endorse the book in its entirety, for it offers some
theories with which I am not in accord. If you read
it, do so with an open mind and take from it only that
which you feel you can use to advantage in achieving
the object of your *definite chief aim*. The book will
stimulate *thought,* which is the greatest service that
any book can render. As a matter of fact the chief
object of this Reading Course on the Law of Success
is to stimulate deliberate *thought*: particularly that
brand of *thought* that is free from bias and prejudice

and is seeking *truth* no matter where or how or when it may be found.

During the World War I was fortunate enough to listen to a great soldier's analysis of how to be a *leader*. This analysis was given to the student-officers of the Second Training Camp at Fort Sheridan, by Major C. A. Bach, a quiet, unassuming army officer acting as an instructor. I have preserved a copy of this address because I believe it to be one of the finest lessons on *leadership* ever recorded.

The wisdom of Major Bach's address is so vital to the business man aspiring to *leadership*, or to the section boss, or to the stenographer, or to the foreman of the shop, or to the president of the works, that I have preserved it as a part of this Reading Course. It is my earnest hope that through the agency of this course this remarkable dissertation on *leadership* will find its way into the hands of every employer and every worker and every ambitious person who aspires to *leadership* in any walk of life. The principles upon which the address is based are as applicable to *leadership* in business and industry and finance as they are in the successful conduct of warfare.

Major Bach spoke as follows:

In a short time each of you men will control the lives of a certain number of other men. You will have in your charge loyal but untrained citizens, who look to you for instruction and guidance. Your word will be their law. Your most casual remark will be remembered. Your mannerisms will be aped. Your clothing, your carriage, your vocabulary, your manner of command will be imitated.

When you join your organization you will find there

a willing body of men who ask from you nothing more than the qualities that will command their respect, their loyalty and their obedience.

They are perfectly ready and eager to follow you so long as you can convince them that you have these qualities. When the time comes that they are satisfied you do not possess them you might as well kiss yourself good-bye. Your usefulness in that organization is at an end.

[How remarkably true this is in all manner of *leadership*.]

From the standpoint of society, the world may be divided into leaders and followers. The professions have their leaders, the financial world has its leaders. In all this leadership it is difficult, if not impossible, to separate from the element of pure leadership that selfish element of personal gain or advantage to the individual, without which any leadership would lose its value.

It is in military service only, where men freely sacrifice their lives for a faith, where men are willing to suffer and die for the right or the prevention of a wrong, that we can hope to realize leadership in its most exalted and disinterested sense. Therefore, when I say *leadership*, I mean *military leadership*.

In a few days the great mass of you men will receive commissions as officers. These commissions will not make you leaders; they will merely make you officers. They will place you in a position where you can become leaders if you possess the proper attributes. But you must make good, not so much with the men over you as with the men under you.

MAKE excuses for t h e shortcomings of others, if you wish, but hold yourself to a strict accountability i f y o u would attain leadership in any undertaking.

Men must and will follow into battle officers who are not leaders, but the driving power behind these men is not enthusiasm but discipline. They go with doubt and trembling that prompts the unspoken question, "What will he do next?" Such men obey the letter of their orders but no more. Of devotion to their commander, of exalted enthusiasm which scorns personal risk, of *self-sacrifice* to insure his personal safety, they know nothing. Their legs carry them forward because their brain and their training tell them they *must* go. Their spirit does not go with them.

Great results are not achieved by cold, passive, unresponsive soldiers. They don't go very far and they stop as soon as they can. Leadership not only demands but receives the willing, unhesitating, unfaltering obedience and loyalty of other men; and a devotion that will cause them, when the time comes, to follow their uncrowned king to hell and back again, if necessary.

You will ask yourselves: "Of just what, then, does *leadership* consist? What must I do to become a leader? What are the attributes of leadership, and how can I cultivate them?"

Leadership is a composite of a number of qualities. [Just as *success* is a composite of the fifteen factors out of which this Reading Course was built.] Among the most important I would list Self-confidence, Moral Ascendency, Self-Sacrifice, Paternalism, Fairness, Initiative, Decision, Dignity, Courage.

Self-confidence results, first, from exact knowledge; second, the ability to impart that knowledge; and third, the feeling of superiority over others that naturally follows. All these give the officer poise. To lead, you must *know!* You may bluff all of your men some of the time, but you can't do it all the time. Men will not have confidence in an officer unless he knows his business, and he must know it from the ground up.

The officer should know more about paper work than his first sergeant and company clerk put together; he should know more about messing than his mess sergeant; more about diseases of the horse than his troop farrier. He should be at least as good a shot as any man in his company.

If the officer does not know, and demonstrates the fact that he does not know, it is entirely human for the soldier to say to himself, "To hell with him. He doesn't know as much about this as I do," and calmly disregard the instructions received.

There is no substitute for accurate knowledge!

Become so well informed that men will hunt you up to ask questions; that your brother officers will say to one another, "Ask Smith—he knows."

And not only should each officer know thoroughly the duties of his own grade, but he should study those of the two grades next above him. A two-fold benefit attaches to this. He prepares himself for duties which may fall to his lot any time during battle; he further gains a broader viewpoint which enables him to appreciate the necessity for the issuance of orders and join more intelligently in their execution.

Not only must the officer know but he must be able to put what he knows into grammatical, interesting, forceful English. He must learn to stand on his feet and speak without embarrassment.

I am told that in British training camps student-officers are required to deliver ten minute talks on any subject they choose. That is excellent practice. For to speak clearly one must think clearly, and clear, logical thinking expresses itself in definite, positive orders.

While self-confidence is the result of knowing more than your men, Moral Ascendency over them is based upon your belief that you are the better man. To gain and maintain this ascendency you must have self-control, physical vitality and endurance and moral force. You must have yourself so well in hand that, even though in battle you be scared stiff, you will never show fear. For if by so much as a hurried movement or a trembling of the hands, or a change of expression, or a hasty order hastily revoked, you indicate your mental condition it will be reflected in your men in a far greater degree.

In garrison or camp many instances will arise to try your temper and wreck the sweetness of your disposition. If at such times you "fly off the handle" you have no business to be in charge of men. For men in anger say and do things that they almost invariably regret afterward.

An officer should never apologize to his men; also an officer should never be guilty of an act for which his sense of justice tells him he should apologize.

Another element in gaining Moral Ascendency lies in the possession of enough physical vitality and endurance to withstand the hardships to which you and your men are subjected, and a dauntless spirit that enables you not only to accept them cheerfully but to minimize their magnitude.

Make light of your troubles, belittle your trials and you will help vitally to build up within your organization an esprit whose value in time of stress cannot be measured.

Moral force is the third element in gaining Moral Ascendency. To exert moral force you must live clean; you must have sufficient brain power to see the right and the will to do right.

Be an example to your men!

An officer can be a power for good or a power for evil. Don't preach to them—that will be worse than useless. Live the kind of life you would have them lead, and you will be surprised to see the number that will imitate you.

A loud-mouthed, profane captain who is careless of his personal appearance will have a loud-mouthed, profane, dirty company. *Remember what I tell you. Your company will be the reflection of yourself!* If you have a rotten company it will be because you are a rotten captain.

Self-sacrifice is essential to leadership. You will give, give, all the time. You will give of yourself physically, for the longest hours, the hardest work and the greatest responsibility are the lot of the captain. He is the first man up in the morning and the last man in at night. He works while others sleep.

You will give of yourself mentally, in sympathy and appreciation for the troubles of men in your charge. This one's mother has died, and that one has lost all his savings in a bank failure. They may desire help, but more than anything else they desire *sympathy*. Don't make the mistake of turning such men down with the statement that you have troubles of your own, for every time you do that you *knock a stone out of the foundation of your house.*

Your men are your foundation, and your house of *leadership* will tumble about your ears unless it rests securely upon them. Finally, you will give of your own slender financial resources. You will frequently spend your own money to conserve the health and well-being of your men or to assist them when in trouble. Generally you get your money back. Very frequently you must charge it off to profit and loss.

Even so, it is worth the cost.

When I say that paternalism is essential to leadership I use the term in its better sense. I do not now refer to that form of paternalism which robs men of *initiative, self-reliance* and *self-respect.* I refer to the paternalism that manifests itself in a watchful care for the comfort and welfare of those in your charge.

Soldiers are much like children. You must see that they have shelter, food and clothing, the best that your utmost efforts can provide. You must see that they have food to eat before you think of your own; that they have each as good a bed as can be provided before you consider where you will sleep. You must be far more solicitous of their comfort than of your own. You must look after their health. You must conserve their strength by not demanding needless exertion or useless labor.

And by doing all these things you are breathing life into what would be otherwise a mere machine. You are creating a soul in your organization that will make the mass respond to you as though it were one man. And that is esprit.

No accurate thinker will judge another person by that which the other person's enemies say about him.

And when your organization has this esprit you will wake up some morning and discover that the tables have been turned; that instead of your constantly looking out for them they have, without even a hint from you, taken up the task of looking out for you. You will find that a detail is always there to see that your tent, if you have one, is promptly pitched; that the most and the cleanest bedding is brought to your tent; that from some mysterious source two eggs have been added to your supper when no one else has any; that an extra man is helping your men give your horse a supergrooming; that your wishes are anticipated; that every man is "Johnny-on-the-spot." And then you have *arrived!*

You cannot treat all men alike! A punishment that would be dismissed by one man with a shrug of the shoulders is mental anguish for another. A company commander who, for a given offense, has a standard punishment that applies to all is either too indolent or too stupid to study the personality of his men. In his case justice is certainly blind.

Study your men as carefully as a surgeon studies a difficult case. And when you are sure of your diagnosis apply the remedy. And remember that you apply the remedy to effect a cure, not merely to see the victim squirm. It may be necessary to cut deep, but when you are satisfied as to your diagnosis don't be diverted from your purpose by any false sympathy for the patient.

Hand in hand with fairness in awarding punishment walks fairness in giving credit. Everybody hates a human hog. When one of your men has accomplished an especially creditable piece of work see that he gets the proper reward. *Turn heaven and earth upside down to get it for him.* Don't try to take it away from him and hog it for yourself. You may do this and get away with it, but you have lost the respect and loyalty of your men. Sooner or later your brother officers will hear of it and shun you like a leper. In war there is glory enough for all. Give the man under you his due. *The man who always takes and never gives is not a leader.* He is a parasite.

There is another kind of fairness—that which will prevent an officer from abusing the privileges of his rank. When you exact respect from soldiers be sure you treat them with equal respect. Build up their manhood and self-respect. Don't try to pull it down.

For an officer to be overbearing and insulting in the treatment of enlisted men is the act of a coward. He ties the man to a tree with the ropes of discipline and then strikes him in the face knowing full well that the man cannot strike back.

Consideration, courtesy and respect from officers toward enlisted men are not incompatible with discipline. They are parts of our discipline. Without initiative and decision no man can expect to lead.

In maneuvers you will frequently see, when an emergency arises, certain men calmly give instant orders which later, on analysis, prove to be, if not exactly the right thing, very nearly the right thing to have done. You will see other men in emergency become badly rattled; their brains refuse to work, or they give a hasty order, revoke it; give another, revoke that; in short, show every indication of being in a blue funk.

Regarding the first man you may say: "That man

is a genius. He hasn't had time to reason this thing out. He acts intuitively." Forget it! Genius is merely the capacity for taking infinite pains. The man who was ready is the man who has prepared himself. He has studied beforehand the possible situations that might arise; he has made tentative plans covering such situations. When he is confronted by the emergency he is ready to meet it. He must have sufficient mental alertness to appreciate the problem that confronts him and the power of quick reasoning to determine what changes are necessary in his already formulated plan. He must also have the decision to order the execution and stick to his orders.

Any reasonable order in an emergency is better than no order. The situation is there. Meet it. It is better to do something and do the wrong thing than to hesitate, hunt around for the right thing to do and wind up by doing nothing at all. And, having decided on a line of action, stick to it. Don't vacillate. Men have no confidence in an officer who doesn't know his own mind.

Occasionally you will be called upon to meet a situation which no reasonable human being could anticipate. If you have prepared yourself to meet other emergencies which you could anticipate, the mental training you have thereby gained will enable you to act promptly and with calmness.

You must frequently act without orders from higher authority. Time will not permit you to wait for them. Here again enters the importance of studying the work of officers above you. If you have a comprehensive grasp of the entire situation and can form an idea of the general plan of your superiors, that and your previous emergency training will enable you to determine that the responsibility is yours and to issue the necessary orders without delay.

The element of *personal dignity* is important in military leadership. Be the friend of your men, but do not become their intimate. Your men should stand in awe of you—not *fear!* If your men presume to become familiar it is your fault, and not theirs. Your actions have encouraged them to do so. And, above all things, don't cheapen yourself by courting their friendship or currying their favor. They will despise you for it. If you are worthy of their loyalty and respect and devotion they will surely give all these without asking. If you are not, nothing that you can do will win them.

It is exceedingly difficult for an officer to be dignified while wearing a dirty, spotted uniform and a three days' stubble of whiskers on his face. Such a man lacks self-respect, and self-respect is an essential of dignity.

There may be occasions when your work entails dirty clothes and an unshaved face. Your men all look that way. At such times there is ample reason for your appearance. In fact, it would be a mistake to look too clean—they would think that you were not doing your share. But as soon as this unusual occasion has passed set an example for personal neatness.

And then I would mention *courage.* Moral courage you need as well as mental courage—that kind of moral courage which enables you to adhere without faltering to a determined course of action, which your judgment has indicated is the one best suited to secure the desired results.

You will find many times, especially in action, that, after having issued your orders to do a certain thing, you will be beset by misgivings and doubts; you will see, or think you see, other and better means for accomplishing the object sought. You will be strongly tempted to change your orders. Don't do it until it is clearly manifested that your first orders were radically wrong. For, if you do, you will be again worried by doubts as to the efficacy of your second orders.

Every time you change your orders without obvious reason you weaken your authority and impair the confidence of your men. Have the moral courage to stand by your order and see it through.

Moral courage further demands that you assume the responsibility for your own acts. If your subordinates have loyally carried out your orders and the movement you directed is a failure the failure is *yours,* not theirs. Yours would have been the honor had it been successful. Take the blame if it results in disaster. Don't try to shift it to a subordinate and make him the goat. That is a cowardly act. Furthermore, you will need moral courage to determine the fate of those under you. You will frequently be called upon for recommendations for promotion or demotion of officers and non-commissioned officers in your immediate command.

Keep clearly in mind your *personal integrity* and the duty you owe your country. Do not let yourself be deflected from a strict sense of justice by feelings of personal friendship. If your own brother is your sec-

THERE is some-
thing wrong about
the man whose wife and
children do not greet him
affectionately o n h i s
homecoming.

ond lieutenant, and you find him unfit to hold his commission, eliminate him. If you don't your lack of moral courage may result in the loss of valuable lives.

If, on the other hand, you are called upon for a recommendation concerning a man whom, for personal reasons, you thoroughly dislike, do not fail to do him full justice. Remember that your aim is the general good, not the satisfaction of an individual grudge.

I am taking it for granted that you have physical courage. I need not tell you how necessary that is. Courage is more than bravery. Bravery is fearlessness —the absence of fear. The merest dolt may be brave, because he lacks the mentality to appreciate his danger; he doesn't know enough to be afraid.

Courage, however, is that firmness of spirit, that moral backbone which, while fully appreciating the danger involved, nevertheless goes on with the undertaking. Bravery is physical; courage is mental and moral. You may be cold all over; your hands may tremble; your legs may quake; your knees be ready to give way—that is fear. If, nevertheless, you go forward; if, in spite of this physical defection you continue to lead your men against the enemy, you have courage. The physical manifestations of fear will pass away. You may never experience them but once. They are the "buck fever" of the hunter who tries to shoot his first deer. You must not give way to them.

A number of years ago, while taking a course in demolitions, the class of which I was a member was handling dynamite. The instructor said, regarding its manipulation: "I must caution you gentlemen to be careful in the use of these explosives. One man has but one accident." And so I would caution you. If you give way to fear that will doubtless beset you in your first action; if you show the white feather; if you let your men go forward while you hunt a shell crater, you will never again have the opportunity of leading those men.

Use judgment in calling on your men for displays of physical courage or bravery. *Don't ask any man to go where you would not go yourself.* If your common sense tells you that the place is too dangerous for you to venture into, then it is too dangerous for him. You know his life is as valuable to him as yours is to you.

Occasionally some of your men must be exposed to danger which you cannot share. A message must be taken across a fire-swept zone. You call for volunteers. If your men know you and know that you are "right" you will never lack volunteers, for they will know your heart is in your work, that you are giving your country the best you have, that you would willingly carry the message yourself if you could. Your example and enthusiasm will have inspired them.

And, lastly, if you aspire to leadership, I would urge you to study men.

Get under their skins and find out what is inside. Some men are quite different from what they appear to be on the surface. Determine the workings of their mind.

Much of General Robert E. Lee's success as a leader may be ascribed to his ability as a *psychologist*. He knew most of his opponents from West Point days; knew the workings of their minds; and he believed that they would do certain things under certain circumstances. In nearly every case he was able to anticipate their movements and block the execution.

You cannot know your opponent in this war in the same way. But you can know your own men. You can study each to determine wherein lies his strength and his weakness; which man can be relied upon to the last gasp and which cannot.

Know your men, know your business, know yourself!

. . . .

In all literature you will not find a better description of *leadership* than this. Apply it to yourself, or to your business, or to your profession, or to the place where you are employed, and you will observe how well it serves as your guide.

Major Bach's address is one that might well be delivered to every boy and girl who graduates in high school. It might well be delivered to every college graduate. It might well become the book of rules for every man who is placed in a position of leadership over other men, no matter in what calling, business or profession.

In Lesson Two you learned the value of a *definite chief aim*. Let it be here emphasized that your aim must be active and not passive. A *definite aim* will never be anything else but a mere wish unless you become a person of initiative and *aggressively* and *persistently* pursue that aim until it has been fulfilled.

You can get nowhere without persistence, a fact which cannot be too often repeated.

The difference between persistence and lack of it is the same as the difference between wishing for a thing and positively determining to get it.

To become a person of initiative you must form the habit of *aggressively* and *persistently* following the object of your *definite chief aim* until you acquire it, whether this requires one year or twenty years. You might as well have no *definite chief aim* as to have such an aim without *continuous* effort to achieve it.

You are not making the most of this course if you do not take some step each day that brings you nearer realization of your *definite chief aim*. Do not fool yourself, or permit yourself to be misled to believe that the object of your *definite chief aim* will materialize if you only wait. The materialization will come through your own determination, backed by your own carefully laid plans and your own initiative in putting those plans into action, or it will not come at all.

One of the major requisites for Leadership is the power of quick and firm DECISION!

Analysis of more than 16,000 people disclosed the fact that Leaders are always men of ready decision, even in matters of small importance, while the follower is NEVER a person of quick decision.

This is worth remembering!

The follower, in whatever walk of life you find him, is a man who seldom knows what he wants. He vacillates, procrastinates, and actually refuses to reach a decision, even in matters of the smallest importance, unless a Leader induces him to do so.

To know that the majority of people cannot and will not reach decisions quickly, if at all, is of great help to the Leader who knows what he wants and has a plan for getting it.

Here it will be observed how closely allied are the two laws covered by Lesson Two and this lesson. The

Leader not only works with A DEFINITE CHIEF AIM, but he has a very definite plan for attaining the object of that aim. It will be seen, also, that the Law of Self-confidence becomes an important part of the working equipment of the Leader.

The chief reason why the follower does not reach decisions is that he lacks the Self-confidence to do so. Every Leader makes use of the Law of a Definite Purpose, the Law of Self-confidence and the Law of Initiative and Leadership. And if he is an outstanding, successful Leader he makes use, also, of the Laws of Imagination, Enthusiasm, Self-Control, Pleasing Personality, Accurate Thinking, Concentration and Tolerance. Without the combined use of all these Laws no one may become a really great Leader. Omission of a single one of these Laws lessens the power of the Leader proportionately.

A salesman for the LaSalle Extension University called on a real estate dealer, in a small western town, for the purpose of trying to sell the real estate man a course in Salesmanship and Business Management.

When the salesman arrived at the prospective student's office he found the gentleman pecking out a letter by the two-finger method, on an antiquated typewriter. The salesman introduced himself, then proceeded to state his business and describe the course he had come to sell.

The real estate man listened with apparent interest.

After the sales talk had been completed the salesman hesitated, waiting for some signs of "yes" or "no" from his prospective client. Thinking that perhaps he had not made the sales talk quite strong enough, he briefly went over the merits of the course he was

NO man may become

an accurate thinker

until he learns how to sep-

arate mere gossip and in-

formation from facts.

selling, a second time. Still there was no response from the prospective student.

The salesman then asked the direct question, "You want this course, do you not?"

In a slow, drawling tone of voice, the real estate man replied:

"Well, I hardly know whether I do or not."

No doubt he was telling the truth, because he was one of the millions of men who find it hard to reach decisions.

Being an able judge of human nature the salesman then arose, put on his hat, placed his literature back in his brief case and made ready to leave. Then he resorted to tactics which were somewhat drastic, and took the real estate man by surprise with this startling statement:

"I am going to take it upon myself to say something to you that you will not like, but it may be of help to you.

"Take a look at this office in which you work! The floor is dirty; the walls are dusty; the typewriter you are using looks as if it might be the one Mr. Noah used in the Ark during the big flood; your pants are bagged at the knees; your collar is dirty; your face is unshaved, and you have a look in your eyes that tells me you are defeated.

"Please go ahead and get mad—that's just what I want you to do, because it may shock you into doing some thinking that will be helpful to you and to those who are dependent upon you.

"I can see, in my imagination, the home in which you live. Several little children, none too well dressed, and perhaps none too well fed; a mother whose dress is three seasons out of style, whose eyes carry the same look of defeat that yours do. This little woman whom you married has stuck by you but you have not made good in life as she had hoped, when you were first married, that you would.

"Please remember that I am not now talking to a prospective student, because I would not sell you this course at THIS PARTICULAR MOMENT if you offered to pay cash in advance, because if I did you would not have the initiative to complete it, and we want no failures on our student list.

"The talk I am now giving you will make it impossible, perhaps, for me ever to sell you anything, but it is going to do something for you that has never been done before, providing it makes you think.

"Now, I will tell you in a very few words exactly why you are defeated; why you are pecking out letters on an old typewriter, in an old dirty office, in a little town: IT IS BECAUSE YOU DO NOT HAVE THE POWER TO REACH A DECISION!

"All your life you have been forming the habit of dodging the responsibility of reaching decisions, until you have come, now, to where it is well-nigh impossible for you to do so.

"If you had told me that you wanted the course, or that you did not want it, I could have sympathized with you, because I would have known that lack of funds was what caused you to hesitate, but what did you say? Why, you admitted you did not know whether you wanted it or not.

"If you will think over what I have said I am sure you will acknowledge that it has become a habit with you to dodge the responsibility of reaching clear-cut decisions on practically all matters that affect you."

The real estate man sat glued in his chair, with his under jaw dropped, his eyes bulged in astonishment, but he made no attempt to answer the biting indictment.

The salesman said good-bye and started for the door.

After he had closed the door behind him he again opened it, walked back in, with a smile on his face, took his seat in front of the astonished real estate man, and explained his conduct in this way:

"I do not blame you at all if you feel hurt at my remarks. In fact I sort of hope that you have been offended, but now let me say this, man to man, that I think you have intelligence and I am sure you have ability, but you have fallen into a habit that has whipped you. No man is ever down and out until he is under the sod. You may be temporarily down, but you can get up again, and I am just sportsman enough to give you my hand and offer you a lift, if you will accept my apologies for what I have said.

"You do not belong in this town. You would starve to death in the real estate business in this place, even if you were a Leader in your field. Get yourself a new suit of clothes, even if you have to borrow the money with which to do it, then go over to St. Louis with me and I will introduce you to a real estate man who will give you a chance to earn some money and at the same time teach you some of the important things about this line of work that you can capitalize later on.

"If you haven't enough credit to get the clothes you need I will stand good for you at a store in St. Louis where I have a charge account. I am in earnest and my offer to help you is based upon the highest motive that can actuate a human being. I am successful in my own field, but I have not always been so. I went through just what you are now going through, but, the important thing is that I WENT THROUGH IT, and got it over with, JUST AS YOU ARE GOING TO DO IF YOU WILL FOLLOW MY ADVICE.

"Will you come with me?"

The real estate man started to arise, but his legs wobbled and he sank back into his chair. Despite the fact that he was a great big fellow, with rather pronounced manly qualities, known as the "he-man" type, his emotions got the better of him and he actually wept.

He made a second attempt and got on his feet, shook hands with the salesman, thanked him for his kindness, and said he was going to follow the advice, but he would do so in his own way.

Calling for an application blank he signed for the course on Salesmanship and Business Management, made the first payment in nickels and dimes, and told the salesman he would hear from him again.

Three years later this real estate man had an organization of sixty salesmen, and one of the most successful real estate businesses in the city of St. Louis. The author of this course (who was advertising manager of the LaSalle Extension University at the time this incident happened) has been in this real estate man's office many times and has observed him over a period of more than fifteen years. He is an entirely different man from the person interviewed by the La-Salle salesman over fifteen years ago, and the thing that made him different is the same that will make

YOU different: it is the power of DECISION which is so essential to Leadership.

This real estate man is now a Leader in the real estate field. He is directing the efforts of other salesmen and helping them to become more efficient. This one change in his philosophy has turned temporary defeat into success. Every new salesman who goes to work for this man is called into his private office, before he is employed, and told the story of his own transformation, word for word just as it occurred when the LaSalle salesman first met him in his shabby little real estate office.

.   .   .   .

Some eighteen years ago the author of this course made his first trip to the little town of Lumberport, W. Va. At that time the only means of transportation leading from Clarksburg, the largest near-by center, to Lumberport, was the Baltimore & Ohio Railroad and an interurban electric line which ran within three miles of the town; one could walk the three miles if he chose.

Upon arrival at Clarksburg I found that the only train going to Lumberport in the forenoon had already gone, and not wishing to wait for the later afternoon train I made the trip by trolley, with the intention of walking the three miles. On the way down the rain began to pour, and those three miles had to be navigated on foot, through deep yellow mud. When I arrived at Lumberport my shoes and pants were muddy, and my disposition was none the better for the experience.

The first person I met was V. L. Hornor, who was

MASTERY of the Fifteen Laws of Success is the equivalent of an insurance policy against failure.

—Samuel Gompers.

then cashier of the Lumberport Bank. In a rather loud tone of voice I asked of him, "Why do you not get that trolley line extended from the junction over to Lumberport so your friends can get in and out of town without drowning in mud?"

"Did you see a river with high banks, at the edge of the town, as you came in?" he asked. I replied that I had seen it. "Well," he continued, "that's the reason we have no street cars running into town. The cost of a bridge would be about $100,000.00, and that is more than the company owning the trolley line is willing to invest. We have been trying for ten years to get them to build a line into town."

"Trying!" I exploded. "How hard have you tried?"

"We have offered them every inducement we could afford, such as free right of way from the junction into the town, and free use of the streets, but that bridge is the stumbling block. They simply will not stand the expense. Claim they cannot afford such an expense for the small amount of revenue they would receive from the three mile extension."

Then the Law of Success philosophy began to come to my rescue!

I asked Mr. Hornor if he would take a walk over to the river with me, that we might look at the spot that was causing so much inconvenience. He said he would be glad to do so.

When we got to the river I began to take inventory of everything in sight. I observed that the Baltimore & Ohio Railroad tracks ran up and down the river banks, on both sides of the river; that the county road crossed the river on a rickety wooden bridge, both approaches to which were over several strands of railroad track, as the railroad company had its switching yards at that point.

While we were standing there a freight train blocked the crossing and several teams stopped on both sides of the train, waiting for an opportunity to get through. The train kept the road blocked for about twenty-five minutes.

With this combination of circumstances in mind it required but little imagination to see that THREE DIFFERENT PARTIES were or could be interested in the building of the bridge such as would be needed to carry the weight of a street car.

It was obvious that the Baltimore & Ohio Railroad Company would be interested in such a bridge, because that would remove the county road from their switching tracks, and save them a possible accident on the crossing, to say nothing of much loss of time and expense in cutting trains to allow teams to pass.

It was also obvious that the County Commissioners would be interested in the bridge, because it would raise the county road to a better level and make it more serviceable to the public. And, of course the street railway company was interested in the bridge, but IT DID NOT WISH TO PAY THE ENTIRE COST.

All these facts passed through my mind as I stood there and watched the freight train being cut for the traffic to pass through.

A DEFINITE CHIEF AIM took place in my mind. Also, a definite plan for its attainment. The next day I got together a committee of townspeople, consisting of the mayor, councilmen and some leading citizens, and called on the Division Superintendent of the Baltimore & Ohio Railroad Company, at Grafton. We convinced him that it was worth one third of the cost of the bridge to get the county road off his company's tracks. Next we went to the County Commissioners and found them to be quite enthusiastic over the possibility of getting a new bridge by paying for only one third of it. They promised to pay their one third providing we could arrange for the other two thirds.

We then went to the president of the Traction Company that owned the trolley line, at Fairmont, and laid before him an offer to donate all the rights of way and pay for two thirds of the cost of the bridge providing he would begin building the line into town promptly. We found him receptive, also.

Three weeks later a contract had been signed between the Baltimore & Ohio Railroad Company, the Monongahela Valley Traction Company and the County Commissioners of Harrison County, providing for the construction of the bridge, one third of its cost to be paid by each.

Two months later the right of way was being graded and the bridge was under way, and three months after that street cars were running into Lumberport on regular schedule.

This incident meant much to the town of Lumberport, because it provided transportation that enabled people to get in and out of the town without undue effort.

It also meant a great deal to me, because it served to introduce me as one who "got things done." Two very definite advantages resulted from this transaction. The Chief Counsel for the Traction Company gave me a position as his assistant, and later on it was the means of an introduction which led to my appointment as the advertising manager of the LaSalle Extension University.

Lumberport, W. Va., was then, and still is a small town, and Chicago was a large city and located a considerable distance away, but news of Initiative and Leadership has a way of taking on wings and traveling.

Four of the Fifteen Laws of Success were combined in the transaction described, namely: A DEFINITE CHIEF AIM, SELF-CONFIDENCE, IMAGINATION and INITIATIVE and LEADERSHIP. The Law of DOING MORE THAN PAID FOR also entered, somewhat, into the transaction, because I was not offered anything and in fact did not expect pay for what I did.

To be perfectly frank I appointed myself to the job of getting the bridge built more as a sort of challenge to those who said it could not be done than I did with the expectation of getting paid for it. By my attitude I rather intimated to Mr. Hornor that I could get the job done, and he was not slow to snap me up and put me to the test.

It may be helpful to call attention here to the part which IMAGINATION played in this transaction. For ten years the townspeople of Lumberport had been trying to get a street car line built into town. It must not be concluded that the town was without men of ability, because that would be inaccurate. In fact there were many men of ability in the town, but they had been making the mistake which is so commonly made by us all, of trying to solve their problem through one single source, whereas there were actually THREE SOURCES of solution available to them.

$100,000.00 was too much for one company to assume, for the construction of a bridge, but when the cost was distributed between three interested parties the amount to be borne by each was more reasonable.

The question might be asked: "Why did not some of the local townsmen think of this three-way solution?"

In the first place they were so close to their problem that they failed to take a perspective, bird's-eye view of it, which would have suggested the solution. This, also, is a common mistake, and one that is always avoided by great Leaders. In the second place these townspeople had never before co-ordinated their efforts or worked as an organized group with the sole purpose in mind of finding a way to get a street car line built into town. This, also, is another common error made by men in all walks of life—that of failure to work in unison, in a thorough spirit of co-operation.

I, being an outsider, had less difficulty in getting co-operative action than one of their own group might have had. Too often there is a spirit of selfishness in small communities which prompts each individual to think that his ideas should prevail. It is an important part of the Leader's responsibility to induce people to subordinate their own ideas and interests for the good of the whole, and this applies to matters of a civic, business, social, political, financial or industrial nature.

Success, no matter what may be one's conception of that term, is nearly always a question of one's ability to get others to subordinate their own individualities and follow a Leader. The Leader who has the Personality and the Imagination to induce his follow-

TIME is the mighty hand that rocks the eternal cradle of progress and nurses struggling humanity through that period when man needs protection against his own ignorance.

ers to accept his plans and carry them out faithfully is always an able Leader.

The next lesson, on IMAGINATION, will take you still further into the art of tactful Leadership. In fact Leadership and Imagination are so closely allied and so essential for success that one cannot be successfully applied without the other. Initiative is the moving force that pushes the Leader ahead, but Imagination is the guiding spirit that tells him which way to go.

Imagination enabled the author of this course to analyze the Lumberport bridge problem, break it up into its three component parts, and assemble these parts in a practical working plan. Nearly every problem may be so broken up into parts which are more easily managed, as parts, than they are when assembled as a whole. Perhaps one of the most important advantages of Imagination is that it enables one to separate all problems into their component parts and to reassemble them in more favorable combinations.

It has been said that all battles in warfare are won or lost, not on the firing line, after the battle begins, but back of the lines, through the sound strategy, or the lack of it, used by the generals who plan the battles.

What is true of warfare is equally true in business, and in most other problems which confront us throughout life. We win or lose according to the nature of the plans we build and carry out, a fact which serves to emphasize the value of the Laws of Initiative and Leadership, Imagination, Self-confidence and a Definite Chief Aim. *With the intelligent use of these four laws one may build plans, for any purpose whatsoever, which cannot be defeated by any person or group of*

persons who do not employ or understand these laws.
There is no escape from the truth here stated!

ORGANIZED EFFORT is effort which is directed according to a plan that was conceived with the aid of Imagination, guided by a Definite Chief Aim, and given momentum with Initiative and Self-confidence. These four laws blend into one and become a power in the hands of a Leader. Without their aid effective leadership is impossible.

.   .   .   .

You are now ready for the lesson on Imagination. Read that lesson with the thought in mind of all that has been here stated and it will take on a deeper meaning.

L IFE IS NOT A
GOBLET TO BE
DRAINED; IT IS A
MEASURE TO BE
FILLED.

—*Hadley.*

INTOLERANCE
An After-the-Lesson Visit With the Author

INTOLERANCE

If you must give expression to prejudice and hatred and intolerance, do not speak it, but write it; write it in the sands, near the water's edge.

When the dawn of Intelligence shall spread over the eastern horizon of human progress, and Ignorance and Superstition shall have left their last footprints on the sands of time, it will be recorded in the last chapter of the book of man's crimes that his most grievous sin was that of Intolerance.

The bitterest intolerance grows out of religious, racial and economic prejudices and differences of opinion. How long, O God, until we poor mortals will understand the folly of trying to destroy one another because we are of different religious beliefs and racial tendencies?

Our allotted time on this earth is but a fleeting moment. Like a candle, we are lighted, shine for a moment, and flicker out. Why can we not learn to so live during this brief earthly visit that when the great Caravan called Death draws up and announces this visit completed we will be ready to fold our tents and silently follow out into the great unknown without fear and trembling?

I am hoping that I will find no Jews or Gentiles, Catholics or Protestants, Germans, Englishmen or Frenchmen when I shall have crossed the bar to the other side. I am hoping that I will find there only human Souls, Brothers and Sisters all, unmarked by race, creed or color, for I shall want to be done with intolerance so I may rest in peace throughout eternity.

YOU will see at the top of the previous page a picture which describes the futility of combat.

The two male deer have engaged in a fight to the finish, each believing that he will be the winner. Off at the side the female awaits the victor, little dreaming that tomorrow the bones of both combatants will be bleaching in the sun.

"Poor foolish animals," someone will say. Perhaps, but not very different from the man family. Man engages his brothers in mortal combat because of competition. The three major forms of competition are sex, economic and religious in nature.

.   .   .   .

Twenty years ago a great educational institution was doing a thriving business and rendering a worthy service to thousands of students. The two owners of the school married two beautiful and talented young women, who were especially accomplished in the art of piano playing. The two wives became involved in an argument as to which one was the more accomplished in this art. The disagreement was taken up

by each of the husbands. They became bitter enemies. Now the bones of that once prosperous school
"lie bleaching in the sun."

The two bucks shown in the picture above locked
horns over the attention of the doe. The two "man
bucks" locked horns over the selfsame impulse.

.   .   .   .

In one of the great industrial plants two young foremen "locked horns" because one received a promotion which the other believed he should have had. For
more than five years the silent undertow of hatred
and intolerance showed itself. The men under each
of the foremen became inoculated with the spirit of
dislike which they saw cropping out in their superiors. Slowly the spirit of retaliation began to spread
over the entire plant. The men became divided into
little cliques. Production began to fall off. Then
came financial difficulty and finally bankruptcy for the
company.

Now the bones of a once prosperous business "lie
bleaching in the sun," and the two foremen and several thousand others were compelled to start all over
again, in another field.

.   .   .   .

Down in the mountains of West Virginia lived two
peaceful families of mountain-folk—the Hatfields and
the McCoys. They had been friendly neighbors for
three generations. A razor-back pig belonging to the
McCoy family crawled through the fence into the Hat-
field family's corn field. The Hatfields turned their
hound loose on the pig. The McCoys retaliated by
killing the dog. Then began a feud that has lasted

for three generations and cost many lives of the Hatfields and McCoys.

In a fashionable suburb of Philadelphia certain
gentlemen of wealth have built their homes. In front
of each house the word "INTOLERANCE" is written.
One man builds a high steel fence in front of his
house. The neighbor next to him, not to be outdone,
builds a fence twice as high. Another buys a new
motor car and the man next door goes him one better
by purchasing two new cars. One remodels his house
adding a colonial style porch. The man next door
adds a new porch and a Spanish style garage for good
measure. The big mansion on top of the hill gives a
reception which brings a long line of motor cars filled
with people who have nothing in particular in common
with the host. Then follows a series of "receptions"
all down the "gold-coast" line, each trying to out-
shine all the others.

The "Mister" (but they don't call him that in fashionable neighborhoods) goes to business in the back
seat of a Rolls Royce that is managed by a chauffeur
and a footman. Why does he go to business? To
make money, of course! Why does he want more
money when he already has millions of dollars? So
he can keep on out-doing his wealthy neighbors.

Poverty has some advantages—it never drives
those who are poverty-stricken to "lock horns" in the
attempt to out-poverty their neighbors.

Wherever you see men with their "horns locked"
in conflict you may trace the cause of the combat to
one of the three causes of intolerance—religious difference of opinion, economic competition or sex competition.

The next time you observe two men engaged in any sort of hostility toward each other, just close your eyes and THINK for a moment and you may see them, in their transformed nature, very much resembling the male deer shown in the picture above. Off at one side you may see the object of the combat—a pile of gold, a religious emblem or a female (or females).

Remember, the purpose of this essay is to tell some of the TRUTH about human nature, with the object of causing its readers to THINK. Its writer seeks no glory or praise, and likely he will receive neither in connection with this particular subject.

Andrew Carnegie and Henry C. Frick did more than any other two men to establish the steel industry. Both made millions of dollars for themselves. Came the day when economic intolerance sprang up between them. To show his contempt for Frick, Carnegie built a tall sky-scraper and named it the "Carnegie Building." Frick retaliated by erecting a much taller building, alongside of the Carnegie Building, naming it the "Frick Building."

These two gentlemen "locked horns" in a fight to the finish, Carnegie lost his mind, and perhaps more, for all we of this world know. What Frick lost is known only to himself and the keeper of the Great Records. In memory their "bones lie bleaching in the sun" of posterity.

The steel men of today are managing things differently. Instead of locking horns they now "interlock directorates," with the result that each is practically a solidified, strong unit of the whole industry. The steel men of today understand the dif-

ference between the meaning of the words COMPE-
TITION and CO-OPERATION; a difference which
the remainder of us would do well to understand, also.

.   .   .   .

In England the men who own the mines and those
who run the labor unions "locked horns." Had not
the cooler heads unlocked those horns the bones of
the British empire (including both the owners of industry and the labor unions) should soon have lain
"bleaching in the sun." One year of open combat between the unions and the owners of industry, in Great
Britain, would have meant annihilation of the British
empire. The other nations of the world would have
grabbed all the economic machinery now controlled by
Britain.

Let the leaders of American industry and unionism
not forget!

.   .   .   .

Fifteen factors enter into the attainment of SUC-
CESS. One of these is TOLERANCE. The other
fourteen are mentioned many times in this series of
lessons.

Intolerance binds man's legs with the shackles of
IGNORANCE and covers his eyes with the scales of
FEAR AND SUPERSTITION. Intolerance closes
the book of knowledge and writes on the cover "Open
not this book again. The last word has been herein
written."

It is not your DUTY to be tolerant; it is your
PRIVILEGE!

Remember, as you read this article, that sowing

the seed of INTOLERANCE is the sole and exclusive
business of some men. All wars and all strikes and
all other forms of human suffering bring profit to
SOME. If this were not true there would be no wars
or strikes or other similar forms of hostility.

In the United States today there is a well organized system of propaganda, the object of which is to
stir up strife and hostility between the owners of industries and those who work in those industries.
Take another look at the picture at the beginning of
this article and you may see what will happen to all
who lock horns in labor disagreements, and remember
that it is always the bones of the workers (and not
those of the leaders of either the unions or the industries) that "lie bleaching in the sun" after the fight
is over.

.   .   .   .

When you feel yourself preparing to "lock horns"
with someone remember that it will be more profitable
if you LOCK HANDS instead! A warm, hearty
hand-shake leaves no bones bleaching in the sun.

"LOVE is the only bow on life's dark cloud. It is
the Morning and the Evening Star. It shines upon the
cradle of the babe, and sheds its radiance upon the
quiet tomb. It is the mother of Art, inspirer of poet,
patriot and philosopher. It is the air and light of every
heart, builder of every home, kindler of every fire on
every hearth. It was the first to dream of immortal-
ity. It fills the world with melody, for Music is the
voice of Love. Love is the magician, the enchanter,
that changes worthless things to Joy, and makes right
royal kings and queens of common clay. It is the per-

fume of the wondrous flower—the heart—and without that sacred passion, that divine swoon, we are less than beasts; but with it, earth is heaven and we are gods."

—INGERSOLL.

Cultivate LOVE for your fellow man and you will no longer want to lock horns with him in futile combat. Love makes every man his brother's keeper.

> Love, indeed, is light from heaven;
> A spark of that immortal fire
> With angels shared, by Allah given,
> To lift from earth our low desire.
> Devotion wafts the mind above,
> But heaven itself descends in love;
> A feeling from the Godhead caught,
> To wean from self each sordid thought;
> A ray of Him who form'd the whole;
> A glory circling round the soul:
> —BYRON.

No ONE HAS GIVEN YOU AN OPPORTUNITY? HAS IT EVER OCCURRED TO YOU TO CREATE OPPORTUNITY FOR YOURSELF?

Treat Yourself to This Fun, Inspirational Book and Discover
How to Find Happiness and Serenity . . .
No Matter What Life Dishes Out

The Dragon Slayer
With a Heavy Heart

---

*This new book by best-selling author Marcia Powers promises to be
one of the most important you will ever read—and one of the most
entertaining, uplifting, and memorable.*

*It brings the Serenity Prayer—which for years has been the guiding
light of 12-step programs worldwide—to everyone . . . and teaches
both new and longtime devotees how to apply it most effectively to
their lives.*

Sometimes things happen we wish hadn't. Sometimes things *don't*
happen we wish *would*. In the course of living, problems arise, both
big and small. We might wish our past had been different or that *we*
could be different. We struggle through disappointments and
frustrations, losses and other painful experiences.

As hard as we may try to be strong, to have a good attitude, not to
let things get us down, we don't always succeed. We get upset. We
worry. We feel stressed. We get depressed. We get angry. We do the
best we can and wait for things to *get* better so we can *feel* better. In
the meantime, our hearts may grow heavy . . . perhaps very heavy.

That's what happened to Duke the Dragon Slayer. In fact, *his*
heart grew *so* heavy with all that was wrong, with all that was not the
way it should be, with all that was unfair, that he became desperate to
lighten it—and set forth on the Path of Serenity to find out how.

Accompany Duke on this life-changing adventure. His guides will
be your guides. His answers will be your answers. His tools will be
your tools. His success will be your success. And by the time he is
heading home, both Duke and you will know how to take life's
inevitable lumps and bumps in stride—and find happiness and
serenity anytime . . . even when you really, REALLY wish some things
were different.

"A BEAUTIFUL, EXCEPTIONALLY WELL-WRITTEN STORY THAT CAN HELP
EVERYONE TO BE EMOTIONALLY STRONGER AND BETTER ABLE TO COPE
WITH ADVERSITY." Albert Ellis, Ph.D.
President, Albert Ellis Institute
Author of *A Guide to Rational Living*

THE
LAW OF
SUCCESS

IN SIXTEEN LESSONS

Teaching, for the First Time in the
History of the World, the True Philosophy upon which all Personal Success
is Built.

⚬⚬❀⚬⚬

BY

NAPOLEON HILL

⚬⚬❀⚬⚬

1 9 2 8

PUBLISHED BY
The RALSTON UNIVERSITY PRESS
MERIDEN, CONN.

Lesson Six

IMAGINATION

I CALL THAT MAN
  I D L E W H O
MIGHT BE BETTER
EMPLOYED.

—*Socrates.*

"You Can Do It if You Believe You Can!"

MAGINATION is the workshop of the human mind wherein old ideas and established facts may be reassembled into new combinations and put to new uses. The modern dictionary defines *imagination* as follows:

"The act of constructive intellect in grouping the materials of knowledge or thought into new, original and rational systems; the constructive or creative faculty; embracing poetic, artistic, philosophic, scientific and ethical imagination.

"The picturing power of the mind; the formation of mental images, pictures, or mental representation of objects or ideas, particularly of objects of sense perception and of mathematical reasoning! also the reproduction and combination, usually with more or less irrational or abnormal modification, of the images or ideas of memory or recalled facts of experience."

Imagination has been called the creative power of the soul, but this is somewhat abstract and goes more deeply into the meaning than is necessary from the

5

viewpoint of a student of this course who wishes to use the course only as a means of attaining material or monetary advantages in life.

If you have mastered and thoroughly understood the preceding lessons of this Reading Course you know that the materials out of which you built your *definite chief aim* were assembled and combined in your imagination. You also know that *self-confidence* and *initiative* and *leadership* must be created in your imagination before they can become a reality, for it is in the workshop of your imagination that you will put the principle of Auto-suggestion into operation in creating these necessary qualities.

This lesson on imagination might be called the "hub" of this Reading Course, because every lesson of the course leads to this lesson and makes use of the principle upon which it is based, just as all the telephone wires lead to the exchange office for their source of power. You will never have a *definite purpose* in life, you will never have *self-confidence,* you will never have *initiative* and *leadership* unless you first create these qualities in your *imagination* and see yourself in possession of them.

Just as the oak tree develops from the germ that lies in the acorn, and the bird develops from the germ that lies asleep in the egg, so will your material achievements grow out of the *organized* plans that you create in your *imagination.* First comes the thought; then organization of that thought into ideas and plans; then transformation of those plans into reality. The beginning, as you will observe, is in your *imagination.*

The imagination is both interpretative and creative in nature. It can examine facts, concepts and ideas, and it can create new combinations and plans out of these.

Through its interpretative capacity the imagination has one power not generally attributed to it; namely, the power to register vibrations and thought waves that are put into motion from outside sources, just as the radio-receiving apparatus picks up the vibrations of sound. The principle through which this interpretative capacity of the imagination functions is called telepathy; the communication of thought from one mind to another, at long or short distances, without the aid of physical or mechanical appliances, in the manner explained in the Introductory Lesson of this course.

Telepathy is an important factor to a student who is preparing to make effective use of imagination, for the reason that this telepathic capacity of the imagination is constantly picking up thought waves and vibrations of every description. So-called "snap-judgment" and "hunches," which prompt one to form an opinion or decide upon a course of action that is not in harmony with logic and reason, are usually the result of stray thought waves that have registered in the imagination.

The recently developed radio apparatus has enabled us to understand that the elements of the ether are so sensitive and alive that all manner of sound waves are constantly flying here and there with lightning-like speed. You have only to understand the modern radio outfit to understand, also, the principle of telepathy. So well has this principle been established, through psychological research, that we have abundance of proof that two minds which are properly attuned and in harmony with each other may send and receive thought at long distances without the aid of mechanical apparatus of any sort. Rarely have two minds become so well attuned that unbroken chains of thought could be registered in this manner, but there is evidence sufficient to establish the fact that parts of organized thought have been picked up.

That you may understand how closely interwoven are the fifteen factors upon which this Reading Course is based, consider, for example, what happens when a salesman who lacks confidence in himself, and in his goods, walks in to see a prospective buyer. Whether the prospective buyer is conscious of it or not, his imagination immediately "senses" that lack of confidence in the salesman's mind. The salesman's own *thoughts* are actually undermining his efforts. This will explain, from another angle, why *self-confidence* is one of the most important factors entering into the great struggle for success.

The principle of telepathy and the law of attraction, through which like attracts like, explain many a failure. If the mind has a tendency to attract from the ether those thought vibrations which harmonize with the dominating thoughts of a given mind, you can easily understand why a negative mind that dwells upon failure and lacks the vitalizing force of self-confidence would not attract a positive mind that is dominated by thoughts of *success*.

Perhaps these explanations are somewhat abstract to the student who has not made any particular study of the functioning processes of the mind, but it seems necessary to inject them into this lesson as a means of enabling the student to understand and make practical use of the subject of this lesson. The imagination is too often regarded merely as an indefinite, untraceable, indescribable something that does nothing but create fiction. It is this popular disregard of the powers of the imagination that has made necessary these more or less abstract references to one of the most important subjects of this course. Not only is the subject of imagination an important factor in this course; but, it is one of the most interesting subjects, as you will observe when you begin to see how it affects all that you do toward the achievement of your *definite chief aim.*

You will see how important is the subject of *imagination* when you stop to realize that it is the only thing in the world over which you have absolute control. Others may deprive you of your material wealth and cheat you in a thousand ways, but no man can deprive you of the control and use of your *imagination.* Men may deal with you unfairly, as men often do; they may deprive you of your liberty, but *they cannot* take from you the privilege of using your *imagination* as you wish.

The most inspiring poem in all literature was written by Leigh Hunt, while he was a poverty-stricken prisoner in an English prison, where he had been unjustly confined because of his advanced views on politics. This poem is entitled Abou Ben Adhem, and it is here re-printed as a reminder that one of the great things a man may do, in his own imagination, is to forgive those who have dealt unjustly with him:

Abou Ben Adhem (may his tribe increase)
Awoke one night from a deep dream of peace,

THE MAN WHO
SLANDERS HIS
FELLOWMAN UN-
WITTINGLY UNCOV-
ERS THE REAL NA-
TURE OF HIS INNER
SELF.

And saw within the moonlight of his room,
Making it rich and like a lily in bloom,
An angel writing in a book of gold,
Exceeding peace had made Ben Adhem bold,
And to the presence in the room he said:
"What writest thou?"—the vision raised its head,
And, with a look made of all sweet accord,
Answered, "The names of those who love the Lord."
"And is mine one?" said Abou. "Nay, not so,"
Replied the angel,—Abou spoke more low,
But cheerily still; and said, "I pray thee, then,
Write me as one that loves his fellow men."
The angel wrote, and vanished. The next night
It came again, with a great wakening light,
And showed the names whom love of God had blessed,
And, lo! Ben Adhem's name led all the rest!

Civilization, itself, owes its existence to such men as Leigh Hunt, in whose fertile *imaginations* have been pictured the higher and nobler standards of human relationship. Abou Ben Adhem is a poem that will never die, thanks to this man who pictured in his *imagination* the hope of an ideal that is constructive.

The major trouble with this world today lies in our lack of understanding of the power of *imagination,* for if we understood this great power we could use it as a weapon with which to wipe out poverty and misery and injustice and persecution, and this could be done in a single generation. This is a rather broad statement, and no one understands better than the author of this course how useless such a statement would be if the principle upon which it is founded were not explained in terms of the most practical, workaday nature; therefore, let us proceed to describe what is meant.

To make this description understandable we must accept as a reality the principle of telepathy, through the operation of which every thought we release is registering itself in the minds of other people. We need devote no time to proving that telepathy is a reality, for the reason that this lesson on *imagination* cannot be of the slightest value to the student who has not sufficiently informed himself to understand and accept telepathy as an established principle. We will take it for granted that you are one who accepts and understands this principle.

You have often heard of "mob psychology," which is nothing more nor less than some strong, dominating idea that has been created in the mind of one or more persons and registers itself in the minds of other persons, through the principle of telepathy. So strong is the power of mob psychology that two men fighting in the street will often start a "free-for-all" fight in which by-standers will engage each other in battle without even knowing what they are fighting about, or with whom they are fighting.

On armistice day, 1918, we had evidence in abundance to prove the reality of the principle of telepathy, on a scale such as the world had never before witnessed. I remember, distinctly, the impression made on my mind on that eventful day. So strong was this impression that it awakened me at about 3:00 o'clock in the morning, just as effectively as if someone had aroused me by physical force. As I sat up in bed I knew that something out of the ordinary had happened, and so strange and impelling was the effect of this experience that I got up, dressed myself and went out in the streets of Chicago, where I was met by thousands of others who had felt the touch of the same influence. Everyone was asking: *"What has happened?"*

What had happened was this:

Millions of men had received instructions to cease fighting, and their combined joy set into motion a thought wave that swept the entire world and made itself felt in every normal mind that was capable of registering this thought wave. Perhaps never in the history of the world had so many millions of people *thought of the same thing, in the same manner, at the same time.* For once in the history of the world *everybody* felt something in common, and the effect of this harmonized thought was the world-wide "mob psychology" that we witnessed on armistice day. In connection with this statement it will be helpful if you recall what was said about the method of creating a "Master Mind," through the harmony of thought of two or more persons, in the Introductory Lesson of this course.

We will bring the application of this principle a little nearer home by showing how it may be made to make or break the harmonious working relationship of a business or industry. You may not have satisfied yourself that it was the harmony of thought of millions of soldiers that registered in the minds of the people of the world and caused the "mob" psychological condition that was everywhere in evidence on armistice day, but you will need no proof that a disgruntled person always disturbs everyone with whom he comes in contact. It is a well established fact that one such person in a place of employment will disrupt the entire organization. The time is almost at hand when neither the workers nor the employers will tolerate the typical "grouch" inside of a place of employment, for the reason that his state of mind registers itself in the minds of those about him, resulting in distrust, suspicion and lack of harmony. The time is near at hand when the workers in a place of employment will no more tolerate one of their own rank and file who is a typical "grouch" than they would a poisonous snake.

Apply the principle in another way: Place among a group of workers one person whose personality is of the positive, optimistic type, and who makes it his business to sow the seeds of harmony around the place where he works, and his influence will reflect itself in every person who works with him.

If every business is "the extended shadow of one man" as Emerson stated, then it behooves that one man to reflect a shadow of confidence and good cheer and optimism and harmony, that these qualities may, in turn, reflect themselves in all who are connected with the business.

In passing to the next step in our application of the power of *imagination* in the attainment of success we will cite some of the most recent and modern examples of its use in the accumulation of material wealth and the perfection of some of the leading inventions of the world.

In approaching this next step it should be borne in mind that "there is nothing new under the sun." Life on this earth may be likened to a great kaleidoscope before which the scenes and facts and material substances are ever shifting and changing, and all any man can do is to take these facts and substances and re-arrange them in new combinations.

The process through which this is done is called *imagination*.

We have stated that the *imagination* is both interpretative and creative in its nature. It can receive impressions or ideas and out of these it can form new combinations.

As our first illustration of the power of *imagination* in modern business achievement, we will take the case of Clarence Saunders, who organized the Piggly-Wiggly system of self-help grocery stores.

Saunders was a grocery clerk in a small southern retail store. One day he was standing in a line, with a tin tray in his hands, waiting his turn to secure food in a cafeteria. He had never earned more than $20.00 a week before that time, and no one had ever noticed anything about him that indicated unusual ability, but something took place in his mind, as he stood in that line of waiting people, that put his *imagination* to work. With the aid of his *imagination* he lifted that "self-help" idea out of the cafeteria in which he found it (not creating anything new, merely shifting an old idea into a new use) and set it down in a grocery store. In an instant the Piggly-Wiggly chain-store grocery plan had been created and Clarence Saunders the twenty-dollar-a-week grocery clerk rapidly became the million-dollar chain-store groceryman of America.

Where, in that transaction, do you see the slightest indication of a performance that you could not duplicate?

I T will make a big dif-

ference to you whether

you are a person with a

message or a person with

a grievance.

Analyze this transaction and measure it by the previous lessons of this course and you will see that Clarence Saunders created a very *definite purpose.* He supported this purpose with sufficient *self-confidence* to cause him to take the *initiative* to transform it into reality. His *imagination* was the workshop in which these three factors, *definite purpose, self-confidence* and *initiative* were brought together and made to supply the momentum for the first step in the organization of the Piggly-Wiggly plan.

Thus are great ideas changed into realities.

When Thomas A. Edison invented the incandescent electric light bulb he merely brought together two old, well known principles and associated them in a new combination. Mr. Edison and practically all others who were informed on the subject of electricity, knew that a light could be produced by heating a small wire with electricity, but the difficult problem was to do this without burning the wire in two. In his experimental research Mr. Edison tried out every conceivable sort of wire, hoping to find some substance that would withstand the tremendous heat to which it had to be subjected before a light could be produced.

His invention was half completed, but it was of no practical value until he could find the missing link that would supply the other half. After thousands of tests and much combining of old ideas in his *imagination,* Edison finally found this missing link. In his study of physics he had learned, as all other students of this subject learn, that there can be no combustion without the presence of oxygen. He of course knew that the difficulty with his electric light apparatus was the lack of a method through which to control the heat.

When it occurred to him that there could be *no* combustion where there was *no* oxygen he placed the little wire of his electric light apparatus inside of a glass globe, shut out *all* the oxygen, and lo! the mighty incandescent light was a reality.

When the sun goes down tonight you step to the wall, press a button and bring it back again, a performance that would have mystified the people of a few generations ago, and yet there is no mystery back of your act. Thanks to the use of Edison's *imagination,* you have simply brought together two principles both of which were in existence since the beginning of time.

No one who knew him intimately ever accredited Andrew Carnegie with unusual ability, or the power of genius, except in one respect, and that was his ability to select men who *could* and *would* co-operate in a spirit of harmony, in carrying out his wishes. But what additional ability did he need in the accumulation of his millions of dollars?

Any man who understands the principle of *organized effort,* as Carnegie understood it, and knows enough about men to be able to select just those types that are needed in the performance of a given task, could duplicate all that Carnegie accomplished.

Carnegie was a man of *imagination.* He first created a *definite purpose* and then surrounded himself with men who had the training and the vision and the capacity necessary for the transformation of that purpose into reality. Carnegie did not always create his own plans for the attainment of his *definite purpose.* He made it *his* business to know what he wanted, then found the men who could create plans through which to procure it. And that was not only *imagination,* it was genius of the highest order.

But it should be made clear that men of Mr. Carnegie's type are not the only ones who can make profitable use of *imagination.* This great power is as available to the beginner in business as it is to the man who has "arrived."

One morning Charles M. Schwab's private car was backed on the side-track at his Bethlehem Steel plant. As he alighted from his car he was met by a young man stenographer who announced that he had come to make sure that any letters or telegrams Mr. Schwab might wish to write would be taken care of promptly. No one told this young man to be on hand, but he had enough *imagination* to see that his being there would not hurt his chances of advancement. From that day on, this young man was "marked" for promotion. Mr. Schwab singled him out for promotion because he had done that which any of the dozen or so other stenographers in the employ of the Bethlehem Steel Company might have done, but didn't. Today this same man is the president of one of the largest drug concerns in the world and has all of this world's goods and wares that he wants and much more than he needs.

A few years ago I received a letter from a young man who had just finished Business College, and who wanted to secure employment in my office. With his letter he sent a crisp ten-dollar bill that had never been folded. The letter read as follows:

"I have just finished a commercial course in a first-class business college and I want a position in your office because I realize how much it would be worth to a young man, just starting out on his business career, to have the privilege of working under the direction of a man like you.

"If the enclosed ten-dollar bill is sufficient to pay for the time you would spend in giving me my first week's instructions I want you to accept it. I will work the first month without pay and you may set my wages after that at whatever I prove to be worth.

"I want this job more than I ever wanted anything in my life and I am willing to make any reasonable sacrifice to get it.   Very cordially,"

This young man got his chance in my office. His *imagination* gained for him the opportunity that he wanted, and before his first month had expired the president of a life insurance company who heard of this incident offered the young man a private secretaryship at a substantial salary. He is today an official of one of the largest life insurance companies in the world.

Some years ago a young man wrote to Thomas A. Edison for a position. For some reason Mr. Edison did not reply. By no means discouraged on this account the young man made up his mind that he would not only get a reply from Mr. Edison, but what was more important still, he would actually secure the position he sought. He lived a long distance from West Orange, New Jersey, where the Edison industries are located, and he did not have the money with which to pay his railroad fare. But *he did have imagination*. He went to West Orange in a freight car, got his interview, told his story in person and got the job he sought.

Today this same man lives in Bradentown, Florida.

He has retired from active business, having made all the money he needs. His name, in case you wish to confirm my statements, is Edwin C. Barnes.

By using his *imagination,* Mr. Barnes saw the advantage of close association with a man like Thomas A. Edison. He saw that such an association would give him the opportunity to study Mr. Edison, and at the same time it would bring him in contact with Mr. Edison's friends, who are among the most influential people of the world.

These are but a few cases in connection with which I have personally observed how men have climbed to high places in the world and accumulated wealth in abundance by making practical use of their *imagination.*

Theodore Roosevelt engraved his name on the tablets of time by one single act during his tenure of office as President of the United States, and after all else that he did while in that office will have been forgotten this one transaction will record him in history as a man of *imagination.*

He started the steam shovels to work on the Panama Canal.

Every President, from Washington on up to Roosevelt, could have started the canal and it would have been completed, but it seemed such a colossal undertaking that it required not only *imagination* but daring courage as well. Roosevelt had both, and the people of the United States have the canal.

At the age of forty—the age at which the average man begins to think he is too old to start anything new —James J. Hill was still sitting at the telegraph key, at a salary of $30.00 per month. He had no capital.

THE reason most people do not like to hear the story of your troubles is that they have a big flock of their own.

He had no influential friends with capital, but he did have that which is more powerful than either—*imagination*.

In his mind's eye he saw a great railway system that would penetrate the undeveloped northwest and unite the Atlantic and Pacific oceans. So vivid was his *imagination* that he made others see the advantages of such a railway system, and from there on the story is familiar enough to every school-boy. I would emphasize the part of the story that most people never mention—that Hill's Great Northern Railway system became a reality in his own *imagination* first. The railroad was built with steel rails and wooden cross ties, just as other railroads are built, and these things were paid for with capital that was secured in very much the same manner that capital for all railroads is secured, but if you want the real story of James J. Hill's success you must go back to that little country railway station where he worked at $30.00 a month and there pick up the little threads that he wove into a mighty railroad, with materials no more visible than the thoughts which he organized in his *imagination*.

What a mighty power is *imagination*, the workshop of the soul, in which *thoughts* are woven into railroads and skyscrapers and mills and factories and all manner of material wealth.

"I hold it true that thoughts are things;
  They're endowed with bodies and breath and wings;
  And that we send them forth to fill
  The world with good results or ill.
  That which we call our secret thought

Speeds forth to earth's remotest spot,
Leaving its blessings or its woes,
Like tracks behind it as it goes.
We build our future, thought by thought,
For good or ill, yet know it not,
Yet so the universe was wrought.
Thought is another name for fate;
Choose, then, thy destiny and wait,
For love brings love and hate brings hate."

If your *imagination* is the mirror of your soul, then you have a perfect right to stand before that mirror and see yourself as you wish to be. You have the right to see reflected in that magic mirror the mansion you intend to own, the factory you intend to manage, the bank of which you intend to be president, the station in life you intend to occupy. *Your imagination* belongs to you! Use it! The more you use it the more efficiently it will serve you.

At the east end of the great Brooklyn Bridge, in New York City, an old man conducts a cobbler shop. When the engineers began driving stakes and marking the foundation place for that great steel structure this man shook his head and said *"It can't be done!"*

Now he looks out from his dingy little shoe-repair shop, shakes his head and asks himself: *"How did they do it?"*

He saw the bridge grow before his very eyes and still he lacks the *imagination* to analyze that which he saw. The engineer who planned the bridge saw it a reality long before a single shovel of dirt had been removed for the foundation stones. The bridge became a reality in his *imagination* because he had trained that *imagination* to weave new combinations out of old ideas.

Through recent experiments in the department of electricity one of our great educational institutions of America has discovered how to put flowers to sleep and wake them up again, with electric "sunlight." This discovery makes possible the growth of vegetables and flowers without the aid of sunshine. In a few more years the city dweller will be raising a crop of vegetables on his back porch, with the aid of a few boxes of dirt and a few electric lights, with some new vegetable maturing every month of the year.

This new discovery, plus a little *imagination*, plus Luther Burbank's discoveries in the field of horticulture, and lo! the city dweller will not only grow vegetables all the year around, within the confines of his back porch, but he will grow bigger vegetables than any which the modern gardener grows in the open sunlight.

In one of the cities on the coast of California all of the land that was suitable for building lots had been developed and put into use. On one side of the city there were some steep hills that could not be used for building purposes, and on the other side the land was unsuitable for buildings because it was so low that the back-water covered it once a day.

A man of *imagination* came to this city. Men of *imagination* usually have keen minds, and this man was no exception. The first day of his arrival he saw the possibilities for making money out of real estate. He secured an option on those hills that were unsuitable for use because of their steepness. He also secured an option on the ground that was unsuitable for use because of the back-water that covered it daily. He secured these options at a very low price because the ground was supposed to be without substantial value.

With the use of a few tons of explosives he turned those steep hills into loose dirt. With the aid of a few tractors and some road scrapers he leveled the ground down and turned it into beautiful building lots, and with the aid of a few mules and carts he dumped the surplus dirt on the low ground and raised it above the water level, thereby turning it into beautiful building lots.

He made a substantial fortune, *for what?*

For removing some dirt from where it was not needed to where it was needed! *For mixing some useless dirt with imagination!*

The people of that little city gave this man credit for being a genius; and he was—the same sort of genius that any one of them could have been had he used his *imagination* as this man used his.

In the field of chemistry it is possible to mix two or more chemical ingredients in such proportions that the mere act of mixing gives each of the ingredients a tremendous amount of energy that it did not possess. It is also possible to mix certain chemical ingredients in such proportions that *all the ingredients of the combination take on an entirely different nature,* as in the case of H_2O, which is a mixture of two parts hydrogen and one part oxygen, creating water.

Chemistry is not the only field in which a combination of various physical materials can be so assembled that each takes on a greater value, or the result is a product entirely foreign in nature to that of its component parts. The man who blew up those useless hills of dirt and stone and removed the surplus from where it was not needed over to the low-land, where it was needed, gave that dirt and stone a value that it did not have before.

A ton of pig-iron is worth but little. Add to that pig-iron carbon, silicon, manganese, sulphur and phosphorus, in the right proportions, and you have transformed it into steel, which is of much greater value. Add still other substances, in the right proportion, including some skilled labor, and that same ton of steel is transformed into watch-springs worth a small fortune. But, in all these transformation processes the one ingredient that is worth most is the one that has no material form—*imagination!*

Here lie great piles of loose brick, lumber, nails and glass. In its present form it is worse than useless for it is a nuisance and an eye-sore. But mix it with the architect's *imagination* and add some skilled labor and lo! it becomes a beautiful mansion worth a king's ransom.

On one of the great highways between New York and Philadelphia stood an old ramshackle, time-worn barn, worth less than fifty dollars. With the aid of a little lumber and some cement, plus *imagination,* this old barn has been turned into a beautiful automobile supply station that earns a small fortune for the man who supplied the *imagination.*

Across the street from my office is a little print-shop that earns coffee and rolls for its owner and his helper, but no more. Less than a dozen blocks away stands one of the most modern printing plants in the world, whose owner spends most of his time traveling and has far more wealth than he will ever use. Twenty-two

I KNOW I am here. I know I had nothing to do with my coming, and I shall have but little, if anything, to do with my going, therefore I will not worry because worries are of no avail.

years ago those two printers were in business together.

The one who owns the big print-shop had the good judgment to ally himself with a man who mixed *imagination* with printing. This man of *imagination* is a writer of advertisements and he keeps the printing plant with which he is associated supplied with more business than it can handle by analyzing its clients' business, creating attractive advertising features and supplying the necessary printed material with which to make these features of service. This plant receives top-notch prices for its printing because the *imagination* mixed with that printing produces a product that most printers cannot supply.

In the city of Chicago the level of a certain boulevard was raised, which spoiled a row of beautiful residences because the side-walk was raised to the level of the second story windows. While the property owners were bemoaning their ill-fortune a man of *imagination* came along, purchased the property for a "song," converted the second stories into business property, and now enjoys a handsome income from his rentals.

As you read these lines please keep in mind all that was stated in the beginning of this lesson; especially the fact that the greatest and most profitable thing you can do with your *imagination* is the act of rearranging old ideas in new combinations.

If you properly use your imagination it will help you convert your failures and mistakes into assets of priceless value; it will lead you to discovery of a truth known only to those who use their *imagination;* namely, that the greatest reverses and misfortunes of life often open the door to golden opportunities.

One of the finest and most highly paid engravers in the United States was formerly a mail-carrier. One day he was fortunate enough to be on a street car that met with an accident and had one of his legs cut off. The street railway company paid him $5,000.00 for his leg. With this money he paid his way through school and became an engraver. The product of his hands, plus his *imagination*, is worth much more than he could earn with his legs, as a mail-carrier. He discovered that he had *imagination* when it became necessary to re-direct his efforts, as a result of the street car accident.

You will never know what is your capacity for achievement until you learn how to mix your efforts with *imagination*. The products of your hands, minus *imagination*, will yield you but a small return, but those selfsame hands, when properly guided by *imagination*, can be made to earn you all the material wealth you can use.

There are two ways in which you can profit by *imagination*. You can develop this faculty in your own mind, or you can ally yourself with those who have already developed it. Andrew Carnegie did both. He not only made use of his own fertile *imagination*, but he gathered around him a group of other men who also possessed this essential quality, for his *definite* purpose in life called for specialists whose *imagination* ran in numerous directions. In that group of men that constituted Mr. Carnegie's "master mind" were men whose *imaginations* were confined to the field of chemistry. He had other men in the group whose *imaginations* were confined to finances. He had still others whose *imaginations* were confined to salesmanship, one of whom was Charles M. Schwab, who is said to have been the most able salesman on Mr. Carnegie's staff.

If you feel that your own *imagination* is inadequate you should form an alliance with someone whose *imagination* is sufficiently developed to supply your deficiency. There are various forms of alliance. For example, there is the alliance of marriage and the alliance of a business partnership and the alliance of friendship and the alliance of employer and employee. Not all men have the capacity to serve their own best interests as employers, and those who haven't this capacity may profit by allying themselves with men of *imagination* who have such capacity.

It is said that Mr. Carnegie made more millionaires of his employees than any other employer in the steel business. Among these was Charles M. Schwab, who displayed evidence of the soundest sort of *imagination* by his good judgment in allying himself with Mr. Carnegie. It is no disgrace to serve in the capacity of employee. To the contrary, it often proves to be the most profitable side of an alliance since not all men are fitted to assume the responsibility of directing other men.

Perhaps there is no field of endeavor in which *imagination* plays such an important part as it does in salesmanship. The master salesman sees the merits of the goods he sells or the service he is rendering, in his own *imagination,* and if he fails to do so he will not make the sale.

A few years ago a sale was made which is said to have been the most far-reaching and important sale of its kind ever made. The object of the sale was not merchandise, but the freedom of a man who was confined in the Ohio penitentiary and the development of a prison reform system that promises a sweeping change in the method of dealing with unfortunate men and women who have become entangled in the meshes of the law.

That you may observe just how *imagination* plays the leading part in salesmanship I will analyze this sale for you, with due apologies for personal references, which cannot be avoided without destroying much of the value of the illustration.

A few years ago I was invited to speak before the inmates of the Ohio penitentiary. When I stepped upon the platform I saw in the audience before me a man whom I had known as a successful business man, more than ten years previously. That man was B——, whose pardon I later secured, and the story of whose release has been spread upon the front page of practically every newspaper in the United States. Perhaps you will recall it.

After I had completed my address I interviewed Mr. B—— and found out that he had been sentenced for forgery, for a period of twenty years. After he had told me his story I said:

"I will have you out of here in less than sixty days!"

With a forced smile he replied: "I admire your spirit but question your judgment. Why, do you know that at least twenty influential men have tried every means at their command to get me released, without success? *It can't be done!*"

I suppose it was that last remark—*It can't be done* —that challenged me to show him that it could be done. I returned to New York City and requested my wife to pack her trunks and get ready for an indefinite stay in the city of Columbus, where the Ohio penitentiary is located.

I had a *definite purpose* in mind! That purpose was to get B—— out of the Ohio penitentiary. Not only did I have in mind securing his release, but I intended to do it in such a way that his release would erase from his breast the scarlet letter of "convict" and at the same time reflect credit upon all who helped to bring about his release.

Not once did I doubt that I would bring about his release, for no salesman can make a sale if he doubts that he can do it. My wife and I returned to Columbus and took up permanent headquarters.

The next day I called on the governor of Ohio and stated the object of my visit in about these words:

"Governor: I have come to ask you to release B—— from the Ohio penitentiary. I have sound reason for asking his release and I hope you will give him his freedom at once, but I have come prepared to stay until he is released, no matter how long that may be.

"During his imprisonment B—— has inaugurated a system of correspondence instruction in the Ohio penitentiary, as you of course know. He has influenced 1729 of the 2518 prisoners of the Ohio penitentiary to take up courses of instruction. He has managed to beg sufficient textbooks and lesson materials with which to keep these men at work on their lessons, and has done this without a penny of expense to the state of Ohio. The warden and the chaplain of the penitentiary tell me that he has carefully observed the prison rules. Surely a man who can influence 1729 men to turn

IF you have been wise
and successful I con-
gratulate you; unless you
are unable to forget how
successful you have been,
then I pity you.

their efforts toward self-betterment cannot be a very bad sort of fellow.

"I have come to ask you to release B—— because I wish to place him at the head of a prison school that will give the 160,000 inmates of the other penitentiaries of the United States a chance to profit by his influence. I am prepared to assume full responsibility for his conduct after his release.

"That is my case, but, before you give me your answer, I want you to know that I am not unmindful of the fact that your enemies will probably criticize you if you release him; in fact if you release him it may cost you many votes if you run for office again."

With his fist clinched and his broad jaw set firmly Governor Vic Donahey of Ohio said:

"If that is what you want with B—— I will release him if it costs me five thousand votes. However, before I sign the pardon I want you to see the Clemency Board and secure its favorable recommendation. I want you also to secure the favorable recommendation of the warden and the chaplain of the Ohio penitentiary. You know a governor is amenable to the Court of Public Opinion, and these gentlemen are the representatives of that Court."

The sale had been made! and the whole transaction had required less than five minutes.

The next day I returned to the governor's office, accompanied by the chaplain of the Ohio penitentiary, and notified the governor that the Clemency Board, the Warden and the Chaplain all joined in recommending the release. Three days later the pardon was signed and B—— walked through the big iron gates, a free man.

I have cited the details to show you that there was nothing difficult about the transaction. The groundwork for the release had all been prepared before I came upon the scene. B—— had done that, by his good conduct and the service he had rendered those 1729 prisoners. When he created the world's first prison correspondence school system he created the key that unlocked the prison doors for himself.

Why, then, had the others who asked for his release failed to secure it?

They failed because they used no *imagination!*

Perhaps they asked the governor for B——'s release on the ground that his parents were prominent people, or on the ground that he was a college graduate and not a bad sort of fellow. *They failed to supply the governor of Ohio with a sufficient motive to justify him in granting a pardon,* for had this not been so he would undoubtedly have released B—— long before I came upon the scene and asked for his release.

Before I went to see the governor I went over all the facts and in my own *imagination* I saw myself in the governor's place and made up my mind what sort of a presentation would appeal most strongly to me if I were in reality in his place.

When I asked for B——'s release I did so in the name of the 160,000 unfortunate men and women inmates of the prisons of the United States who would enjoy the benefits of the correspondence school system that he had created. I said nothing about his prominent parents. I said nothing about my friendship with him during former years. I said nothing about his being a deserving fellow. All these matters might have been used as sound reasons for his release, but they seemed insignificant when compared with the bigger and sounder reason that his release would be of help to 160,000 other people who would feel the influence of his correspondence school system after his release.

When the governor of Ohio came to a decision I doubt not that B—— was of secondary importance as far as his decision was concerned. The governor no doubt saw a possible benefit, not to B—— alone, but to 160,000 other men and women who needed the influence that B—— could supply, if released.

And that was imagination!

It was also salesmanship! In speaking of the incident after it was over, one of the men who had worked diligently for more than a year in trying to secure B——'s freedom, asked:

"How did you do it?"

And I replied: "It was the easiest task I ever performed, because most of the work had been done before I took hold of it. In fact I didn't do it— B—— did it himself."

This man looked at me in bewilderment. He did not see that which I am here trying to make clear; namely, that practically all difficult tasks are easily performed if one approaches them from the right angle. There were two important factors entering B——'s release. The first was the fact that he had supplied the material for a good case before I took it in charge; and the second was the fact that before I called on the governor of Ohio I so completely convinced myself that I had a right to ask for B——'s release that I had no difficulty in presenting my case effectively.

Go back to what was stated in the beginning of this lesson, on the subject of telepathy, and apply it to this case. The governor could tell, long before I had stated my mission, that *I knew I had a good case*. If my brain did not telegraph this thought to his brain, then the look of self-confidence in my eyes and the positive tone of my voice made obvious my belief in the merits of my case.

Again I apologize for these personal references with the explanation that I have used them only because the whole of America was familiar with the B—— case that I have described. I disclaim all credit for the small part I played in the case, for I did nothing except use my *imagination* as an assembly room in which to piece together the factors out of which the sale was made. I did nothing except that which any salesman of *imagination* could have done.

It requires considerable courage to prompt one to use the personal pronoun as freely as it has been used in relating the facts connected with this case, but justification lies in the value of application of the principle of *imagination* to a case with which nearly everybody is familiar.

I cannot recall an incident in my entire life in connection with which the soundness of the fifteen factors that enter into this Reading Course was more clearly manifested than it was in securing the release of B——.

It is but another link in a long chain of evidence that proves to my entire satisfaction the power of *imagination* as a factor in salesmanship. There are endless millions of approaches to every problem, but there is *only one* best approach. Find this one best approach and your problem is easily solved. No matter how much merit your goods may have, there are millions of *wrong* ways in which to offer them. Your *imagination* will assist you in finding the *right* way.

In your search for the *right* way in which to offer your merchandise or your services, remember this peculiar trait of mankind:

Men will grant favors that you request for the benefit of a third person when they would not grant them if requested for your benefit.

Compare this statement with the fact that I asked the governor of Ohio to release B——, not as a favor to me, and not as a favor to B——, but, for the benefit of 160,000 unfortunate inmates of the prisons of America.

Salesmen of *imagination* always offer their wares in such terminology that the advantages of those wares to the prospective purchaser are obvious. It is seldom that any man makes a purchase of merchandise or renders another a favor just to accommodate the salesman. It is a prominent trait of human nature that prompts us all to do that which advances our own interests. This is a cold, indisputable fact, claims of the idealist to the contrary notwithstanding.

To be perfectly plain, *men are selfish!*

To understand the truth is to understand how to present your case, whether you are asking for the release of a man from prison or offering for sale some commodity. In your own *imagination* so plan your presentation of your case that the strongest and most impelling advantages to the buyer are made plain.

This is *imagination!*

I NEVER see a person trying to disclose the scarlet letter on another's breast that I do not wonder if he doesn't carry some mark of disgrace which would have ruined him had he been overtaken by justice.

A farmer moved to the city, taking with him his well trained shepherd dog. He soon found that the dog was out of place in the city, so he decided to "get rid of him." (Note the words in quotation.) Taking the dog with him he went out into the country and rapped on the door of a farm-house. A man came hobbling to the door, on crutches. The man with the dog greeted the man in the house in these words:

"You wouldn't care to buy a fine shepherd dog, that I wish to get rid of, would you?"

The man on crutches replied, *"No!"* and closed the door.

The man with the dog called at half a dozen other farm-houses, asking the same question, and received the same answer. He made up his mind that no one wanted the dog and returned to the city. That evening he was telling of his misfortune, to a man of *imagination*. The man heard how the owner of the dog had tried in vain to "get rid of him."

"Let me dispose of the dog for you," said the man of *imagination*. The owner was willing. The next morning the man of *imagination* took the dog out into the country and stopped at the first farm-house at which the owner of the dog had called the day before. The same old man hobbled out on crutches and answered the knock at the door.

The man of *imagination* greeted him in this fashion:

"I see you are all crippled with rheumatism. What you need is a fine dog to run errands for you. I have a dog here that has been trained to bring home the cows, drive away wild animals, herd the sheep and perform other useful services. You may have this dog for a hundred dollars."

"All right," said the crippled man, "I'll take him!"
That, too, was *imagination!*

No one wants a dog that someone else wants to "get rid of," but most anyone would like to own a dog that would herd sheep and bring home the cows and perform other useful services.

The dog was the same one that the crippled buyer had refused the day before, but the man who sold the dog was not the man who had tried to "get rid of him." If you use your *imagination* you will know that no one wants anything that someone else is trying to "get rid of."

Remember that which was said about the Law of Attraction through the operation of which "like attracts like." If you look and act the part of a failure you will attract nothing but failures.

Whatever your life-work may be, it calls for the use of *imagination*.

Niagara Falls was nothing but a great mass of roaring water until a man of *imagination* harnessed it and converted the wasted energy into electric current that now turns the wheels of industry. Before this man of *imagination* came along millions of people had seen and heard those roaring falls, but lacked the *imagination* to harness them.

The first Rotary Club of the world was born in the fertile *imagination* of Paul Harris, of Chicago, who saw in this child of his brain an effective means of cultivating prospective clients and the extension of his law practice. The ethics of the legal profession forbid advertising in the usual way, but Paul Harris' *imagination* found a way to extend his law practice without advertising in the usual way.

If the winds of Fortune are temporarily blowing against you, remember that you can harness them and make them carry you toward your *definite purpose,* through the use of your *imagination.* A kite rises against the wind—not with it!

Dr. Frank Crane was a struggling "third-rate" preacher until the starvation wages of the clergy forced him to use his *imagination.* Now he earns upward of a hundred thousand dollars a year for an hour's work a day, writing essays.

Bud Fisher once worked for a mere pittance, but he now earns seventy-five thousand dollars a year by making folks grin, with his Mutt and Jeff comic strip. No art goes into his drawings, therefore he must be selling his *imagination.*

Woolworth was a poorly paid clerk in a retail store —poorly paid, perhaps, because he had not yet found out that he had *imagination.* Before he died he built the tallest office building in the world and girdled the United States with Five and Ten Cent Stores, through the use of his *imagination.*

You will observe, by analyzing these illustrations, that a close study of human nature played an important part in the achievements mentioned. To make profitable use of your *imagination* you must make it give you a keen insight into the motives that cause men to do or refrain from doing a given act. If your *imagination* leads you to understand how quickly people grant your requests when those requests appeal to their self-interest, you can have practically anything you go after.

I saw my wife make a very clever sale to our baby not long ago. The baby was pounding the top of our mahogany library table with a spoon. When my wife reached for the spoon the baby refused to give it up, but being a woman of *imagination* she offered the baby a nice stick of red candy; he dropped the spoon immediately and centered his attention on the more desirable object.

That was *imagination!* It was also salesmanship. She won her point without using force.

I was riding in an automobile with a friend who was driving beyond the speed limit. An officer rode up on a motorcycle and told my friend he was under arrest for speeding. The friend smiled pleasantly at the officer and said: "I'm sorry to have brought you out in all this rain, but I wanted to make the ten o'clock train with my friend here, and I was hitting it up around thirty-five miles an hour."

"No, you were only going twenty-eight miles an hour," replied the officer, "and as long as you are so nice about it I will let you off this time if you will watch yourself hereafter."

And that, too, was *imagination!* Even a traffic cop will listen to reason when approached in the right manner, but woe unto the motorist who tries to bully the cop into believing his speedometer was not registering properly.

There is one form of *imagination* against which I would caution you. It is the brand which prompts some people to *imagine* that they can get something for nothing, or that they can force themselves ahead in the world without observing the rights of others. There are more than 160,000 prisoners in the penal institutions of the United States, practically every one of whom is in prison because he *imagined* he could play the game of life without observing the rights of his fellow men.

There is a man in the Ohio penitentiary who has served more than thirty-five years of time for forgery, and the largest amount he ever got from his misapplication of *imagination* was twelve dollars.

There are a few people who direct their *imaginations* in the vain attempt to work out a way to show what happens when "an immovable body comes in contact with an irresistible force," but these types belong in the psychopathic hospitals.

There is also another form of misapplied *imagination;* namely, that of the young boy or girl who knows more about life than his or her "Dad." But this form is subject to modification with *time*. My own boys have taught me many things that my "Dad" tried, in vain, to teach me when I was their age.

Time and *imagination* (which is often but the product of time) teach us many things, but nothing of more importance than this:

That all men are much alike in many ways.

If you would know what your customer is thinking, Mr. Salesman, study yourself and find out what *you* would be thinking if you were in your customer's place.

Study yourself, find out what are the motives which actuate you in the performance of certain deeds and cause you to refrain from performing other deeds, and you will have gone far toward perfecting yourself in the accurate use of *imagination*.

The detective's biggest asset is *imagination*. The first question he asks, when called in to solve a crime is: *"What was the motive?"* If he can find out the

WE all like commen-
dation and many of
us like flattery, but it is a
debatable question as to
whether the indulgence
of these tendencies builds
character and strength
and individuality.

motive he can usually find the perpetrator of the crime.

A man who had lost a horse posted a reward of five dollars for its return. Several days later a boy who was supposed to have been "weak-minded" came leading the horse home and claimed the reward. The owner was curious to know how the boy found the horse. "How did you ever think where to look for the horse?" he asked, and the boy replied, "Well, I just thought where I would have gone if I had been a horse and went there, and he had." Not so bad for a "weak-minded" fellow. Some who are not accused of being weak-minded go all the way through life without displaying as much evidence of *imagination* as did this boy.

If you want to know what the other fellow will do, use your *imagination,* put yourself in his place and find out what you would have done. That's *imagination.*

Every person should be somewhat of a dreamer. Every business needs the dreamer. Every industry and every profession needs him. But, the dreamer must be, also, a doer; or else he must form an alliance with someone who can and does translate dreams into reality.

The greatest nation upon the face of this earth was conceived, born and nurtured through the early days of its childhood, as the result of *imagination* in the minds of men who combined dreams with *action!*

Your mind is capable of creating many new and useful combinations of old ideas, but the most important thing it can create is a *definite chief aim* that will give you that which you most desire.

Your *definite chief aim* can be speedily translated

into reality after you have fashioned it in the cradle of your *imagination*. If you have faithfully followed the instructions set down for your guidance in Lesson Two you are now well on the road toward success, because you know what it is that you want, and you have a plan for getting that which you want.

The battle for the achievement of success is half won when one knows definitely what is wanted. The battle is all over except the "shouting" when one knows what is wanted and has made up his mind to get it, whatever the price may be.

The selection of a *definite chief aim* calls for the use of both *imagination* and decision! The power of decision grows with use. Prompt decision in forcing the *imagination* to create a *definite chief aim* renders more powerful the capacity to reach decisions in other matters.

Adversities and temporary defeat are generally blessings in disguise, for the reason that they force one to use both *imagination* and decision. This is why a man usually makes a better fight when his back is to the wall and he knows there is no retreat. He then reaches the decision to fight instead of running.

The *imagination* is never quite so active as it is when one faces some emergency calling for quick and definite decision and action.

In these moments of emergency men have reached decisions, built plans, used their *imagination* in such a manner that they became known as geniuses. Many a genius has been born out of the necessity for unusual stimulation of the *imagination,* as the result of some trying experience which forced quick thought and prompt decision.

It is a well known fact that the only manner in which an overpampered boy or girl may be made to become useful is by forcing him or her to become self-sustaining. This calls for the exercise of both *imagination* and decision, neither of which would be used except out of necessity.

The Reverend P. W. Welshimer is the pastor of a church in Canton, Ohio, where he has been located for nearly a quarter of a century. Ordinarily pastors do not remain at the head of one church for so great a length of time, and Reverend Welshimer would have been no exception to this rule if he had not mixed *imagination* with his pastoral duties.

Three years constitute the usual time that one pastor may remain in a given pastorate without wearing out his welcome.

The church of which Reverend Welshimer is the leader has a Sunday School of over 5,000 members— the largest membership enjoyed by any church in the United States.

No pastor could have remained at the head of one church for a quarter of a century, with the full consent of his followers, and have built up a Sunday School of this size, without employing the Laws of Initiative and Leadership, a Definite Chief Aim, Self-confidence and Imagination.

The author of this course made it his business to study the methods employed by Reverend Welshimer, and they are here described for the benefit of the students of this philosophy.

It is a well known fact that church factions, jealousy, etc., often lead to disagreements which make a change in leaders essential. Reverend Welshimer has steered around this common obstacle by a unique application of the Law of Imagination. When a new member comes into his church he immediately assigns a DEFINITE task to that member—one that suits the temperament, training and business qualifications of the individual, as nearly as possible—and, to use the minister's own words, he "keeps each member so busy pulling for the church that there is no time left for kicking or disagreeing with other members."

Not a bad policy for application in the field of business, or in any other field. The old saying that "idle hands are the devil's best tools" is more than a mere play upon words, for it is true.

Give any man something to do that he likes to do, and keep him busy doing it, and he will not be apt to degenerate into a disorganizing force. If any member of the Sunday School misses attendance twice in succession a committee from the church calls to find out the reason for the failure to attend. There is a "committee" job for practically every member of the church. In this way Reverend Welshimer delegates to the members, themselves, the responsibility of rounding up the delinquents and keeping them interested in church affairs. He is an organizer of the highest type. His efforts have attracted the attention of business men throughout the country, and times too numerous to be mentioned he has been offered positions, at fancy salaries, by banks, steel plants, business houses, etc., that recognized in him a real Leader.

In the basement of the church Reverend Welshimer operates a first-class printing plant where he publishes, weekly, a very creditable church paper that goes to all the members. The production and distribution of this paper is another source of employment which keeps the church members out of mischief, as practically all of them take some sort of an active interest in it. The paper is devoted exclusively to the affairs of the church as a whole, and those of the individual members. It is read by each member, line by line, because there is always a chance that each member's name may be mentioned in the news locals.

The church has a well trained choir and an orchestra that would be a credit to some of the largest theaters. Here Reverend Welshimer serves the double purpose of supplying entertainment and at the same time keeping the more "temperamental" members who are artists employed so they, also, remain out of mischief, incidentally giving them a chance to do that which they like best.

The late Dr. Harper, who was formerly president of the University of Chicago, was one of the most efficient college presidents of his time. He had a penchant for raising funds in large amounts. It was he who induced John D. Rockefeller to contribute millions of dollars to the support of the University of Chicago.

It may be helpful to the student of this philosophy to study Dr. Harper's technique, because he was a Leader of the highest order. Moreover, I have his own word for it that his leadership was never a matter of chance or accident, but always the result of carefully planned procedure.

The following incident will serve to show just how Dr. Harper made use of *imagination* in raising money in large sums:

He needed an extra million dollars for the construc-

WE cannot sow this-
tles and reap clover.
Nature simply does not
run things that way. She
goes by cause and effect.

tion of a new building. Taking inventory of the wealthy men of Chicago to whom he might turn for this large sum, he decided upon two men, each of whom was a millionaire, and both were bitter enemies.

One of these men was, at that time, the head of the Chicago Street Railway system. Choosing the noon hour, when the office force and this man's secretary, in particular, would be apt to be out at lunch, Dr. Harper nonchalantly strolled into the office, and, finding no one on guard at the outer door, walked into the office of his intended "victim," whom he surprised by his appearance unannounced.

"My name is Harper," said the doctor, "and I am president of the University of Chicago. Pardon my intrusion, but I found no one in the outer office (which was no mere accident) so I took the liberty of walking on in.

"I have thought of you and your street railway system many many times. You have built up a wonderful system, and I understand that you have made lots of money for your efforts. I never think of you, however, without its occurring to me that one of these days you will be passing out into the Great Unknown, and after you are gone there will be nothing left as a monument to your name, because others will take over your money, and money has a way of losing its identity very quickly, as soon as it changes hands.

"I have often thought of offering you the opportunity to perpetuate your name by permitting you to build a new Hall out on the University grounds, and naming it after you. I would have offered you this opportunity long ago had it not been for the fact that one of the members of our Board wishes the honor to go to Mr. X—— (the street car head's enemy). Personally, however, I have always favored you and I still favor you, and if I have your permission to do so I am going to try to swing the opposition over to you.

"I have not come to ask for any decision today, however, as I was just passing and thought it a good time to drop in and meet you. Think the matter over and if you wish to talk to me about it again, telephone me at your leisure.

"Good day, sir! I am happy to have had this opportunity of meeting you."

With this he bowed himself out without giving the head of the street car company a chance to say either yes or no. In fact the street car man had very little chance to do any talking. Dr. Harper did the talking. That was as he planned it to be. He went into the office merely to plant the seed, believing that it would germinate and spring into life in due time.

His belief was not without foundation. He had hardly returned to his office at the University when the telephone rang. The street car man was on the other end of the wire. He asked for an appointment with Dr. Harper, which was granted, and the two met in Dr. Harper's office the next morning, and the check for a million dollars was in Dr. Harper's hands an hour later.

Despite the fact that Dr. Harper was a small, rather insignificant-looking man it was said of him that "he had a way about him that enabled him to get everything he went after."

And as to this "way" that he was reputed to have had—what was it?

It was nothing more nor less than his understanding of the power of Imagination. Suppose he had gone to the office of the street car head and asked for an appointment. Sufficient time would have elapsed between the time he called and the time when he would have actually seen his man, to have enabled the latter to anticipate the reason for his call, and also to formulate a good, logical excuse for saying, "No!"

Suppose, again, he had opened his interview with the street car man something like this:

"The University is badly in need of funds and I have come to you to ask your help. You have made lots of money and you owe something to the community in which you have made it. (Which, perhaps, was true.) If you will give us a million dollars we will place your name on a new Hall that we wish to build."

What might have been the result?

In the first place, there would have been no motive suggested that was sufficiently appealing to sway the mind of the street car man. While it may have been true that he "owed something to the community from which he had made a fortune," he probably would not have admitted that fact. In the second place, he would have enjoyed the position of being on the offensive instead of the defensive side of the proposal.

But Dr. Harper, shrewd in the use of Imagination as he was, provided for just such contingencies by the way he stated his case. First, he placed the street car man on the defensive by informing him that it was not certain that he (Dr. Harper) could get the permission of his Board to accept the money and name the Hall after the street car man. In the second place, he intensified the desire of the street car man to have his name on that building because of the thought that his enemy and competitor might get the honor if it got away from him. Moreover (and this was no accident, either), Dr. Harper had made a powerful appeal to one of the most common of all human weaknesses by showing this street car man how to perpetuate his own name.

All of which required a practical application of the Law of Imagination.

Dr. Harper was a Master Salesman. When he asked men for money he always paved the way for success by planting in the mind of the man of whom he asked it a good sound reason why the money should be given; a reason which emphasized some advantage accruing to the man as the result of the gift. Often this would take on the form of a business advantage. Again it would take on the nature of an appeal to that part of man's nature which prompts him to wish to perpetuate his name so it will live after him. But, always, the request for money was carried out according to a plan that had been carefully thought out, embellished and smoothed down with the use of Imagination.

.   .   .   .

While the Law of Success philosophy was in the embryonic stage, long before it had been organized into a systematic course of instruction and reduced to textbooks, the author was lecturing on this philosophy in a small town in Illinois.

One of the members of the audience was a young life insurance salesman who had but recently taken up that line of work. After hearing what was said on the subject of Imagination he began to apply what he had heard to his own problem of selling life insurance. Something was said, during the lecture, about the value of allied effort, through which men may enjoy greater success by co-operative effort, through a working arrangement under which each "boosts" the interests of the other.

Taking this suggestion as his cue, the young man in question immediately formulated a plan whereby he gained the co-operation of a group of business men who were in no way connected with the insurance business.

Going to the leading grocer in his town he made arrangements with that grocer to give a thousand dollar insurance policy to every customer purchasing no less than fifty dollars' worth of groceries each month. He then made it a part of his business to inform people of this arrangement and brought in many new customers. The groceryman had a large neatly lettered card placed in his store, informing his customers of this offer of free insurance, thus helping himself by offering all his customers an inducement to do ALL their trading in the grocery line with him.

This young life insurance man then went to the leading gasoline filling station owner in the town and made arrangements with him to insure all customers who purchased all their gasoline, oil and other motor supplies from him.

Next he went to the leading restaurant in the town and made a similar arrangement with the owner. Incidentally, this alliance proved to be quite profitable to the restaurant man, who promptly began an advertis-

CHARLES CHAP-
LIN makes a mil-
lion dollars a year out of
a funny, shuffling walk
and a pair of baggy trou-
sers, because he does
"something different."
Take the hint and "indi-
vidualize" yourself with
some distinctive idea.

ing campaign in which he stated that his food was so pure, wholesome and good that all who ate at his place regularly would be apt to live much longer, therefore he would insure the life of each regular customer for $1,000.00.

The life insurance salesman then made arrangements with a local builder and real estate man to insure the life of each person buying property from him, for an amount sufficient to pay off the balance due on the property in case the purchaser died before payments were completed.

The young man in question is now the General Agent for one of the largest life insurance companies in the United States, with headquarters in one of the largest cities in Ohio, and his income now averages well above $25,000.00 a year.

The turning-point in his life came when he discovered how he might make practical use of the Law of Imagination.

There is no patent on his plan. It may be duplicated over and over again by other life insurance men who know the value of *imagination*. Just now, if I were engaged in selling life insurance, I think I should make use of this plan by allying myself with a group of automobile distributors in each of several cities, thus enabling them to sell more automobiles and at the same time providing for the sale of a large amount of life insurance, through their efforts.

.   .   .   .

Financial success is not difficult to achieve after one learns how to make practical use of creative imagination. Someone with sufficient *initiative* and *leadership,* and the necessary *imagination*, will duplicate the fortunes being made each year by the owners of Five and Ten Cent Stores, by developing a system of marketing the same sort of goods now sold in these stores, with the aid of vending machines. This will save a fortune in clerk hire, insure against theft, and cut down the overhead of store operation in many other ways. Such a system can be conducted just as successfully as food can be dispensed with the aid of automatic vending machines.

The seed of the idea has been here sown. It is yours for the taking!

Someone with an inventive turn of the mind is going to make a fortune and at the same time save thousands of lives each year, by perfecting an automatic railroad crossing "control" that will reduce the number of automobile accidents on crossings.

The system, when perfected, will work somewhat after this fashion: A hundred yards or so before reaching the railroad crossing the automobile will cross a platform somewhat on the order of a large scale platform used for weighing heavy objects, and the weight of the automobile will lower a gate and ring a gong. This will force the automobile to slow down. After the lapse of one minute the gate will again rise and the car may continue on its way. Meanwhile, there will have been plenty of time for observation of the track in both directions, to make sure that no trains are approaching.

Imagination, plus some mechanical skill, will give the motorist this much needed safe-guard, and make the man who perfects the system all the money he needs and much more besides.

Some inventor who understands the value of *imagination* and has a working knowledge of the radio principle, may make a fortune by perfecting a burglar alarm system that will signal police headquarters and at the same time switch on lights and ring a gong in the place about to be burglarized, with the aid of apparatus similar to that now used for broadcasting.

Any farmer with enough *imagination* to create a plan, plus the use of a list of all automobile licenses issued in his state, may easily work up a clientele of motorists who will come to his farm and purchase all the vegetables he can produce and all the chickens he can raise, thus saving him the expense of hauling his products to the city. By contracting with each motorist for the season the farmer may accurately estimate the amount of produce he should provide. The advantage to the motorist, accruing under the arrangement, is that he will be sure of direct-from-the-farm produce, at less cost than he could purchase it from local dealers.

The roadside gasoline filling station owner can make effective use of *imagination* by placing a lunch stand near his filling station, and then doing some attractive advertising along the road in each direction, calling attention to his "barbecue," "home-made sandwiches" or whatever else he may wish to specialize on. The lunch stand will cause the motorists to stop, and many of them will purchase gasoline before starting on their way again.

These are simple suggestions, involving no particular amount of complication in connection with their use, yet it is just such uses of *imagination* that bring financial success.

The Piggly-Wiggly self-help store plan, which made millions of dollars for its originator, was a very simple idea which anyone could have adopted, yet considerable *imagination* was required to put the idea to work in a practical sort of way.

The more simple and easily adapted to a need an idea is, the greater is its value, as no one is looking for ideas which are involved with great detail or in any manner complicated.

.　　.　　.　　.　　.　　.　　.

Imagination is the most important factor entering into the art of selling. The Master Salesman is always one who makes systematic use of *imagination*. The outstanding merchant relies upon *imagination* for the ideas which make his business excel.

Imagination may be used effectively in the sale of even the smallest articles of merchandise, such as ties, shirts, hosiery, etc. Let us proceed to examine just how this may be done.

I walked into one of the best known haberdasheries in the city of Philadelphia, for the purpose of purchasing some shirts and ties.

As I approached the tie counter a young man stepped forward and inquired:

"Is there something you want?"

Now if I had been the man behind the counter I would not have asked that question. He ought to have known, by the fact that I had approached the tie counter, that I wanted to look at ties.

I picked up two or three ties from the counter, examined them briefly, then laid down all but one light blue which somewhat appealed to me. Finally I laid this one down, also, and began to look through the remainder of the assortment.

The young man behind the counter then had a happy idea. Picking up a gaudy-looking yellow tie he wound it around his fingers to show how it would look when tied, and asked:

"Isn't this a beauty?"

Now I hate yellow ties, and the salesman made no particular hit with me by suggesting that a gaudy yellow tie is pretty. If I had been in that salesman's place I would have picked up the blue tie for which I had shown a decided preference, and I would have wound it around my fingers so as to bring out its appearance after being tied. I would have known what my customer wanted by watching the kinds of ties that he picked up and examined. Moreover, I would have known the particular tie that he liked best by the time he held it in his hands. A man will not stand by a counter and fondle a piece of merchandise which he does not like. If given the opportunity, any customer will give the alert salesman a clue as to the particular merchandise which should be stressed in an effort to make a sale.

I then moved over to the shirt counter. Here I was met by an elderly gentleman who asked:

"Is there something I can do for you today?"

Well, I thought to myself that if he ever did anything for me it would have to be today, as I might never come back to that particular store again. I told him I wanted to look at shirts, and described the style and color of shirt that I wanted.

The old gentleman made quite a hit with me when he replied by saying:

THE man who is afraid to give credit to those who help him do a piece of creditable work is so small that Opportunity will pass by without seeing him some day.

"I am sorry, sir, but they are not wearing that style this season, so we are not showing it."

I said I knew "they" were not wearing the style for which I had asked, and for that very reason, among others, I was going to wear it providing I could find it in stock.

If there is anything which nettles a man—especially that type of man who knows exactly what he wants and describes it the moment he walks into the store—it is to be told that "they are not wearing it this season."

Such a statement is an insult to a man's intelligence, or to what he thinks is his intelligence, and in most cases it is fatal to a sale. If I were selling goods I might think what I pleased about a customer's taste, but I surely would not be so lacking in tact and diplomacy as to tell the customer that I thought he didn't know his business. Rather I would prefer to manage tactfully to show him what I believed to be more appropriate merchandise than that for which he had called, if what he wanted was not in stock.

One of the most famous and highly paid writers in the world has built his fame and fortune on the sole discovery that it is profitable to write about that which people already know and with which they are already in accord. The same rule might as well apply to the sale of merchandise.

The old gentleman finally pulled down some shirt boxes and began laying out shirts which were not even similar to the shirt for which I had asked. I told him that none of these suited, and as I started to walk out he asked if I would like to look at some nice suspenders.

Imagine it!   To begin with I do not wear suspenders, and, furthermore, there was nothing about my manner or bearing to indicate that I might like to look at suspenders.

It is proper for a salesman to try to interest a customer in wares for which he makes no inquiry, but judgment should be used and care taken to offer something which the salesman has reason to believe the customer may want.

I walked out of the store without having bought either shirts or ties, and feeling somewhat resentful because I had been so grossly misjudged as to my tastes for colors and styles.

A little further down the street I went into a small, one-man shop which had shirts and ties on display in the window.

Here I was handled differently!

The man behind the counter asked no unnecessary or stereotyped questions. He took one glance at me as I entered the door, sized me up quite accurately and greeted me with a very pleasant "Good morning, sir!"

He then inquired, "Which shall I show you first, shirts or ties?"   I said I would look at the shirts first. He then glanced at the style of shirt I was wearing, asked my size, and began laying out shirts of the very type and color for which I was searching, without my saying another word. He laid out six different styles and watched to see which I would pick up first. I looked at each shirt, in turn, and laid them all back on the counter, but the salesman observed that I examined one of the shirts a little more closely than the others, and that I held it a little longer. No sooner had I laid this shirt down than the salesman picked it up and began to explain how it was made. He then went to the tie counter and came back with three very beautiful blue ties, of the very type for which I had been looking, tied each and held it in front of the shirt, calling attention to the perfect harmony between the colors of the ties and the shirt.

Before I had been in the store five minutes I had purchased three shirts and three ties, and was on my way with the package under my arm, feeling that here was a store to which I would return when I needed more shirts and ties.

I learned, afterwards, that the merchant who owns the little shop where I made these purchases pays a monthly rental of $500.00 for the small store, and makes a handsome income from the sale of nothing but shirts, ties and collars. He would have to go out of business, with a fixed charge of $500.00 a month for rent, if it were not for his knowledge of human nature which enables him to make a very high percentage of sales to all who come into his store.

.   .   .   .

I have often observed women when they were trying on hats, and have wondered why salespeople did not read the prospective buyer's mind by watching her manner of handling the hats.

A woman goes into a store and asks to be shown some hats. The salesperson starts bringing out hats and the prospective buyer starts trying them on. If a hat suits her, even in the slightest sort of way, she will keep it on a few seconds, or a few minutes, but if she does not like it she will pull it right off her head the moment the salesperson takes her hands off the hat.

Finally, when the customer is shown a hat that she likes she will begin to announce that fact, in terms which no well informed salesperson will fail to understand, by arranging her hair under the hat, or pulling it down on her head to just the angle which she likes best, and by looking at the hat from the rear, with the aid of a hand-mirror. The signs of admiration are unmistakable. Finally, the customer will remove the hat from her head, and begin to look at it closely; then she may lay it aside and permit another hat to be tried on her, in which event the clever salesperson will lay aside the hat just removed, and at the opportune time she will bring it back and ask the customer to try it on again.

By careful observation of the customer's likes and dislikes a clever saleswoman may often sell as many as three or four hats to the same customer, at one sitting, by merely watching what appeals to the customer and then concentrating upon the sale of that.

The same rule applies in the sale of other merchandise. The customer will, if closely observed, clearly indicate what is wanted, and, if the clue is followed, very rarely will a customer walk out without buying.

I believe it a conservative estimate when I say that fully seventy-five per cent of the "walk-outs," as the non-purchasing customers are called, are due to lack of tactful showing of merchandise.

.   .   .   .

Last Fall I went into a hat store to purchase a felt hat. It was a busy Saturday afternoon and I was approached by a young "extra" rush-hour salesman who had not yet learned how to size people up at a glance. For no good reason whatsoever the young man pulled down a brown derby and handed it to me, or rather tried to hand it to me. I thought he was trying to be funny, and refused to take the hat into my hands, saying to him, in an attempt to return his compliment and be funny in turn, "Do you tell bed-time stories also?" He looked at me in surprise, but didn't take the cue which I had offered him.

If I had not observed the young man more closely than he had observed me, and sized him up as an earnest but inexperienced "extra," I would have been highly insulted, for if there is anything I hate it is a derby of any sort, much less a brown derby.

One of the regular salesmen happened to see what was going on, walked over and snatched the brown derby out of the young man's hands, and, with a smile on his face intended as a sort of sop to me, said, "What the hell are you trying to show this gentleman, anyway?"

That spoiled my fun, and the salesman who had immediately recognized me as a gentleman sold me the first hat he brought out.

The customer generally feels complimented when a salesman takes the time to study the customer's personality and lay out merchandise suited to that personality.

.   .   .   .

I went into one of the largest men's clothing stores in New York City, a few years ago, and asked for a suit, describing exactly what was wanted, but not

HOT HEADS" go

with "cold feet."

He who loses his temper

is usually a bluffer and

when "called" is a quitter.

mentioning price. The young man, who purported to be a salesman, said he did not believe they carried such a suit, but I happened to see exactly what I wanted hanging on a model, and called his attention to the suit. He then made a hit with me by saying, "Oh, that one over there? That's a high-priced suit!"

His reply amused me; it also angered me, so I inquired of the young man what he saw about me which indicated that I did not come in to purchase a high-priced suit? With embarrassment he tried to explain, but his explanations were as bad as the original offense, and I started toward the door, muttering something to myself about "dumb-bells." Before I reached the door I was met by another salesman who had sensed by the way I walked and the expression on my face that I was none too well pleased.

With tact well worth remembering, this salesman engaged me in conversation while I unburdened my woes and then managed to get me to go back with him and look at the suit. Before I left the store I purchased the suit I came in to look at, and two others which I had not intended purchasing.

That was the difference between a salesman and one who drove customers away. Moreover, I later introduced two of my friends to this same salesman and he made sizable sales to each of them.

. . . .

I was once walking down Michigan Boulevard, in Chicago, when my eye was attracted to a beautiful gray suit in the window of a men's store. I had no notion of buying the suit, but I was curious to know the price, so I opened the door, and, without entering, merely pushed my head inside and asked the first man I saw how much the suit in the window was.

Then followed one of the cleverest bits of sales maneuvering I have ever observed. The salesman knew he could not sell me the suit unless I came into the store, so he said, "Will you not step inside, sir, while I find out the price of the suit?"

Of course he knew the price, all the time, but that was his way of disarming me of the thought that he intended trying to sell me the suit. Of course I had to be as polite as the salesman, so I said, "Certainly," and walked inside.

The salesman said, "Step right this way, sir, and I will get the information for you."

In less than two minutes I found myself standing in front of a case, with my coat off, getting ready to try on a coat like the one I had observed in the window.

After I was in the coat, which happened to fit almost perfectly (which was no accident, thanks to the accurate eyes of an observing salesman) my attention was called to the nice, smooth touch of the material. I rubbed my hand up and down the arm of the coat, as I had seen the salesman do while describing the material, and, sure enough, it was a very fine piece of material. By this time I had again asked the price, and when I was told that the suit was only fifty dollars I was agreeably surprised, because I had been led to believe that it might have been priced much higher. However, when I first saw the suit in the window my guess was that it was priced at about thirty-five dollars, and I doubt that I would have paid that much for it had I not fallen into the hands of a man who knew

how to show the suit to best advantage. If the first
coat tried on me had been about two sizes too large,
or a size too small, I doubt that any sale would have
been made, despite the fact that all ready-to-wear
suits sold in the better stores are altered to fit the
customer.

I bought that suit "on the impulse of the moment,"
as the psychologist would say, and I am not the only
man who buys goods on that same sort of impulse. A
single slip on the part of the salesman would have lost
him the sale of that suit. If he had replied, "Fifty
dollars," when I asked the price I would have said,
"Thank you," and have gone my way without looking
at the suit.

Later in the season I purchased two more suits
from this same salesman, and if I now lived in Chicago the chances are that I would buy still other suits
from him, because he always showed me suits that
were in keeping with my personality.

·   ·   ·   ·   ·   ·   ·

The Marshall Field store, in Chicago, gets more for
merchandise than does any other store of its kind in
the country. Moreover, people knowingly pay more
at this store, and feel better satisfied than if they
bought the merchandise at another store for less
money.

Why is this?

Well, there are many reasons, among them the fact
that anything purchased at the Field store which is not
entirely satisfactory may be returned and exchanged
for other merchandise, or the purchase price may be
refunded, just as the customer wishes. An implied

guarantee goes with every article sold in the Field
store.

Another reason why people will pay more at the
Field store is the fact that the merchandise is displayed and shown to better advantage than it is at
most other stores. The Field window-displays are
truly works of art, no less than if they were created
for the sake of art alone, and not merely to sell merchandise. The same is true of the goods displayed
in the store. There is harmony and proper grouping
of merchandise throughout the Field establishment,
and this creates an "atmosphere" that is more—much
more—than merely an imaginary one.

Still another reason why the Field store can get
more for merchandise than most other merchants is
due to the careful selection and supervision of salespeople. One would seldom find a person employed in
the Field store whom one would not be willing to
accept as a social equal, or as a neighbor. Not a few
men have made the acquaintance of girls in the Field
store who later became their wives.

Merchandise purchased in the Field store is packed
or wrapped more artistically than is common in other
stores, which is still another reason why people go
out of their way and pay higher prices to trade there.

.   .   .   .

While we are on the subject of artistic wrapping of
merchandise I wish to relate the experience of a friend
of mine which will not fail to convey a very definite
meaning to those engaged in the business of selling,
as it shows how *imagination* may be used even in
wrapping merchandise.

This friend had a very fine silver cigarette case which he had carried for years, and of which he was very proud because it was a gift from his wife.

Constant usage had banged the case up rather badly. It had been bent, dented, the hinges warped, etc., until he decided to take it to Caldwell the jeweler, in Philadelphia, to be repaired. He left the case and asked them to send it to his office when it was ready.

About two weeks later a splendid-looking new delivery wagon with the Caldwell name on it drew up in front of his office, and a nice-looking young man in a neat uniform stepped out with a package that was artistically wrapped and tied with a ribbon tape string.

The package happened to be delivered to my friend on his birthday, and, having forgotten about leaving the cigarette case to be repaired, and observing the beauty and size of the package that was handed to him, he naturally imagined that someone had sent him a birthday present.

His secretary and other workers in his office gathered around his desk to watch him open up his "present." He cut the ribbon and removed the outer covering. Under this was a covering of tissue paper, fastened with beautiful gold seals bearing the Caldwell initials and trade-mark. This paper was removed and behold! a most beautiful plush-lined box met his eyes. The box was opened, and, after removing the tissue paper packing, there was a cigarette case which he recognized, after careful examination, as the one he had left to be repaired, but it did not look like the same case, thanks to the *imagination* of the Caldwell manager.

E. M. STATLER BE-
CAME THE MOST
SUCCESSFUL HOTEL
MAN IN THE WORLD
BY RENDERING
MORE SERVICE and
BETTER SERVICE
THAN HIS GUESTS
WERE ASKED TO
PAY FOR.

Every dent had been carefully straightened out. The hinges had been trued and the case had been polished and cleaned so it shone as it did when it was first purchased.

Simultaneously a prolonged "Oo-o-o-o-o-o-Oh!" of admiration came from the onlookers, including the owner of the cigarette case.

And the bill! Oh, it was a plenty, and yet the price charged for the repair did not seem too high. As a matter of fact everything that entered into the transaction from the packing of the case, with the fine tissue paper cover, the gold seals, the ribbon tape string, the delivery of the package by a neatly uniformed boy, from a well appointed new delivery wagon, was based upon carefully calculated psychology which laid the foundation for a high price for the repair.

People, generally, do not complain of high prices, providing the "service" or embellishment of the merchandise is such as to pave the way for high prices. What people do complain of, and rightly so, is high prices and "sloppy" service.

To me there was a great lesson in this cigarette case incident, and I think there is a lesson in it for any person who makes a business of selling any sort of merchandise.

The goods you are selling may actually be worth all you are asking for them, but if you do not carefully study the subjects of advantageous display and artistic packing you may be accused of overcharging your customers.

. . . .

On Broad Street, in the city of Philadelphia, there is a fruit shop where those who patronize the store are met at the door by a man in uniform who opens the door for them. He does nothing else but merely open the door, but he does it with a smile (even though it be a carefully studied and rehearsed smile) which makes the customer feel welcome even before he gets inside of the store. This fruit merchant specializes on specially prepared baskets of fruit. Just outside the store is a big blackboard on which are listed the sailing dates of the various ocean liners leaving New York City. This merchant caters to people who wish baskets of fruit delivered on board departing boats on which friends are sailing. If a man's sweetheart, or perhaps his wife or a very dear friend, happens to be sailing on a certain date he naturally wants the basket of fruit he purchases for her to be embellished with frills and "trimmings." Moreover, he is not necessarily looking for something "cheap" or even inexpensive.

All of which the fruit merchant capitalizes! He gets from $10.00 to $25.00 for a basket of fruit which one could purchase just around the corner, not more than a block away, for from $3.00 to $7.50, with the exception that the latter would not be embellished with the seventy-five cents' worth of frills which the former contains.

This merchant's store is a small affair, no larger than the average small fruit-stand store, but he pays a rent of at least $15,000.00 a year for the place and makes more money than half a hundred ordinary fruit stands combined, merely because he knows how to display and deliver his wares so they appeal to the vanity of the buyers. This is but another proof of the value of *imagination*.

The American people—and this means all of them, not merely the so-called rich—are the most extravagant spenders on earth, but they insist on "class" when it comes to appearances such as wrapping and delivery and other embellishments which add no real value to the merchandise they buy. The merchant who understands this, and has learned how to mix IMAGINATION with his merchandise, may reap a rich harvest in return for his knowledge.

And a great many are doing it, too.

The salesman who understands the psychology of proper display, wrapping and delivery of merchandise, and who knows how to show his wares to fit the whims and characteristics of his customers, can make ordinary merchandise bring fancy prices, and what is more important still, he can do so and still retain the patronage of his customers more readily than if he sold the same merchandise without the "studied" appeal and the artistic wrapping and delivery service.

In a "cheap" restaurant, where coffee is served in heavy, thick cups and the silverware is tarnished or dirty, a ham sandwich is only a ham sandwich, and if the restaurant keeper gets fifteen cents for it he is doing well; but just across the street, where the coffee is served in dainty thin cups, on neatly covered tables, by neatly dressed young women, a much smaller ham sandwich will bring a quarter, to say nothing of the cost of the tip to the waitress. The only difference in the sandwiches is merely in appearances; the ham comes from the same butcher and the bread from the same baker, whether purchased from the former or the latter restaurant. The difference in price is very considerable, but the difference in the merchandise is not a difference of either quality or quantity so much as it is of "atmosphere," or appearances.

People love to buy "appearance" or atmosphere! which is merely a more refined way of saying that which P. T. Barnum said about "one being born every minute."

It is no overstatement of fact to say that a master of sales psychology could go into the average merchant's store, where the stock of goods was worth, let us say, $50,000.00, and at very slight additional expense make the stock bring $60,000.00 to $75,000.00. He would do nothing except coach the salespeople on the proper showing of the merchandise, after having purchased a small amount of more suitable fixtures, perhaps, and re-packed the merchandise in more suitable coverings and boxes.

A man's shirt, packed one to the box, in the right sort of a box, with a piece of ribbon and a sheet of tissue paper added for embellishment, can be made to bring a dollar or a dollar and a half more than the same shirt would bring without the more artistic packing. I know this is true, and I have proved it more times than I can recall, to convince some skeptical merchant who had not studied the effect of "proper displays."

Conversely stated, I have proved, many times, that the finest shirt made cannot be sold for half its value if it is removed from its box and placed on a bargain counter, with inferior looking shirts, both of which examples prove that people do not know what they are buying—that they go more by appearances than they do by actual analysis of the merchandise they purchase.

This is noticeably true in the purchase of automobiles. The American people want, and DEMAND, style in the appearance of automobiles. What is under the hood or in the rear axle they do not know and really do not care, as long as the car looks the part.

Henry Ford required nearly twenty years of experience to learn the truth of the statement just made, and even then, despite all of his analytical ability, he only acknowledged the truth when forced to do so by his competitors. If it were not true that people buy "appearances" more than they buy "reality" Ford never would have created his new automobile. That car is the finest sort of example of a psychologist who appeals to the tendency which people have to purchase "appearance," although, of course, it must be admitted that in this particular example the real value of the car actually exists.

GREAT ACHIEVE-
MENT IS USU-
ALLY BORN OF
GREAT SACRIFICE,
AND IS NEVER THE
RESULT OF SELF-
ISHNESS.

Lesson Seven

ENTHUSIASM

I GAVE a beggar a dime with the suggestion that he invest it in a copy of Elbert Hubbard's Message to Garcia.

THE LAW OF SUCCESS
Lesson Seven
ENTHUSIASM

"You Can Do It if You Believe You Can!"

NTHUSIASM is a state of mind that inspires and arouses one to put *action* into the task at hand. It does more than this —it is contagious, and vitally affects not only the enthusiast, but all with whom he comes in contact.

Enthusiasm bears the same relationship to a human being that steam does to the locomotive—it is the vital moving force that impels *action*. The greatest leaders of men are those who know how to inspire enthusiasm in their followers. Enthusiasm is the most important factor entering into salesmanship. It is, by far, the most vital factor that enters into public speaking.

If you wish to understand the difference between a man who is enthusiastic and one who is not, compare Billy Sunday with the average man of his profession. The finest sermon ever delivered would fall upon deaf ears if it were not backed with enthusiasm by the speaker.

HOW ENTHUSIASM WILL AFFECT YOU

Mix enthusiasm with your work and it will not seem hard or monotonous. Enthusiasm will so energize your entire body that you can get along with less than half the usual amount of sleep and at the same time it will enable you to perform from two to three times as much work as you usually perform in a given period, without fatigue.

For many years I have done most of my writing at night. One night, while I was enthusiastically at work over my typewriter, I looked out of the window of my study, just across the square from the Metropolitan tower, in New York City, and saw what seemed to be the most peculiar reflection of the moon on the tower. It was of a silvery gray shade, such as I had never seen before. Upon closer inspection I found that the reflection was that of the early morning sun and not that of the moon. It was daylight! I had been at work all night, but I was so engrossed in my work that the night had passed as though it were but an hour. I worked at my task all that day and all the following night without stopping, except for a small amount of light food.

Two nights and one day without sleep, and with but little food, without the slightest evidence of fatigue, would not have been possible had I not kept my body energized with *enthusiasm* over the work at hand.

Enthusiasm is not merely a figure of speech; it is a vital force that you can harness and use with profit. Without it you would resemble an electric battery without electricity.

Enthusiasm is the vital force with which you re-charge your body and develop a dynamic personality. Some people are blessed with natural *enthusiasm,* while others must acquire it. The procedure through which it may be developed is simple. It begins by the doing of the work or rendering of the service which one likes best. If you should be so situated that you cannot conveniently engage in the work which you like best, for the time being, then you can proceed along another line very effectively by adopting a *definite chief aim* that contemplates your engaging in that particular work at some future time.

Lack of capital and many other circumstances over which you have no immediate control may force you to engage in work which you do not like, but no one can stop you from determining in your own mind what your *definite chief aim* in life shall be, nor can anyone stop you from planning ways and means for translating this aim into reality, nor can anyone stop you from mixing *enthusiasm* with your plans.

Happiness, the final object of all human effort, is a state of mind that can be maintained only through the hope of future achievement. Happiness lies always in the future and never in the past. The happy person is the one who dreams of heights of achievement that are yet unattained. The home you intend to own, the money you intend to earn and place in the bank, the trip you intend to take when you can afford it, the position in life you intend to fill when you have pre-pared yourself, and the preparation, itself—these are the things that produce happiness. Likewise, these are the materials out of which your *definite chief aim* is formed; these are the things over which you may become *enthusiastic,* no matter what your present station in life may be.

More than twenty years ago I became enthusiastic over an idea. When the idea first took form in my mind I was unprepared to take even the first step toward its transformation into reality. But I nursed it in my mind—I became *enthusiastic* over it as I looked ahead, in my imagination, and saw the time when I would be prepared to make it a reality.

The idea was this: I wanted to become the editor of a magazine, based upon the Golden Rule, through which I could inspire people to keep up courage and deal with one another squarely.

Finally my chance came! and, on armistice day, 1918, I wrote the first editorial for what was to become the material realization of a hope that had lain dormant in my mind for nearly a score of years.

With *enthusiasm* I poured into that editorial the emotions which I had been developing in my heart over a period of more than twenty years. My dream had come true. My editorship of a national magazine had become a reality.

As I have stated, this editorial was written with *enthusiasm.* I took it to a man of my acquaintance and with *enthusiasm* I read it to him. The editorial ended in these words: "At last my twenty-year-old dream is about to come true. It takes money, and a lot of it, to publish a national magazine, and I haven't the slightest idea where I am going to get this essential factor, but this is worrying me not at all because *I know I am going to get it somewhere!*" As I wrote those lines, I mixed *enthusiasm* and faith with them.

I had hardly finished reading this editorial when

the man to whom I read it—the first and only person to whom I had shown it—said:

"I can tell you where you are going to get the money, for I am going to supply it."

And he did!

Yes, *enthusiasm* is a vital force; so vital, in fact, that no man who has it highly developed can begin even to approximate his power of achievement.

Before passing to the next step in this lesson, I wish to repeat and to emphasize the fact that you may develop *enthusiasm* over your *definite chief aim* in life, no matter whether you are in position to achieve that purpose at this time or not. You may be a long way from realization of your *definite chief aim,* but if you will kindle the fire of *enthusiasm* in your heart, and keep it burning, before very long the obstacles that now stand in the way of your attainment of that purpose will melt away as if by the force of magic, and you will find yourself in possession of power that you did not know you possessed.

HOW YOUR ENTHUSIASM WILL AFFECT OTHERS

We come, now, to the discussion of one of the most important subjects of this Reading Course, namely, *suggestion.*

In the preceding lessons we have discussed the subject of *Auto-suggestion,* which is self-suggestion. You saw, in Lesson Three, what an important part *Auto-suggestion* played.

Suggestion is the principle through which your words and your acts and even *your state of mind* influence

ONE of the most valuable things any man can learn is the art of using the knowledge and experience of others.

others. That you may comprehend the far-reaching power of *suggestion,* let me refer to the Introductory Lesson, in which the principle of telepathy is described. If you now understand and accept the principle of telepathy (the communication of thought from one mind to another without the aid of signs, symbols or sounds) as a reality, you of course understand why *enthusiasm* is contagious, and why it influences all within its radius.

When your own mind is vibrating at a high rate, because it has been stimulated with *enthusiasm,* that vibration registers in the minds of all within its radius, and especially in the minds of those with whom you come in close contact. When a public speaker "senses" the feeling that his audience is "en rapport" with him he merely recognizes the fact that his own *enthusiasm* has influenced the minds of his listeners until their minds are vibrating in harmony with his own.

When the salesman "senses" the fact that the "psychological" moment for closing a sale has arrived, he merely feels the effect of his own *enthusiasm* as it influences the mind of his prospective buyer and places that mind "en rapport" (in harmony) with his own.

The subject of *suggestion* constitutes so vitally an important part of this lesson, and of this entire course, that I will now proceed to describe the three mediums through which it usually operates; namely, what you say, what you do and what you *think!*

When you are *enthusiastic* over the goods you are selling or the services you are offering, or the speech you are delivering, your state of mind becomes obvious to all who hear you, *by the tone of your voice.* Whether you have ever thought of it in this way or not, it is the tone in which you make a statement, more than it is the statement itself, that carries conviction or fails to convince. No mere combination of words can ever take the place of a deep belief in a statement that is expressed with burning *enthusiasm*. Words are but devitalized sounds unless colored with feeling that is born of *enthusiasm*.

Here the printed word fails me, for I can never express with mere type and paper the difference between words that fall from unemotional lips, without the fire of *enthusiasm* back of them, and those which seem to pour forth from a heart that is bursting with eagerness for expression. The difference is there, however.

Thus, *what you say,* and the way in which you say it, conveys a meaning that may be just the opposite to what is intended. This accounts for many a failure by the salesman who presents his arguments in words which seem logical enough, but lack the coloring that can come only from *enthusiasm* that is born of sincerity and belief in the goods he is trying to sell. His words said one thing, but the tone of his voice *suggested* something entirely different; therefore, no sale was made.

That which you *say* is an important factor in the operation of the principle of *suggestion,* but not nearly so important as that which you *do. Your acts will count for more than your words,* and woe unto you if the two fail to harmonize.

If a man preach the Golden Rule as a sound rule of conduct his words will fall upon deaf ears if he does not practice that which he preaches. The most effective sermon that any man can preach on the soundness of the Golden Rule is that which he preaches, by *suggestion,* when he applies this rule in his relationships with his fellow men.

If a salesman of Ford automobiles drives up to his prospective purchaser in a Buick, or some other make of car, all the arguments he can present in behalf of the Ford will be without effect. Once I went into one of the offices of the Dictaphone Company to look at a dictaphone (dictating machine). The salesman in charge presented a logical argument as to the machine's merits, while the stenographer at his side was transcribing letters from a shorthand note-book. His arguments in favor of a dictating machine, as compared with the old method of dictating to a stenographer, did not impress me, because his actions were not in harmony with his words.

Your *thoughts* constitute the most important of the three ways in which you apply the principle of *suggestion,* for the reason that they control the tone of your words and, to some extent at least, your actions. If your *thoughts* and your *actions* and your *words* harmonize, you are bound to influence those with whom you come in contact, more or less toward your way of thinking.

We will now proceed to analyze the subject of *suggestion* and to show you exactly how to apply the principle upon which it operates. As we have already seen, *suggestion* differs from *Auto-suggestion* only in one way—we use it, consciously or unconsciously, when we influence others, while we use *Auto-suggestion* as a means of influencing ourselves.

Before you can influence another person through *suggestion,* that person's mind must be in a state of neutrality; that is, it must be open and receptive to

your method of *suggestion*. Right here is where most
salesmen fail—they try to make a sale before the mind
of the prospective buyer has been rendered receptive
or neutralized. This is such a vital point in this lesson
that I feel impelled to dwell upon it until there can be
no doubt that you understand the principle that I am
describing.

When I say that the salesman must neutralize the
mind of his prospective purchaser before a sale can be
made I mean that the prospective purchaser's mind
must be credulous. A state of confidence must have
been established and it is obvious that there can be no
set rule for either establishing confidence or neutralizing the mind to a state of openness. Here the in-
genuity of the salesman must supply that which
cannot be set down as a hard and fast rule.

I know a life insurance salesman who sells nothing
but large policies, amounting to $100,000.00 and up-
ward. Before this man even approaches the subject
of insurance with a prospective client he familiarizes
himself with the prospective client's complete history,
including his education, his financial status, his eccen-
tricities if he has any, his religious preferences and
other data too numerous to be listed. Armed with this
information, he manages to secure an introduction
under conditions which permit him to know the prospective client in a social as well as a business way.
Nothing is said about the sale of life insurance during
his first visit, nor his second, and sometimes he does
not approach the subject of insurance until he has become very well acquainted with the prospective client.

All this time, however, he is not dissipating his
efforts. He is taking advantage of these friendly visits

for the purpose of neutralizing his prospective client's mind; that is, he is building up a relationship of confidence so that when the time comes for him to talk life insurance that which he says will fall upon ears that *willingly listen*.

Some years ago I wrote a book entitled How to Sell Your Services. Just before the manuscript went to the publisher, it occurred to me to request some of the well known men of the United States to write letters of endorsement to be published in the book. The printer was then waiting for the manuscript; therefore, I hurriedly wrote a letter to some eight or ten men, in which I briefly outlined exactly what I wanted, but the letter brought back no replies. I had failed to observe two important prerequisites for success—I had written the letter so hurriedly that I had failed to inject the spirit of *enthusiasm* into it, and, I had neglected so to word the letter that it had the effect of neutralizing the minds of those to whom it was sent; therefore, I had not paved the way for the application of the principle of *suggestion*.

After I discovered my mistake, I then wrote a letter that was based upon strict application of the principle of *suggestion,* and this letter not only brought back replies from all to whom it was sent, but many of the replies were masterpieces and served, far beyond my fondest hopes, as valuable supplements to the book. For the purpose of comparison, to show you how the principle of *suggestion* may be used in writing a letter, and what an important part *enthusiasm* plays in giving the written word "flesh," the two letters are here reproduced. It will not be necessary to indicate which letter failed, as that will be quite obvious:

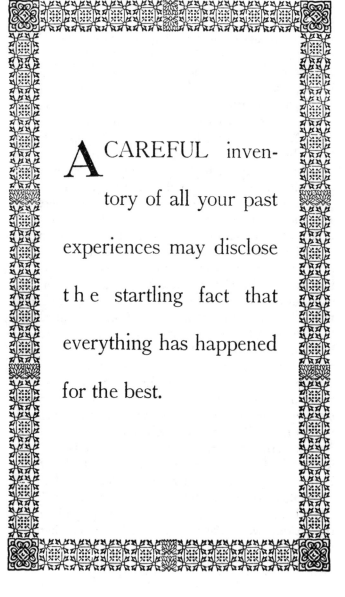

A CAREFUL inventory of all your past experiences may disclose t h e startling fact that everything has happened for the best.

My dear Mr. Ford:

I am just completing a manuscript for a new book entitled How to Sell Your Services. I anticipate the sale of several hundred thousand of these books and I believe those who purchase the book would welcome the opportunity of receiving a message from you as to the best method of marketing personal services.

Would you, therefore, be good enough to give me a few minutes of your time by writing a brief message to be published in my book? This will be a big favor to me personally and I know it would be appreciated by the readers of the book.

Thanking you in advance for any consideration you may care to show me, I am,

Yours very truly,

.   .   .   .

Hon. Thomas R. Marshall,
Vice-President of the United States,
Washington, D. C.
My dear Mr. Marshall:

Would you care for the opportunity to send a message of encouragement, and possibly a word of advice, to a few hundred thousand of your fellow men who have failed to make their mark in the world as successfully as you have done?

I have about completed a manuscript for a book to be entitled How to Sell Your Services. The main point made in the book is that service rendered is *cause* and the pay envelope is *effect;* and that the latter varies in proportion to the efficiency of the former.

The book would be incomplete without a few words

of advice from a few men who, like yourself, have come up from the bottom to enviable positions in the world. Therefore, if you will write me of your views as to the most essential points to be borne in mind by those who are offering personal services for sale I will pass your message on through my book, which will insure its getting into hands where it will do a world of good for a class of earnest people who are struggling to find their places in the world's work.

I know you are a busy man, Mr. Marshall, but please bear in mind that by simply calling in your secretary and dictating a brief letter you will be sending forth an important message to possibly half a million people. In money this will not be worth to you the two cent stamp that you will place on the letter, but, if estimated from the viewpoint of the good it may do others who are less fortunate than yourself, it may be worth the difference between success and failure to many a worthy person who will read your message, believe in it, and be guided by it.

Very cordially yours,

Now, let us analyze the two letters and find out why one failed in its mission while the other succeeded. This analysis should start with one of the most important fundamentals of salesmanship, namely motive. In the first letter it is obvious that the motive is entirely one of self-interest. The letter states exactly what is wanted, but the wording of it leaves a doubt as to *why* the request is made or whom it is intended to benefit. Study the sentence in the second paragraph, "This will be a big favor to me personally, etc." Now it may seem to be a peculiar trait, but the truth is that most people will not grant favors just to please others. If I ask you to render a service that will benefit me, without bringing you some corresponding advantage, you will not show much enthusiasm in granting that favor; you may refuse altogether if you have a plausible excuse for refusing. But if I ask you to render a service that will benefit a third person, even though the service must be rendered through me; and if that service is of such a nature that it is likely to reflect credit on you, the chances are that you will render the service willingly.

We see this psychology demonstrated by the man who pitches a dime to the beggar on the street, or perhaps refuses even the dime, but willingly hands over a hundred or a thousand dollars to the charity worker who is begging in the name of others.

But the most damaging suggestion of all is contained in the last and most important paragraph of the letter, "Thanking you in advance for *any consideration you may care to show me.*" This sentence strongly suggests that the writer of the letter anticipates a refusal of his request. It clearly indicates lack of *enthusiasm*. It paves the way for a refusal of the request. There is not one single word in the entire letter that places in the mind of a man to whom it is sent a satisfactory reason why he should comply with the request. On the other hand, he can clearly see that the object of the letter is to secure from him a letter of endorsement that will help sell the book. The most important selling argument—in fact, the only selling argument available in connection with this request, has been lost because it was not brought out and established as the real motive for making the request. This argument was but faintly mentioned in the sentence, "I believe those who purchase the book would welcome the opportunity of receiving a message from you as to the best method of marketing personal services."

The opening paragraph of the letter violates an important fundamental of salesmanship because it clearly suggests that the object of the letter is to gain some advantage for its writer, and does not even hint at any corresponding advantage that may accrue to the person to whom it is sent. Instead of neutralizing the mind of the recipient of the letter, as it should do, it has just the opposite effect; it causes him to close his mind against all argument that follows; it puts him in a frame of mind that makes it easy for him to say no. It reminds me of a salesman—or, perhaps I should say, a man who wanted to be a salesman— who once approached me for the purpose of selling me a subscription to the Saturday Evening Post. As he held a copy of the magazine in front of me he suggested the answer I should make by this question:

"You wouldn't subscribe for the Post to help me out, would you?"

Of course I said no! He had made it easy for me to say no. There was no *enthusiasm* back of his words, and gloom and discouragement were written all over his face. He needed the commission he would have made on my subscription had I purchased; no doubt about that—but he suggested nothing that appealed to my self-interest motive, therefore he lost a sale. But the loss of this *one sale* was not the sad part of his misfortune; the sad part was that this same attitude was causing him to lose all other sales which he might have made had he changed his approach.

A few weeks later another subscription agent approached me. She was selling a combination of six magazines, one of which was the Saturday Evening Post, but how different was her approach. She glanced at my library table, on which she saw several magazines, then at my book shelves, and exclaimed with *enthusiasm*:

"*Oh! I see you are a lover of books and magazines.*"

I *proudly* pleaded guilty to the charge. Observe the word "*proudly*," for it has an important bearing on this incident. I laid down the manuscript that I was reading when this saleswoman came in, for I could see that she was a woman of intelligence. Just how I came to see this I will leave to your imagination. The important point is that I laid down the manuscript and actually felt myself wanting to hear what she had to say.

With the aid of eleven words, plus a pleasant smile, plus a tone of genuine *enthusiasm,* she had neutralized my mind sufficiently to make me want to hear her. She had performed her most difficult task, with those few words, because I had made up my mind when she was announced that I would keep my manuscript in my hands and thereby convey to her mind, as politely as I could, the fact that I was busy and did not wish to be detained.

Being a student of salesmanship and of *suggestion,* I carefully watched to see what her next move would be. She had a bundle of magazines under her arm and I expected she would unroll it and begin to urge me to purchase, but she didn't. You will recall that I said she was *selling* a combination of six magazines; not merely trying to sell them.

FIRST IMPRESSIONS
REALLY DO COUNT.
DRESS TO LOOK
THE PART YOU IN-
TEND TO PLAY IN
LIFE, BUT TAKE
CARE NOT TO
OVERDO IT.

She walked over to my book shelves, pulled out a copy of Emerson's Essays, and for the next ten minutes she talked about Emerson's essay on Compensation so interestingly that I lost sight of the roll of magazines that she carried. (She was neutralizing my mind some more.)

Incidentally, she gave me a sufficient number of new ideas about Emerson's works to provide material for an excellent editorial.

Then she asked me which magazines I received regularly, and after I told her she smiled as she began to unroll her bundle of magazines and laid them on the table in front of me. She analyzed her magazines one by one, and explained just why I should have each of them. The Saturday Evening Post would bring me the cleanest fiction; Literary Digest would bring me the news of the world in condensed form, such as a *busy man like myself* would demand; the American Magazine would bring me the latest biographies of the men who were leading in business and industry, and so on, until she had covered the entire list.

But I was not responding to her argument as freely as she thought I should have, so she slipped me this gentle *suggestion:*

"A man of your position is bound to be well informed and, if he isn't, it will show up in his own work!"

She spoke the truth! Her remark was both a compliment and a gentle reprimand. She made me feel somewhat sheepish because she had taken inventory of my reading matter—and six of the leading magazines were not on my list. (The six that she was selling.)

Then I began to "slip" by asking her how much the six magazines would cost. She put on the finishing touches of a well presented sales talk by this tactful reply: "The cost? Why, the cost of the entire number is less than you receive for a single page of the typewritten manuscript that you had in your hands when I came in."

Again she spoke the truth. And how did she happen to guess so well what I was getting for my manuscript? The answer is, she didn't guess—*she knew!* She made it a part of her business to draw me out tactfully as to the nature of my work (which in no way made me angry). She became so deeply interested in the manuscript which I had laid down when she came in, that she actually induced me to talk about it. (I am not saying, of course, that this required any great amount of skill or coaxing, for have I not said that *it was my manuscript?*) In my remarks about that manuscript I suspect I *admitted* that I was receiving $250.00 for the fifteen pages; yes, *I am sure I was careless enough to admit that I was being well paid for my work.*

Perhaps she induced me to make the admission. At any rate, the information was valuable to her and she made effective use of it at the psychological moment. For all I know it was a part of her plan to observe carefully all that she saw and heard, with the object of finding out just what my weaknesses were and what I was most interested in discussing. Some salesmen take the time to do this; some do not. She was one of those who did.

Yes, she went away with my order for the six magazines; also my twelve dollars. But that was not all the benefit she derived from tactful *suggestion* plus *enthusiasm;* she got my consent to canvass my office, and before she left she had five other orders from my employees.

At no time during her stay did she leave the impression that I was favoring her by purchasing her magazines. Just to the contrary, she distinctly impressed me with the feeling that she was rendering me a favor. This was tactful suggestion.

Before we get away from this incident, I wish to make an admission—when she drew me into conversation she did it in such a way that I talked with *enthusiasm.* There were two reasons for this. She was one of them; and the other one was the fact that she managed to get me to talk *about my own work!* Of course I am not suggesting that *you* should be meddlesome enough to smile at my carelessness as you read this; or that you should gather from this incident the impression that this tactful saleswoman actually led me to talk of my own work for the purpose of neutralizing my mind so that I would listen to her, when she was ready to talk of her magazines, as patiently as she had listened to me. However, if you should be clever enough to draw a lesson from her method, there is no way for me to stop you from doing so.

As I have stated, when I talked I mixed *enthusiasm* with my conversation. Perhaps I caught the spirit of *enthusiasm* from this clever saleswoman, when she made that opening remark as she came into my study. Yes, I am sure this is where I caught it, and, I am just as sure that her enthusiasm was not a matter of accident. She had trained herself to look for something in her prospective purchaser's office, or his work, or his conversation, over which she could express *enthusiasm*.

Remember, *suggestion* and *enthusiasm* go hand in hand!

I can remember, as though it were yesterday, the feeling that came over me when that would-be salesman pushed that Saturday Evening Post in front of me, as he remarked:

"You wouldn't subscribe for the Post to help me out, would you?"

His words were chilled, they were lifeless; they lacked *enthusiasm;* they registered an impression in my mind, but that impression was one of coldness. I wanted to see the man go out at the door at which he had come in. Mind you, I am not naturally unsympathetic, but the tone of his voice, the look on his face, his general bearing *suggested* that he was there to ask a favor and not to offer one.

Suggestion is one of the most subtle and powerful principles of psychology. You are making use of it in all that you do and say and think, but, unless you understand the difference between negative suggestion and positive suggestion, you may be using it in such a way that it is bringing you defeat instead of success.

Science has established the fact that through the negative use of suggestion life may be extinguished. Some years ago, in France, a criminal was condemned to death, but before the time for his execution an experiment was performed on him which conclusively proved that through the principle of *suggestion* death could be produced. The criminal was brought to the guillotine and his head was placed under the knife, after he had been blindfolded. A heavy, sharp edged plank was then dropped on his neck, producing a shock similar to that of a sharp edged knife. Warm water was then gently poured on his neck and allowed to trickle slowly down his spine, to imitate the flow of warm blood. In seven minutes the doctors pronounced the man dead. His imagination, through the principle of suggestion, had actually turned the sharp edged plank into a guillotine blade and stopped his heart from beating.

In the little town where I was raised, there lived an old lady who constantly complained that she feared death from cancer. During her childhood she had seen a woman who had cancer and the sight had so impressed itself upon her mind that she began to look for the symptoms of cancer in her own body. She was sure that every little ache and pain was the beginning of her long-looked-for symptom of cancer. I have seen her place her hand on her breast and have heard her exclaim, "Oh, I am sure I have a cancer growing here. I can feel it." When complaining of this imaginary disease, she always placed her hand on her left breast, where she believed the cancer was attacking her.

For more than twenty years she kept this up.

A few weeks ago she died—*with cancer on her left breast!* If suggestion will actually turn the edge of a plank into a guillotine blade and transform healthy body cells into parasites out of which cancer will develop, can you not imagine what it will do in destroying disease germs, if properly directed? *Suggestion* is the law through which mental healers work what appear to be miracles. I have personally witnessed the removal of parasitical growths known as warts,

Half the wrecks that strew
life's ocean

If some star had been their
guide,

Might in safety now be
riding,

But they drifted with the
Tide.

through the aid of suggestion, within forty-eight hours.

You—the reader of this lesson—can be sent to bed with *imaginary* sickness of the worst sort, in two hours' time or less, through the use of *suggestion*. If you should start down the street and three or four people in whom you had confidence should meet you and each exclaim that you look ill you would be ready for a doctor. This brings to mind an experience that I once had with a life insurance salesman. I had made application for a policy, but was undecided as to whether I would take ten or twenty thousand dollars. Meanwhile, the agent had sent me to the life insurance company's doctor to be examined. The following day I was called back for another examination. The second time the examination was more searching, and the doctor carried a worried look on his face. The third day I was called back again, and this time two consulting physicians were there to look me over. They gave me the most searching examination I had ever received or even heard of.

The next day the agent called on me and addressed me as follows:

"I do not wish to alarm you! but the doctors who examined you do not agree on your analysis. You have not yet decided whether you will take ten or twenty thousand dollars' worth of insurance, and I do not think it fair for me to give you a report on your medical examination until you make this decision, because if I did you might feel that I was urging you to take the larger amount."

Then I spoke up and said: "Well, I have already decided to take the full amount." True enough; I had decided to take the full twenty thousand dollar policy.

I decided the moment the agent planted the suggestion in my mind that perhaps I had some constitutional weakness that would make it hard for me to get as much insurance as I wanted.

"Very well," said the agent, "now that you have decided I feel it my duty to tell you that two of the doctors believe you have the tubercular germ in your system, while the other two disagree with them." The trick had been turned. Clever suggestion had pushed me over the fence of indecision and we were all satisfied.

Where does *enthusiasm* come in, do you ask? Never mind, it "came in" all right, but if you wish to know who brought it you will have to ask the life insurance agent and his four medical *accomplices,* for I am sure they must have had a hearty laugh at my expense. But the trick was all right. I needed the insurance anyway.

Of course, if you happen to be a life insurance agent you will not grab this idea and work it out on the next prospective client who is slow in making up his mind about taking a policy. Of course you will not!

A few months ago I received one of the most effective pieces of advertising I ever saw. It was a neat little book in which a clever automobile insurance salesman had reprinted press dispatches that he had gathered from all over the country, in which it was shown that sixty-five automobiles had been stolen in a single day. On the back page of the book was this highly *suggestive* statement:

"Your car may be the next one to go. Is it insured?"

At the bottom of the page was the salesman's name and address; also his telephone number. Before I had finished reading the first two pages of the book I called the salesman on the telephone and made inquiry about rates. He came right over to see me, and you know the remainder of the story.

.   .   .   .

Go back, now, to the two letters and let us analyze the second one, which brought the desired replies from all to whom it was sent. Study, carefully, the first paragraph and you will observe that it asks a question which can be answered in but one way. Compare this opening paragraph with that of the first letter, by asking yourself which of the two would have impressed you most favorably. This paragraph is worded as it is for a two-fold purpose; first, it is intended to serve the purpose of neutralizing the mind of the reader so he will read the remainder of the letter in an open-minded attitude; and, second, it asks a question which can be answered in but one way, for the purpose of committing the reader to a viewpoint which harmonizes with the nature of the service that he is to be requested to render in subsequent paragraphs of the letter.

In the second lesson of this course you observed that Andrew Carnegie refused to answer my question, when I asked him to what he attributed his *success*, until he had asked me to define the word *success*. He did this to avoid misunderstanding. The first paragraph of the letter we are analyzing is so worded that it states the object of the letter and at the same time practically forces the reader to accept that object as being sound and reasonable.

Any person who would answer the question asked

in this paragraph of the letter under discussion, in the negative, would, by the same answer, convict himself on the charge of selfishness, and no man wants to face himself with a guilty conscience on such a charge. Just as the farmer first plows his ground, then fertilizes it, and perhaps harrows it and prepares it to receive the seed, in order that he may be sure of a crop, so does this paragraph fertilize the mind of the reader and prepare it for the seed which is to be placed there through the subtle *suggestion* that the paragraph contains.

Study, carefully, the second paragraph of the letter and you will observe that it carries a statement of fact which the reader can *neither question nor deny!* It provides him with no reason for argument because it is obviously based upon a sound fundamental. It takes him the second step of the psychological journey that leads straight toward compliance with the request that is carefully clothed and covered up in the third paragraph of the letter, but you will notice that the third paragraph begins by paying the reader a nice little compliment that was not designed to make him angry. "Therefore, if you will write me of your views as to the most essential points to be borne in mind by those who are offering personal services for sale," etc. Study the wording of this sentence, together with the setting in which it has been placed, and you will observe that it hardly appears to be a request at all, and certainly there is nothing about it to suggest that the *writer of the letter is requesting a favor for his personal benefit*. At most, it can be construed merely as a request for a favor for others.

Now study the closing paragraph and notice how

tactfully concealed is the suggestion that if the reader should refuse the request he is placing himself in the awkward position of one who does not care enough about those who are less fortunate than himself to spend a two cent stamp and a few minutes of time for their benefit.

From start to finish the letter conveys its strongest impressions by mere *suggestion,* yet this suggestion is so carefully covered that it is not obvious except upon careful analysis of the entire letter.

The whole construction of the letter is such that if the reader lays it aside without complying with the request it makes *he will have to reckon with his own conscience!* This effect is intensified by the last sentence of the last paragraph and especially by the last thirteen words of that sentence, "who will *read your message, believe in it, and be guided by it.*"

This letter brings the reader up with a bang and turns his own conscience into an ally of the writer; it corners him, just as a hunter might corner a rabbit by driving it into a carefully prepared net.

The best evidence that this analysis is correct is the fact that the letter brought replies from every person to whom it was sent, despite the fact that every one of these men was of the type that we speak of as being a man of affairs—the type that is generally supposed to be too busy to answer a letter of this nature. Not only did the letter bring the desired replies, but the men to whom it was sent replied in person, with the exception of the late Theodore Roosevelt, who replied under the signature of a secretary.

John Wanamaker and Frank A. Vanderlip wrote two of the finest letters I have ever read, each a mas-

CONCEIT is a fog which envelops a man's real character beyond his own recognition. It weakens his native ability and strengthens all his inconsistencies.

terpiece that might well have adorned the pages of a more dignified volume than the one for which the letters were requested. Andrew Carnegie also wrote a letter that was well worth consideration by all who have personal services for sale. William Jennings Bryan wrote a fine letter, as did, also, the late Lord Northcliffe. None of these men wrote merely to please me, for I was unknown to all of them, with the exception of four. *They did not write to please me—they wrote to please themselves and to render a worthy service.* Perhaps the wording of the letter had something to do with this, but, as to that, I make no point other than to state that all of these men whom I have mentioned, and most others of their type, are generally the most willing men to render service for others when they are properly approached.

I wish to take advantage of this appropriate opportunity to state that all of the really big men whom I have had the pleasure of knowing have been the most willing and courteous men of my acquaintance when it came to rendering service that was of benefit to others. Perhaps that was one reason why they were *really* big men.

The human mind is a marvelous piece of machinery!

One of its outstanding characteristics is noticed in the fact that all impressions which reach it, either through outside *suggestion* or Auto-suggestion, are recorded together in groups which harmonize in nature. The negative impressions are stored away, all in one portion of the brain, while the positive impressions are stored in another portion. When one of these impressions (or past experiences) is called into the conscious mind, through the principle of memory, there is a tendency to recall with it all others of a similar nature, just as the raising of one link of a chain brings up other links with it. For example, anything that causes a feeling of doubt to arise in a person's mind is sufficient to call forth all of his experiences which caused him to become doubtful. If a man is asked by a stranger to cash a check, immediately he remembers having cashed checks that were not good, or of having heard of others who did so. Through the law of association all similar emotions, experiences and sense impressions that reach the mind are filed away together, so that the recalling of one has a tendency to bring back to memory all the others.

To arouse a feeling of distrust in a person's mind has a tendency to bring to the surface every doubt-building experience that person ever had. For this reason successful salesmen endeavor to keep away from the discussion of subjects that may arouse the buyer's "chain of doubt impressions" which he has stored away by reason of previous experiences. The successful salesman quickly learns that "knocking" a competitor or a competing article may result in bringing to the buyer's mind certain negative emotions growing out of previous experiences which may make it impossible for the salesman to "neutralize" the buyer's mind.

This principle applies to and controls every sense impression that is lodged in the human mind. Take the feeling of fear, for example; the moment we permit a single emotion that is related to fear to reach the conscious mind, it calls with it all of its unsavory relations. A feeling of courage cannot claim the attention of the conscious mind while a feeling of fear is there. One or the other must dominate. They make poor room-mates because they do not harmonize in nature. Like attracts like. Every thought held in the conscious mind has a tendency to draw to it other thoughts of a similar nature. You see, therefore, that these feelings, thoughts and emotions growing out of past experiences, which claim the attention of the conscious mind, are backed by a regular army of supporting soldiers of a similar nature, that stand ready to aid them in their work.

Deliberately place in your own mind, through the principle of Auto-suggestion, the ambition to succeed through the aid of a *definite chief aim,* and notice how quickly all of your latent or undeveloped ability in the nature of past experiences will become stimulated and aroused to action in your behalf. Plant in a boy's mind, through the principle of *suggestion,* the ambition to become a successful lawyer or doctor or engineer or business man or financier, and if you plant that suggestion deeply enough, and keep it there, by repetition, it will begin to move that boy toward the achievement of the object of that ambition.

If you would plant a *suggestion* "deeply," mix it generously with *enthusiasm;* for enthusiasm is the fertilizer that will insure its rapid growth as well as its permanency.

When that kind-hearted old gentleman planted in my mind the suggestion that I was a "bright boy" and that I could make my mark in the world if I would educate myself, it was not so much *what* he said, as it was the *way in which he said it* that made such a deep and lasting impression on my mind. It was the way in which he gripped my shoulders and the look of confidence in his eyes that drove his suggestion so deeply into my subconscious mind that it never gave me any peace until I commenced taking the steps that led to the fulfillment of the suggestion.

This is a point that I would stress with all the power at my command. *It is not so much what you say as it is the TONE and MANNER in which you say it that makes a lasting impression.*

It naturally follows, therefore, that sincerity of purpose, honesty and earnestness must be placed back of all that one says if one would make a lasting and favorable impression.

Whatever you successfully sell to others you must first sell to *yourself!*

Not long ago I was approached by an agent of the government of Mexico who sought my services as a writer of propaganda for the administration in charge at that time. His approach was about as follows:

"Whereas, Señor has a reputation as an exponent of the Golden Rule philosophy; and whereas, Señor is known throughout the United States as an independent who is not allied with any political faction, now, therefore, would Señor be gracious enough to come to Mexico, study the economic and political affairs of that country, then return to the United States and write a series of articles to appear in the newspapers, recommending to the people of America the immediate recognition of Mexico by the government of the United States, etc."

For this service, I was offered more money than I shall, perhaps, ever possess during my entire life; but I refused the commission, and for a reason that will fail to impress anyone except those who understand the principle which makes it necessary for all who would influence others to remain on good terms with their own conscience.

I could not write convincingly of Mexico's cause for the reason that I did not believe in that cause; therefore, I could not have mixed sufficient *enthusiasm* with my writing to have made it effective, even though I had been willing to prostitute my talent and dip my pen into ink that I knew to be muddy.

I will not endeavor further to explain my philosophy on this incident for the reason that those who are far enough advanced in the study of Auto-suggestion will not need further explanation, while those who are not far enough advanced would not and could not understand.

No man can afford to express, through words or acts, that which is not in harmony with his own belief, and if he does so he must pay by the loss of his ability to influence others.

Please read, aloud, the foregoing paragraph! It is worth emphasizing by repetition, for lack of observation of the principle upon which it is based constitutes the rocks and reefs upon which many a man's *definite chief aim* dashes itself to pieces.

I do not believe that I can afford to try to deceive anyone, about anything, but *I know that I cannot afford to try to deceive myself.* To do so would destroy the power of my pen and render my words ineffective. It is only when I write with the *fire of enthusiasm* burning in my heart that my writing impresses others favorably; and it is only when I speak from a heart that is bursting with belief in my message, that I can move my audience to accept that message.

IS there not food for thought in the fact that no newspaper has ever published any account of "Wild drinking parties" or other similar scandals in connection with the names of Edison, Ford, Rockefeller a n d most of the other really big fellows?

I would also have you read, aloud, the foregoing paragraph. Yes, I would have you commit it to memory. Even more than this, I would have you write it out and place it where it may serve as a daily reminder of a principle, nay, a *law* as immutable as the law of gravitation, *without which you can never become a power in your chosen life-work.*

There have been times, and many of them, when it *appeared* that if I stood by this principle it would mean starvation!

There have been times when my closest friends and business advisers have strongly urged me to shade my philosophy for the sake of gaining a needed advantage here and there, but somehow I have managed to cling to it, mainly, I suppose, for the reason that I have preferred peace and harmony in my own heart to the material gain that I might have had by a forced compromise with my conscience.

Strange as it may seem, my deliberations and conclusions on this subject of refusing to strangle my own conscience have seldom been based upon what is commonly called "honesty." That which I have done in the matter of refraining from writing or speaking anything that I did not believe has been solely a question of honor between my conscience and myself. I have tried to express that which my heart dictated because I have aimed to give my words "flesh." It might be said that my motive was based more upon self-interest than it was on a desire to be fair with others, although I have never desired to be unfair with others, so far as I am able to analyze myself.

No man can become a master salesman if he compromises with falsehood. Murder will out, and even though no one ever catches him red-handed in expressing that which he does not believe, his words will fail in the accomplishment of their purpose because he cannot give them "flesh," if they do not come from his heart, and if they are not mixed with genuine, unadulterated *enthusiasm.*

I would also have you read, aloud, the foregoing paragraph, for it embraces a great law that you must *understand and apply* before you can become a person of influence in any undertaking.

In making these requests, for the sake of emphasis, I am not trying to take undue liberties with you. I am giving you full credit for being an adult, a thinker, an intelligent person, yet I know how likely you are to skip over these vital laws without being sufficiently impressed by them to make them a part of your own workaday philosophy. *I know your weakness because I know my own.* It has required the better part of twenty-five years of ups and downs—mostly downs—to impress these basic truths upon my own mind so that they influenced me. I have tried both them and their opposites; therefore, I can speak, not as one who merely *believes* in their soundness, but as one who *knows.*

And what do I mean by "these truths"?

So that you cannot possibly misunderstand my meaning, and so that these words of warning cannot possibly convey an abstract meaning, I will state that by "these truths" I mean this:

You cannot afford to suggest to another person, by word of mouth or by an act of yours, that which you do not believe.

Surely that is plain enough.

And, the reason you cannot afford to do so, is this:

If you compromise with your own conscience, it will not be long before you will have no conscience; for your conscience will fail to guide you, just as an alarm clock will fail to awaken you if you do not heed it.

Surely, that is plain enough, also.

And how do I happen to be an authority on this vital subject, do you ask?

I am an authority because I have experimented with the principle until I know how it works!

"But," you may ask, "how do I know that you are telling the truth?"

The answer is that *you will know only by experimenting for yourself, and by observing others who faithfully apply this principle and those who do not apply it.*

If my evidence needs backing, then consult any man whom you know to be a person who has "tried to get by" without observing this principle, and if he will not or cannot give you the truth you can get it, nevertheless, by analyzing the man.

There is but one thing in the world that gives a man real and enduring power, and that is *character! Reputation*, bear in mind, is not *character*. Reputation is that which people are believed to be; character is that which people *are!* If you would be a person of great influence, then be a person of real *character*.

Character is the philosopher's lode-stone through which all who have it may turn the base metals of their life into pure gold. Without *character* you have nothing; you are nothing; and you can be nothing, except a pile of flesh and bone and hair, worth perhaps twenty-five dollars. Character is something that you cannot beg or steal or buy. You can get it only by *building it;* and you can build it by your own *thoughts* and *deeds,* and in no other way.

Through the aid of Auto-suggestion, any person can build a sound character, no matter what his past has been. As a fitting close for this lesson, I wish to emphasize the fact that all who have *character* have *enthusiasm* and personality sufficient to draw to them others who have character.

You will now be instructed as to how you shall proceed in developing *enthusiasm,* in the event that you do not already possess this rare quality.

The instructions will be simple, but you will be unfortunate if you discount their value on that account.

First: Complete the remaining lessons of this course, because other important instructions which are to be co-ordinated with this one will be found in subsequent lessons.

Second: If you have not already done so, write out your *definite chief aim* in clear, simple language, and follow this by writing out the plan through which you intend to transform your *aim* into reality.

Third: Read over the description of your *definite chief aim* each night, just before retiring, and as you read, see yourself (in your imagination) in full possession of the object of your *aim.* Do this with full faith in your ability to transform your *definite chief aim* into reality. *Read aloud, with all the enthusiasm at your command, emphasizing every word. Repeat this reading until the small still voice within you tells you that your purpose will be realized.* Sometimes you will feel the effects of this voice *from within* the first time you read your *definite chief aim;* while at other times, you may have to read it a dozen or fifty times before the assurance comes, but do not stop until you feel it.

If you prefer to do so you may read your *definite chief aim* as a prayer.

The remainder of this lesson is for the person who has not yet learned the power of *faith* and who knows little or nothing of the principle of Auto-suggestion.

To all who are in this class, I would recommend the reading of the seventh and eighth verses of the seventh chapter, and the twentieth verse of the seventeenth chapter of St. Matthew.

One of the greatest powers for good, upon the face of this earth, is faith. To this marvelous power may be traced miracles of the most astounding nature. It offers peace on earth to all who embrace it.

Faith involves a principle that is so far-reaching in its effect that no man can say what are its limitations, or if it has limitations. *Write into the description of your definite chief aim a statement of the qualities that you intend to develop in yourself, and the station in life that you intend to attain, and have faith, as you read this description each night, that you can transform this purpose into reality.* Surely, you cannot miss the suggestion contained in this lesson.

To become successful you must be a person of action. Merely to "know" is not sufficient. It is necessary both to *know* and *do.*

Enthusiasm is the mainspring of the mind which urges one to put knowledge into action.

Billy Sunday is the most successful evangelist this country has ever known. For the purpose of study-

IF you think your lot in life has been hard read "Up From Slavery" by Booker T. Washington, and you may see how fortunate you have been.

ing his technique and checking up on his psychological methods the author of this course went through three campaigns with Reverend Sunday.

His success is based very largely upon one word— ENTHUSIASM!

By making effective use of the law of suggestion Billy Sunday conveys his own spirit of enthusiasm to the minds of his followers and they become influenced by it. He sells his sermons by the use of exactly the same sort of strategy employed by many Master Salesmen.

Enthusiasm is as essential to a salesman as water is to a duck!

All successful sales managers understand the psychology of enthusiasm and make use of it, in various ways, as a practical means of helping their men produce more sales.

Practically all sales organizations have get-together meetings at stated times, for the purpose of revitalizing the minds of all members of the sales force, and injecting the spirit of enthusiasm, which can be best done en masse, through group psychology.

Sales meetings might properly be called "revival" meetings, because their purpose is to revive interest and arouse enthusiasm which will enable the salesman to take up the fight with renewed ambition and energy.

During his administration as Sales Manager of the National Cash Register Company Hugh Chalmers (who later became famous in the motor car industry) faced a most embarrassing situation which threatened to wipe out his position as well as that of thousands of salesmen under his direction.

The company was in financial difficulty. This fact

had become known to the salesmen in the field and the
effect of it was to cause them to lose their Enthusiasm. Sales began to dwindle until finally the conditions became so alarming that a general meeting of
the sales organization was called, to be held at the
company's plant in Dayton, Ohio. Salesmen were
called in from all over the country.

Mr. Chalmers presided over the meeting. He began
by calling on several of his best salesmen to get on their
feet and tell what was wrong out in the field that orders
had fallen off. One by one they got up, as called, and
each man had a most terrible tale of grief to unfold.
Business conditions were bad, money was scarce,
people were holding off buying until after Presidential
election, etc. As the fifth man began to enumerate
the difficulties which had kept him from making his
usual quota of sales Mr. Chalmers jumped up on top
of a table, held up his hands for silence, and said
"STOP! I order this convention to come to a close
for ten minutes while I get my shoes shined."

Then turning to a small colored boy who sat near
by he ordered the boy to bring his shoe-shine outfit
and shine his shoes, right where he stood, on top of
the table.

The salesmen in the audience were astounded!
Some of them thought that Mr. Chalmers had suddenly
lost his mind. They began to whisper among themselves. Meanwhile, the little colored boy shined first
one and then the other shoe, taking plenty of time
and doing a first-class job.

After the job was finished Mr. Chalmers handed
the boy a dime, then went ahead with his speech:

"I want each of you," said he, "to take a good look

at this little colored boy. He has the concession for shoe-shining throughout our plant and offices. His predecessor was a white boy, considerably older than himself, and despite the fact that the company subsidized him with a salary of $5.00 a week he could not make a living in this plant, where thousands of people are employed.

"This little colored boy not only makes a good living, without any subsidy from the company, but he is actually saving money out of his earnings each week, working under the same conditions, in the same plant, for the same people.

"Now I wish to ask you a question: Whose fault was it that the white boy did not get more business? Was it his fault, or the fault of his buyers?"

In a mighty roar from the crowd the answer came back:

"IT WAS THE BOY'S FAULT, OF COURSE!"

"Just so," replied Chalmers, "and now I want to tell you this, that you are selling Cash Registers in the same territory, to the same people, with exactly the same business conditions that existed a year ago, yet you are not producing the business that you were then. Now whose fault is that? Is it yours, or the buyer's?"

And again the answer came back with a roar:

"IT IS OUR FAULT, OF COURSE!"

"I am glad that you are frank to acknowledge your faults," Chalmers continued, "and I now wish to tell you what your trouble is: You have heard rumors about this company being in financial trouble and that has killed off your enthusiasm so that you are not making the effort that you formerly made. If you will go back into your territories with a definite promise to send in five orders each during the next thirty days this company will no longer be in financial difficulty, for that additional business will see us clear. Will you do it?"

They said they would, and they did!

That incident has gone down in the history of the National Cash Register Company under the name of Hugh Chalmers' Million Dollar Shoe Shine, for it is said that this turned the tide in the company's affairs and was worth millions of dollars.

Enthusiasm knows no defeat! The Sales Manager who knows how to send out an army of enthusiastic salespeople may set his own price on his services, and what is more important even than this, he can increase the earning capacity of every person under his direction; thus, his enthusiasm benefits not only himself but perhaps hundreds of others.

Enthusiasm is never a matter of chance. There are certain stimuli which produce enthusiasm, the most important of these being as follows:

1. Occupation in work which one loves best.

2. Environment where one comes in contact with others who are enthusiastic and optimistic.

3. Financial success.

4. Complete mastery and application, in one's daily work, of the Fifteen Laws of Success.

5. Good health.

6. Knowledge that one has served others in some helpful manner.

7. Good clothes, appropriate to the needs of one's occupation.

All of these seven sources of stimuli are self-explanatory with the exception of the last. The psychology of clothes is understood by very few people, and for this reason it will be here explained in detail. Clothes constitute the most important part of the embellishment which every person must have in order to feel self-reliant, hopeful and enthusiastic.

THE PSYCHOLOGY OF GOOD CLOTHES

When the good news came from the theater of war, on November the eleventh, 1918, my worldly possessions amounted to but little more than they did the day I came into the world.

The war had destroyed my business and made it necessary for me to make a new start!

My wardrobe consisted of three well worn business suits and two uniforms which I no longer needed.

Knowing all too well that the world forms its first and most lasting impressions of a man by the clothes he wears, I lost no time in visiting my tailor.

Happily, my tailor had known me for many years, therefore he did not judge me entirely by the clothes I wore. If he had I would have been "sunk."

With less than a dollar in change in my pocket, I picked out the cloth for three of the most expensive suits I ever owned, and ordered that they be made up for me at once.

The three suits came to $375.00!

I shall never forget the remark made by the tailor as he took my measure. Glancing first at the three bolts of expensive cloth which I had selected, and then at me, he inquired:

"Dollar-a-year man, eh?"

ALL anyone really requires, as a capital on which to start a successful career, is a sound mind, a healthy body and a genuine desire to be of as much service as possible to as many people as possible.

"No," said I, "if I had been fortunate enough to get on the dollar-a-year payroll I might now have enough money to pay for these suits."

The tailor looked at me with surprise. I don't think he got the joke.

One of the suits was a beautiful dark gray; one was a dark blue; the other was a light blue with a pin stripe.

Fortunately I was in good standing with my tailor, therefore he did not ask when I was going to pay for those expensive suits.

I knew that I could and would pay for them in due time, but could I have convinced him of that? This was the thought which was running through my mind, with hope against hope that the question would not be brought up.

I then visited my haberdasher, from whom I purchased three less expensive suits and a complete supply of the best shirts, collars, ties, hosiery and underwear that he carried.

My bill at the haberdasher's amounted to a little over $300.00.

With an air of prosperity I nonchalantly signed the charge ticket and tossed it back to the salesman, with instructions to deliver my purchase the following morning. The feeling of renewed self-reliance and success had begun to come over me, even before I had attired myself in my newly purchased outfit.

I was out of the war and $675.00 in debt, all in less than twenty-four hours.

The following day the first of the three suits ordered from the haberdasher was delivered. I put it on at once, stuffed a new silk handkerchief in the outside pocket of my coat, shoved the $50.00 I had borrowed on my ring down into my pants pocket, and walked down Michigan Boulevard, in Chicago, feeling as rich as Rockefeller.

Every article of clothing I wore, from my underwear out, was of the very best. That it was not paid for was nobody's business except mine and my tailor's and my haberdasher's.

Every morning I dressed myself in an entirely new outfit, and walked down the same street, at precisely the same hour. That hour "happened" to be the time when a certain wealthy publisher usually walked down the same street, on his way to lunch.

I made it my business to speak to him each day, and occasionally I would stop for a minute's chat with him.

After this daily meeting had been going on for about a week I met this publisher one day, but decided I would see if he would let me get by without speaking.

Watching him from under my eyelashes I looked straight ahead, and started to pass him when he stopped and motioned me over to the edge of the sidewalk, placed his hand on my shoulder, looked me over from head to foot, and said: "You look damned prosperous for a man who has just laid aside a uniform. Who makes your clothes?"

"Well," said I, "Wilkie & Sellery made this particular suit."

He then wanted to know what sort of business I was engaged in. That "airy" atmosphere of prosperity which I had been wearing, along with a new and different suit every day, had got the better of his curiosity. (I had hoped that it would.)

Flipping the ashes from my Havana perfecto, I said "Oh, I am preparing the copy for a new magazine that I am going to publish."

"A new magazine, eh?" he queried, "and what are you going to call it?"

"It is to be named Hill's Golden Rule."

"Don't forget," said my publisher friend, "that I am in the business of printing and distributing magazines. Perhaps I can serve you, also."

That was the moment for which I had been waiting. I had that very moment, and almost the very spot of ground on which we stood, in mind when I was purchasing those new suits.

But, is it necessary to remind you, that conversation never would have taken place had this publisher observed me walking down that street from day to day, with a "whipped-dog" look on my face, an unpressed suit on my back and a look of poverty in my eyes.

An appearance of prosperity attracts attention always, with no exceptions whatsover. Moreover, a look of prosperity attracts "favorable attention," because the one dominating desire in every human heart is to be prosperous.

.   .   .   .

My publisher friend invited me to his club for lunch. Before the coffee and cigars had been served he had "talked me out of" the contract for printing and distributing my magazine. I had even "consented" to permit him to supply the capital, without any interest charge.

For the benefit of those who are not familiar with

the publishing business may I not offer the information that considerable capital is required for launching a new nationally distributed magazine.

Capital, in such large amounts, is often hard to get, even with the best of security. The capital necessary for launching Hill's Golden Rule Magazine, which you may have read, was well above $30,000.00, and every cent of it was raised on a "front" created mostly by good clothes. True, there may have been some ability back of those clothes, but many millions of men have ability who never have anything else, and who are never heard of outside of the limited community in which they live. This is a rather sad truth!

To some it may seem an unpardonable extravagance for one who was "broke" to have gone in debt for $675.00 worth of clothes, but the psychology back of that investment more than justified it.

The appearance of prosperity not only made a favorable impression on those to whom I had to look for favors, but of more importance still was the effect that proper attire HAD ON ME.

I not only knew that correct clothes would impress others favorably, but I knew also that good clothes would give me an atmosphere of self-reliance, without which I could not hope to regain my lost fortunes.

I got my first training in the psychology of good clothes from my friend Edwin C. Barnes, who is a close business associate of Thomas A. Edison. Barnes afforded considerable amusement for the Edison staff when, some twenty-odd years ago, he rode into West Orange on a freight train (not being able to raise sufficient money for passenger fare) and announced at the Edison offices that he had come to enter into a partnership with Mr. Edison.

Nearly everybody around the Edison plant laughed at Barnes, except Edison himself. He saw something in the square jaw and determined face of young Barnes which most of the others did not see, despite the fact that the young man looked more like a tramp than he did a future partner of the greatest inventor on earth.

Barnes got his start, sweeping floors in the Edison offices!

That was all he sought—just a chance to get a toe-hold in the Edison organization. From there on he made history that is well worth emulation by other young men who wish to make places for themselves.

Barnes has now retired from active business, even though he is still a comparatively young man, and spends most of his time at his two beautiful homes in Bradentown, Florida, and Damariscotta, Maine. He is a multimillionaire, prosperous and happy.

I first became acquainted with Barnes during the early days of his association with Edison, before he had "arrived."

In those days he had the largest and most expensive collection of clothes I had ever seen or heard of one man owning. His wardrobe consisted of thirty-one suits; one for each day of the month. He never wore the same suit two days in succession.

Moreover, all his suits were of the most expensive type. (Incidentally, his clothes were made by the same tailors who made those three suits for me.)

He wore socks which cost six dollars per pair.

THERE is a suitable reward for every virtue and appropriate punishment for every sin a man commits. Both the reward and the punishment are effects over which no man has control, as they come upon him voluntarily.

His shirts and other wearing apparel cost in similar proportion. His cravats were specially made, at a cost of from five to seven dollars and a half each.

One day, in a spirit of fun, I asked him to save some of his old suits which he did not need, for me.

He informed me that he hadn't a single suit which he did not need!

He then gave me a lesson on the psychology of clothes which is well worth remembering. "I do not wear thirty-one suits of clothes," said he, "entirely for the impression they make on other people; I do it mostly for the impression they have on me."

Barnes then told me of the day when he presented himself at the Edison plant, for a position. He said he had to walk around the plant a dozen times before he worked up enough courage to announce himself, because he knew that he looked more like a tramp than he did a desirable employee.

Barnes is said to be the most able salesman ever connected with the great inventor of West Orange. His entire fortune was made through his ability as a salesman, but he has often said that he never could have accomplished the results which have made him both wealthy and famous had it not been for his understanding of the psychology of clothes.

.   .   .   .

I have met many salesman in my time. During the past ten years I have personally trained and directed the efforts of more than 3,000 salespeople, both men and women, and I have observed that, without a single exception, the star producers were all people who understood and made good use of the psychology of clothes.

I have seen a few well dressed people who made no outstanding records as salesmen, but I have yet to see the first poorly dressed man who became a star producer in the field of selling.

I have studied the psychology of clothes for so long, and I have watched its effect on people in so many different walks of life, that I am fully convinced there is a close connection between clothes and success.

.   .   .   .

Personally I feel no need of thirty-one suits of clothes, but if my personality demanded a wardrobe of this size I would manage to get it, no matter how much it might cost.

To be well dressed a man should have at least ten suits of clothes. He should have a different suit for each of the seven days of the week, a full dress suit and a Tuxedo, for formal evening occasions, and a cutaway for formal afternoon occasions.

For summer wear he should have an assortment of at least four appropriate light suits, with blue coat and white flannel trousers for informal afternoon and evening occasions. If he plays golf he should have at least one golf suit.

This, of course, is for the man who is a notch or two above the "mediocre" class. The man who is satisfied with mediocrity needs but few clothes.

It may be true, as a well known poet has said, that "clothes do not make the man," but no one can deny the fact that good clothes go a very long way toward giving him a *favorable start*.

A man's bank will generally loan him all the money he wants when he does not need it—when he is prosperous, but never go to your bank for a loan with a shabby-looking suit on your back and a look of poverty in your eyes, for if you do you'll get the gate.

Success attracts success! There is no escape from this great universal law; therefore, if you wish to attract success make sure that you look the part of success, whether your calling is that of day laborer or merchant prince.

For the benefit of the more "dignified" students of this philosophy who may object to resorting to "stunt" stimuli or "trick clothing" as a means of achieving success, it may be profitably explained that practically every successful man on earth has discovered some form of stimulus through which he can and does drive himself on to greater effort.

It may be shocking to members of the Anti-Saloon League, but it is said to be true, nevertheless, that James Whitcomb Riley wrote his best poems when he was under the influence of alcohol. His stimulus was liquor. (The author wishes it distinctly understood that he does not recommend the use of alcoholic or narcotic stimuli, for any purpose whatsoever, as either will eventually destroy both body and mind of all who use them.) Under the influence of alcohol Riley became imaginative, enthusiastic and an entirely different person, according to close personal friends of his.

Edwin Barnes spurred himself into the necessary action to produce outstanding results, with the aid of good clothes.

Some men rise to great heights of achievement as

the result of love for some woman. Connect this with the brief suggestion to the subject which was made in the Introductory Lesson and you will, if you are a person who knows the ways of men, be able to finish the discussion of this particular phase of enthusiasm stimulus without further comment by the author which might not be appropriate for the younger minds that will assimilate this philosophy.

Underworld characters who are engaged in the dangerous business of highway robbery, burglary, etc., generally "dope" themselves for the occasion of their operations, with cocaine, morphine and other narcotics. Even in this there is a lesson which shows that practically all men need temporary or artificial stimuli to drive them to greater effort than that normally employed in the ordinary pursuits of life.

SUCCESSFUL PEOPLE HAVE DISCOVERED WAYS AND MEANS WHICH THEY BELIEVE BEST SUITED TO THEIR OWN NEEDS, TO PRODUCE STIMULI WHICH CAUSE THEM TO RISE TO HEIGHTS OF ENDEAVOR ABOVE THE ORDINARY.

One of the most successful writers in the world employs an orchestra of beautifully dressed young women who play for him while he writes. Seated in a room that has been artistically decorated to suit his own taste, under lights that have been colored, tinted and softened, these beautiful young ladies, dressed in handsome evening gowns, play his favorite music. To use his own words, "I become drunk with enthusiasm, under the influence of this environment, and rise to heights I never know or feel on other occasions. It is then that I do my work. The thoughts pour in on me as if they were dictated by an unseen and unknown power."

This author gets much of his inspiration from music and art. Once a week he spends at least an hour in an art museum, looking at the works of the masters. On these occasions, again using his own words, "I get enough enthusiasm from one hour's visit in the museum of art to carry me for two days."

Edgar Allan Poe wrote "The Raven" when, it is reported, he was more than half intoxicated. Oscar Wilde wrote his poems under the influence of a form of stimulus which cannot be appropriately mentioned in a course of this nature.

Henry Ford (so it is believed by this author, who admits that this is merely the author's opinion) got his real start as the result of his love for his charming life-companion. It was she who inspired him, gave him faith in himself, and kept him keyed up so that he carried on in the face of adversities which would have killed off a dozen ordinary men.

These incidents are cited as evidence that men of outstanding achievement have, by accident or design, discovered ways and means of stimulating themselves to a high state of enthusiasm.

Associate that which has been here stated with what was said concerning the law of the "Master Mind," in the Introductory Lesson, and you will have an entirely new conception of the modus operandi through which that law may be applied. You will also have a somewhat different understanding of the real purpose of "allied effort, in a spirit of perfect harmony," which constitutes the best known method of bringing into use the Law of the Master Mind.

YOUR employer does not control the sort of service you render. You control that, and it is the thing that makes or breaks you.

At this point it seems appropriate to call your attention to the manner in which the lessons of this course blend. You will observe that each lesson covers the subject intended to be covered, and in addition to this it overlaps and gives the student a better understanding of some other lesson or lessons of the course.

In the light of what has been said in this lesson, for example, the student will better understand the real purpose of the Law of the Master Mind; that purpose being, in the main, a practical method of stimulating the minds of all who participate in the group constituting the Master Mind.

Times too numerous to be here described this author has gone into conference with men whose faces showed the signs of care, who had the appearance of worry written all over them, only to see those same men straighten up their shoulders, tilt their chins at a higher angle, soften their faces with smiles of confidence, and get down to business with that sort of ENTHUSIASM which knows no defeat.

The change took place the moment harmony of purpose was established.

If a man goes about the affairs of life in the same day-in and day-out, prosaic, lackadaisical spirit, devoid of enthusiasm, he is doomed to failure. Nothing can save him until he changes his attitude and learns how to stimulate his mind and body to unusual heights of enthusiasm AT WILL!

The author is unwilling to leave this subject without having stated the principle here described in so many different ways that it is bound to be understood and also respected by the students of this course, who, all will remember, are men and women of all sorts of natures, experiences and degrees of intelligence. For this reason much repetition is essential.

Your business in life, you are reminded once again, is to achieve success!

With the stimulus you will experience from studying this philosophy, and with the aid of the ideas you will gather from it, plus the personal co-operation of the author who will give you an accurate inventory of your outstanding qualities, you should be able to create a DEFINITE PLAN that will lift you to great heights of achievement. However, there is no plan that can produce this desirable result without the aid of some influence that will cause you to arouse yourself, in a spirit of enthusiasm, to where you will exert greater than the ordinary effort which you put into your daily occupation.

You are now ready for the lesson on Self-control!

As you read that lesson you will observe that it has a vital bearing on this lesson, just as this lesson has a direct connection with the preceding lessons on A Definite Chief Aim, Self-confidence, Initiative and Leadership and Imagination.

The next lesson describes the Law which serves as the Balance Wheel of this entire philosophy.

THE SEVEN DEADLY HORSEMEN

An After-the-Lesson Visit With the Author

The "seven horsemen" are labeled, in order shown,—Intolerance, Greed, Revenge, Egotism, Suspicion, Jealously and "?"

The worst enemy that any man has is the one that walks around under his own hat.

If you could see yourself as others see you the enemies that you harbor in your own personality might be discovered and thrown out. The Seven Enemies named in this essay are the commonest which ride millions of men and women to failure without being discovered. Weigh yourself carefully and find out how many of the Seven you are harboring.

YOU see, in this picture, seven deadly warriors! From birth until death every human being must give battle to these enemies. Your success will be measured very largely by the way you manage your battle against these swift riders.

As you look at this picture you will say, of course,

that it is only imagination.   True, the picture is imaginary, but the swift riders of destruction are REAL.

If these enemies rode openly, on real horses, they
would not be dangerous, because they could be
rounded up and put out of commission.   But, they ride
unseen, in the minds of men.   So silently and subtly
do they work that most people never recognize their
presence.

Take inventory of yourself and find out how many
of these seven horsemen you are harboring.

.   .   .   .

In the foreground you will find the most dangerous and the commonest of the riders.   You will be
fortunate if you discover this enemy and protect yourself against it.   This cruel warrior, INTOLERANCE,
has killed more people, destroyed more friendships,
brought more misery and suffering into the world and
caused more wars than all of the other six horsemen
that you see in this picture.

Until you master INTOLERANCE you will never
become an accurate thinker.   This enemy of mankind
closes up the mind and pushes reason and logic and
FACTS into the back-ground.   If you find yourself
hating those whose religious viewpoint is different from
your own you may be sure that the most dangerous
of the seven deadly horsemen still rides in your brain.

.   .   .   .

Next, in the picture, you will observe REVENGE
and GREED!

These riders travel side by side.   Where one is
found the other is always close at hand.   GREED

warps and twists man's brain so that he wants to build
a fence around the earth and keep everyone else on
the outside of it. This is the enemy that drives man
to accumulate millions upon top of millions of dollars
which he does not need and can never use. This is
the enemy that causes man to twist the screw until
he has wrung the last drop of blood from his fellow
man.

And, thanks to REVENGE which rides alongside
of GREED, the unfortunate person who gives brain-
room to these cruel twins is not satisfied to merely
take away his fellow man's earthly belongings; he
wants to destroy his reputation in the bargain.

> "Revenge is a naked sword—
>   It has neither hilt nor guard.
> Would'st thou wield this brand of the Lord:
>   Is thy grasp then firm and hard?
> But the closer thy clutch of the blade,
>   The deadlier blow thou would'st deal,
> Deeper wound in thy hand is made—
>   It is thy blood reddens the steel.
> And when thou hast dealt the blow—
>   When the blade from thy hand has flown—
> Instead of the heart of the foe
>   Thou may'st find it sheathed in thine own."

If you would know how deadly are ENVY and
GREED, study the history of every man who has set
out to become RULER OF THIS WORLD!

If you do not wish to undertake so ambitious a
program of research, then study the people around
you; those who have tried and those who are now try-

ing to "feather their own nests" at the cost of others. GREED and REVENGE stand at the crossroads of life, where they turn aside to failure and misery every person who would take the road that leads to success. It is a part of your business not to permit them to interfere with you when you approach one of these crossroads.

Both individuals and nations rapidly decline where GREED and ENVY ride in the minds of those who dominate. Take a look at Mexico and Spain if you wish to know what happens to the envious and the greedy.

Most important of all, take a look at YOURSELF and make sure that these two deadly enemies are not riding in your brain!

.   .   .   .

Turn your attention, now, to two more twins of destruction—EGOTISM and SUSPICION. Observe that they, also, ride side by side. There is no hope of success for the person who suffers either from too much self-love or lack of confidence in others.

Someone who likes to manipulate figures has estimated that the largest club in the world is the "IT CAN'T BE DONE CLUB." It is claimed that there are approximately ninety-nine million members of this club in the United States of America alone.

If you have no FAITH in other people you have not the seed of success in you. SUSPICION is a prolific germ. If permitted to get a start it rapidly multiplies itself until it leaves no room for FAITH.

Without faith no man may enjoy enduring success.

Running, like a golden cord of illumination throughout the Bible, is the admonition to have FAITH. Before civilization lost itself in its mad rush for dollars men understood the power of FAITH.

"For verily I say unto you, if ye have faith as a grain of mustard seed, ye shall say unto this mountain, Remove hence to yonder place; and it shall remove; and nothing shall be impossible unto you."

The writer of this passage, which appears in the Bible, understood a great law which but few of today understand. Believe in people if you would have them believe in you. Kill off SUSPICION. If you do not it will kill you off.

If you would have power, cultivate FAITH in mankind!

EGOTISM thrives where SUSPICION exists. Interest yourself in others and you will be too busy to indulge in self-love. Observe those around you who begin every sentence with the personal pronoun, "I," and you will notice that they are suspicious of other people.

The man who can forget himself while engaging in useful service to other people is never cursed with SUSPICION. Study those about you who are both SUSPICIOUS and EGOTISTICAL and see how many of this type you can name who are successful in whatever work they may be engaged in.

And, while making this study of OTHERS, study, also, yourself!

Be sure that you are not bound down by EGOTISM and SUSPICION.

Bringing up the rear of this deadly group of riders you see two horsemen. One is JEALOUSY and the name of the other has been purposely omitted.

Each reader of this article may take inventory of himself and give the seventh rider a name that fits whatever he finds in his own mind.

Some will name this rider DISHONESTY. Others will name it PROCRASTINATION. A few will have the courage to name it UNCONTROLLED SEX DESIRE. As for you, name it whatever you please, but be sure to give it a name.

Perhaps your own imagination will supply an appropriate name as a fellow-traveler for JEALOUSY.

You will be better prepared to give the unnamed rider a name if you know that JEALOUSY is a form of insanity! Facts are sometimes cruel things to face. It is a fact that JEALOUSY is a form of insanity, known to the medical fraternity as "dementia praecox."

> "O jealousy,
> Thou ugliest fiend of hell! thy deadly venom
> Preys on my vitals, turns the healthful hue
> Of my fresh cheek to haggard sallowness,
> And drinks my spirit up!"

You will notice that JEALOUSY rides just back of SUSPICION. Some who read this will say that JEALOUSY and SUSPICION should have ridden side by side, as one often leads to the other in man's mind.

JEALOUSY is the most common form of insanity. It rides in the minds of both men and women; sometimes with a real cause, but more often without any cause whatsoever.

This deadly rider is a great friend of the divorce lawyers!

It also keeps detective agencies busy night and day.

It takes its regular toll of murder. It breaks up homes and makes widows of mothers and orphans of innocent little children. Peace and happiness can never be YOURS as long as this rider remains unharnessed in your brain.

Man and wife may go through life together in poverty and still be very happy, if both are free from this child of insanity known as JEALOUSY. Examine yourself carefully and if you find any evidence of JEALOUSY in your mind begin, at once, to master it.

JEALOUSY rides in many forms.

When it first begins to creep into the brain it manifests itself in something after this fashion:

"I wonder where she is and what she is doing while I am away?"

Or, "I wonder if he does not see another woman when he is away from me?"

When these questions begin to arise in your mind do not call in a detective. Instead, go to the psychopathic hospital and have yourself examined, because more than likely you are suffering from a mild form of insanity.

Get your foot on JEALOUSY'S neck before it gets its clutches on your throat.

.   .   .   .

After you have read this essay lay it aside and THINK about it.

At first you may say "This does not apply to me. I have no imaginary horsemen in my brain." And, you may be right—ONE OUT OF EVERY TEN MILLION COULD SAY THIS AND BE RIGHT! The other nine million nine hundred and ninety-nine

thousand nine hundred and ninety-nine would be
wrong.

Do not fool yourself!   You may be in that larger
class.   The purpose of this article is to get you to
see yourself as YOU ARE!   If you are suffering failure and poverty and misery in any of their forms you
are sure to discover one or more of these deadly riders
in your brain.

Make no mistake about it—those who have all they
want, including happiness and good health, have driven
the seven horsemen out of their brains.

Come back to this essay a month from now, after
you have had time to analyze yourself carefully.   Read
it again and it may bring you face to face with FACTS
that will emancipate you from a horde of cruel enemies
that now ride within your brain without your knowing it.